KIDS LOVE Guide ®

Over 200,000 Kids Love Books Sold

KIDS LOVE OHIO

Your Family Travel Guide to Exploring Kid-Friendly Ohio
500 Fun Stops & Unique Spots

Michele Darrall Zavatsky

Dedicated to the Families of Ohio

In a Hundred Years...It will not matter, The size of my bank account...The kind of house that I lived in, the kind of car that I drove...But what will matter is...That the world may be different Because I was important in the life of a child.

- author unknown

For the latest major updates corresponding to the pages in this book visit our website:

www.KidsLoveTravel.com

Although the authors have exhaustively researched all sources to ensure accuracy and completeness of the information contained in this book, we assume no responsibility for errors, inaccuracies, omissions or any other inconsistency herein. Any slights against any entries or organizations are unintentional.

- ***REMEMBER:*** *Museum exhibits change frequently. Check the site's website before you visit to note any changes. Also, HOURS and ADMISSIONS are subject to change at the owner's discretion. If you are tight on time or money, check the attraction's website or call before you visit.*

- ***INTERNET PRECAUTION:*** *All websites mentioned in KIDS LOVE OHIO have been checked for appropriate content. However, due to the fast-changing nature of the Internet, we strongly urge parents to preview any recommended sites and to always supervise their children when on-line.*

- ***EDUCATORS:*** *There are suggestions for finding FREE lessons plans embedded in many listings as helpful notes for educators.*

KIDS ♥ OHIO ™ Kids Love Publications, LLC

TABLE OF CONTENTS

State Detail Map

(With Major Routes and Cities Marked)

Chapter Area Map

(Chapters arranged alphabetically by chapter name)

HOW TO USE THIS BOOK

(a few hints to make your adventures run smoothly:)

BEFORE YOU LEAVE:

- Each chapter represents a two hour radius area of the state or a Day Trip. The chapter begins with an introduction and Quick Tour of favorites within the chapter. The listings are by City and then alphabetical by name, numeric by zip code. Each listing has tons of important details (pricing, hours, website, etc.) and a review noting the most engaging aspects of the place. Our popular Activity Index in back is helpful if you want to focus on a particular type of attraction (i.e. History, Tours, Outdoor Exploring, Animals & Farms, etc.).
- Begin by assigning each family member a different colored highlighter (for example: Daniel gets blue, Jenny gets pink, Mommy gets yellow and Daddy gets green). At your leisure, begin to read each review and put a highlighter "check" mark next to the sites that most interest each family member or highlight the features you most want to see. Now, when you go to plan a quick trip - or a long van ride - you can easily choose different stops in one day to please everyone.
- Know directions and parking. Use a GPS system or print off parking directions from websites.
- Most attractions are closed major holidays unless noted.
- When children are in tow, it is better to make your lodging reservations ahead of time. Every time we've tried to "wing it", we've always ended up at a place that was overpriced, in a unsafe area, or not super clean. We've never been satisfied when we didn't make a reservation ahead of time.
- If you have a large family, or are traveling with extended family or friends, most places offer group discounts. Check out the company's website for details.
- For the latest critical updates corresponding to the pages in this book, visit our website: www.kidslovetravel.com. Click on *News*.

ON THE ROAD:

- Consider the child's age before you stop at an exit. Some attractions and restaurants, even hotels, are too formal for young ones or not enough adventure for teens. Read our trusted reviews first.
- Estimate the duration of the trip and how many stops you can afford to make. From our experience, it is best to stop every two hours to stretch your legs or eat/snack or maybe visit an inexpensive attraction.
- Bring along books and games for "entertainment" in the van. As an added bonus, these "enriching" games also stimulate conversation - you may get to know your family better and create memorable life lessons.

ON THE ROAD: *(cont.)*

- ☐ In between meals, we offer the family snacks like: pretzels, whole grain chips, water bottles, bite-size (dark) chocolates, grapes and apples. None of these are messy.
- ☐ Plan picnics along the way. Many Historical sites and State Parks are scattered along the highway. Allow time for a rest stop or a scenic byway to take advantage of these free picnic facilities.

WHEN YOU GET HOME:

- ☐ Make a family "treasure chest". Decorate a big box or use an old popcorn tin. Store memorabilia from a fun outing, journals, pictures, brochures and souvenirs. Once a year, look through the "treasure chest" and reminisce.

WAYS TO SAVE MONEY:

- ☐ Memberships - many children's museums, science centers, zoos and aquariums are members of associations that provide FREE or Discounted reciprocity to other such museums across the country. AAA Auto Club cards offer discounts to many of the activities and hotels in this book. If grandparents are along for the ride, they can use their AARP card and get discounts. Be sure to carry your member cards with you as proof to receive the discounts.
- ☐ Supermarket Customer Cards - national and local supermarkets often offer good discounted tickets to major attractions in the area.
- ☐ Internet Hotel Reservations - if you're traveling with kids, don't take the risk of being spontaneous with lodging. Make reservations ahead of time. We don't use non-refundable, deep discount hotel "scouting" websites (ex. Hotwire) unless we're traveling on business - just adults. You can't cancel your reservation, or change them, and you can't be guaranteed the type of room you want (ex. non-smoking, two beds). Instead, stick with a national hotel chain you trust and join their rewards program to accumulate points towards FREE night stays.
- ☐ State Travel Centers - as you enter a new state, their welcome centers offer many current promotions.
- ☐ Hotel Lobbies - often have a display of discount coupons to area shops and restaurants. When you check in, ask the clerk for discount pizza coupons they may have at the front desk.
- ☐ Attraction Online Coupons - check the websites listed with each review for possible printable coupons or discounted online tickets good towards the attraction.

General State Agency & Recreational Information

Call *(or visit websites)* for the services of interest. Request to be added to their mailing lists.

Ohio Department of Natural Resources, (877) 4BOATER. (800) WILDLIFE. www.dnr.state.oh.us/odnr

Ohio Campground Owner's Association (614) 764-0279 or www.ohiocamper.com

National Camping Information www.gocampingamerica.com

Ohio State Parks (614) 466-0652 or http://parks.ohiodnr.gov

Ohio State Park Lodges & Resorts (800) 282-7275 or www.dnr.state.oh.us/parks/overnightfacilities

Ohio's Agricultural Fairs, www.ohioagriculture.gov. (614) 728-6200. Schedules available.

Muskingum Watershed Conservancy District (877) 363-8500 or www.mwcdlakes.com.
Well-maintained boating, swimming and fishing lakes in CE Ohio.

- ☐ Ohio Division of Travel & Tourism (800) BUCKEYE or www.discoverohio.com
- ☐ **C** - Greater Columbus CVB (800) 345-4FUN or www.experiencecolumbus.org
- ☐ **CE** - Carroll County CVB (877) 727-0103 or www.carrollcountyohio.com
- ☐ **CE** - Tuscarawas County CVB (800) 527-3387 or www.neohiotravel.com
- ☐ **CE** - Wayne County CVB (800) 362-6474 or www.wooster-wayne.com/wccvb
- ☐ **CW** - Greene County CVB (800) 733-9109 or www.greenecountyohio.org
- ☐ **CW** - Greene County Parks (937) 562-7440 or www.co.greene.oh.us/parks.htm
- ☐ **NC** - Lorain County Metroparks (440) 458-5121 or www.loraincountymetroparks.com
- ☐ **NC** - Ottawa County Visitors Bureau (800) 441-1271 or www.lake-erie.com
- ☐ **NC** - Sandusky/Erie County VCB (800) 255-ERIE or www.buckeyenorth.com
- ☐ **NE** - Convention & Visitors Bureau of Greater Cleveland (800) 321-1001 or www.positivelycleveland.com
- ☐ **SC** - Ross County-Chillicothe CVB (800) 413-4118
- ☐ **SW** - Cincinnati CVB (800) CINCYUSA or www.cincyusa.com

Skiing / Tobogganing - Usually December – early March. Ski Conditions, (800) BUCKEYE. Or contact local MetroParks or Ohio Department of Natural Resources for cross-country skiing.

- **C** - Clearfork – (800) 237-5673, Butler. www.skiclearfork.com.
- **C** - Snow Trails – (800) DEC-SNOW or (800) OHIO-SKI, Mansfield. www.snowtrails.com.
- **CW** - Mad River Mountain – (937) 599-1015 or (800) 231-7669, Bellefontaine. www.skimadriver.com
- **NE** - Alpine Valley - (440) 729-9775, Chesterland. www.alpinevalleyohio.com.
- **NE** - Boston Mills/Brandywine – (800) USKI241, Peninsula or Northfield. www.bmbw.com.
- **SC** - Spicy Run - (740) 493-2599, Latham. www.spicyrun.com
- **CE** - Bear Creek Resort Ranch KOA, 3232 Downing St. S.W., East Sparta. (330) 484-3901. Ohio's longest, fastest, and safest way to toboggan. Newly rebuilt twin half-mile-long refrigerated toboggan chutes operate 40 degrees or colder, snow or no snow. A bus takes riders and toboggans back to the top so there's no walking and hauling the toboggan back up the hill.
- **NE** – Cleveland Metroparks Chalet in Mill Stream Run Reservation, Strongsville. (440) 572-9990. Toboggan chutes 1000 feet long and 42 feet tall.

College Athletics

- **SW** - University of Cincinnati - (513) 556-CATS. www.ucbearcats.com. 18 sports. Fall, Winter, Spring.
- **SW** - Xavier University, Cintas Center - (513) 745-3900 or www.xu.edu. Volleyball, basketball.

Canoeing - **SW**- Morgan's Canoe - SR 350, Oregonia. - (800) WECANOE. www.morgancanoe.com

Check out these businesses / services in your area for tour ideas:

AIRPORTS - All children love to visit the airport! Why not take a tour and understand all the jobs it takes to run an airport? Tour the terminal, baggage claim, gates and security / currency exchange. Maybe you'll even get to board a plane.

ANIMAL SHELTERS - Great for the would-be pet owner. Not only will you see many cats and dogs available for adoption, but a guide will show you the clinic and explain the needs of a pet. Be prepared to have the children "fall in love" with one of the animals while they are there!

BANKS - Take a "behind the scenes" look at automated teller machines, bank vaults and drive-thru window chutes. You may want to take this tour and then open a savings account for your child.

CITY HALLS - Halls of Fame, City Council Chambers & Meeting Room, Mayor's Office and famous statues.

ELECTRIC COMPANY / POWER PLANTS - Modern science has created many ways to generate electricity today, but what really goes on with the "flip of a switch". Because coal can be dirty, wear old, comfortable clothes. Coal furnaces heat water, which produces steam, that propels turbines, that drives generators, that make electricity.

FIRE STATIONS - Many Open Houses in October, Fire Prevention Month. Take a look into the life of the firefighters servicing your area and try on their gear. See where they hang out, sleep and eat. Hop aboard a real-life fire engine truck and learn fire safety too.

HOSPITALS - Some Children's Hospitals offer pre-surgery and general tours.

NEWSPAPERS - You'll be amazed at all the new technology. See monster printers and robotics. See samples in the layout department and maybe try to put together your own page. After seeing a newspaper made, most companies give you a free copy (dated that day) as your souvenir. National Newspaper Week is in October.

PETCO - Various stores. Contact each store manager to see if they participate. The Fur, Feathers & Fins™ program allows children to learn about the characteristics and habitats of fish, reptiles, birds, and small animals. At your local Petco, lessons in science, math and geography come to life through this hands-on field trip. As students develop a respect for animals, they will also develop a greater sense of responsibility.

PIZZA HUT & PAPA JOHN'S - Participating locations. Contact store manager. Best days are Monday, Tuesday and Wednesday mid-afternoon. Min of 10 people. Small charge. All children love pizza – especially when they can create their own! As the children tour the kitchen, they learn how to make a pizza, bake it, and then eat it.

KRISPY KREME DONUTS - Participating locations. Get an "inside look" and learn the techniques that make these donuts some of our favorites! Watch the dough being made in "giant" mixers, being formed into donuts and taking a "trip" through the fryer. Seeing them being iced and topped with colorful sprinkles is always a favorite with the kids. Contact your local store manager. They prefer Monday or Tuesday. Free.

SUPERMARKETS - Kids are fascinated to go behind the scenes of the same store where Mom and Dad shop. Usually you will see them grind meat, walk into large freezer rooms, watch cakes and bread bake and receive free samples along the way. Maybe you'll even get to pet a live lobster!

TV / RADIO STATIONS - Studios, newsrooms, Why do weathermen never wear blue/green clothes on TV? What makes a "DJ's" voice sound deep?

WATER TREATMENT PLANTS - A giant science experiment! You can watch seven stages of water treatment. The favorite is usually the wall of bright buttons flashing as workers monitor the different processes.

U.S. MAIN POST OFFICES - Did you know Ben Franklin was the first Postmaster General? Most interesting is the high-speed automated mail processing equipment. Learn how to address envelopes so they will be sent quicker (there are secrets). To make your tour more interesting, have your children write a letter to themselves and address it with colorful markers. Mail it earlier that day and try to locate the letter in all the high-speed machinery.

GEOCACHING

The object of Geocaching is to find the hidden container filled with a logbook, pencil and sometimes prizes! Where are Caches? Everywhere! But to be safe, be sure you're treading on Public Property. When you find the cache, write your name and the date you found it in the logbook. Larger caches might contain maps, books, toys, even money! When you take something from the cache you are honor-bound to leave something else in its place. Usually cache hunters will report their individual cache experiences on the Internet. (www.geocaching.com)

Chapter 1
Central Ohio

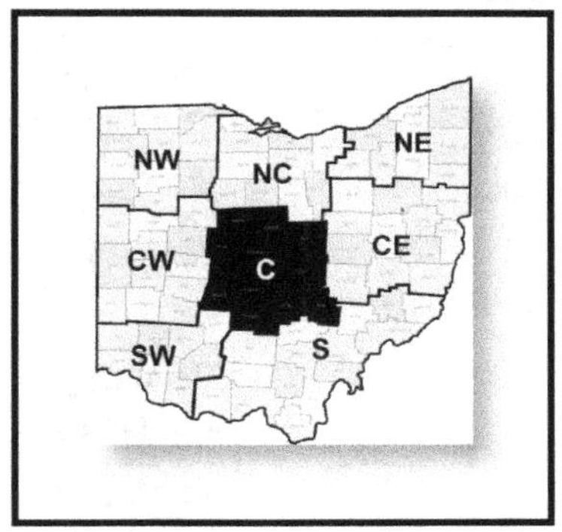

Ashville

- Slate Run Historical Farm

Buckeye Lake

- Buckeye Lake State Park
- Cranberry Bog Annual Open House

Circleville

- A.W. Marion State Park
- Circleville Pumpkin Show

Columbus

- All American Quarterhorse Congress
- Al's Delicious Popcorn (The Popcorn Outlet)
- Anthony Thomas Candy Company
- Balletmet
- Central Ohio Fire Museum & Learning Center
- Columbus Children's Theatre
- Columbus International Festival
- Columbus Museum Of Art
- Columbus Sports
- Columbus Symphony Orchestra
- Cosi
- First Night Columbus
- Franklin Park Conservatory And Botanical Gardens
- Graeter's Ice Cream Factory
- Greek Festival
- Ohio Historical Center
- Ohio State Fair
- Ohio State University Museums
- Ohio Statehouse
- Red, White And Boom
- Thurber House
- Topiary Garden

Columbus (Dublin)

- Irish Festival

Columbus (Groveport)

- Motts Military Museum

Columbus (Hilliard)

- Franklin County Fair

Columbus (Pickerington)

- Motorcycle Hall Of Fame Museum

Columbus (Powell)

- Columbus Zoo And Aquarium
- Zoombezi Bay

Columbus (Reynoldsburg)

- Tomato Festival

Columbus (Westerville)

- Hanby House

Columbus (Worthington)

- American Whistle Corporation
- Ohio Railway Museum
- Orange Johnson House

Delaware

- Alum Creek State Park
- Delaware State Park
- Harvest Festival, Stratford Ecological
- Little Brown Jug & All Horse Parade
- Maple Syrup Festival
- Olentangy Indian Caverns
- Perkins Observatory

Glenford

- Flint Ridge

Grove City

- Fall Fun Days

Heath

- Great Circle Earthworks

Hebron

- Pumpkin Maze Playland (S

Lancaster

- Aha! A Hands-On Adventure Children's Museum
- Sherman House Museum
- Wahkeena Nature Preserve

Lithopolis

- Wagnalls Memorial Library

London

- Madison Lake State Park

Marion

- Apple Festival
- Christmas By Candlelight
- Harding Home
- Marion County Fair
- Mysterious Revolving Ball
- Popcorn Pop-N-Drop
- Wyandot Popcorn Museum

Milford Center

- The Maize At Little Darby Creek

Mt. Gilead

- Mt. Gilead State Park

Mt. Sterling

- Deer Creek State Park Resort

Mt. Vernon

- Knox County Fair
- Knox County Museum

Newark

- Coco Key Water Resort
- Dawes Arboretum
- The Works - Ohio Center Of History, Art & Technology

Ostrander

- Pumpkin Maze Playland

Sugar Grove

- Pumpkin Maze Playland

Sunbury

- Hartman Aviary

Utica

- Velvet Ice Cream: Ye Olde Mill Ice Cream Museum

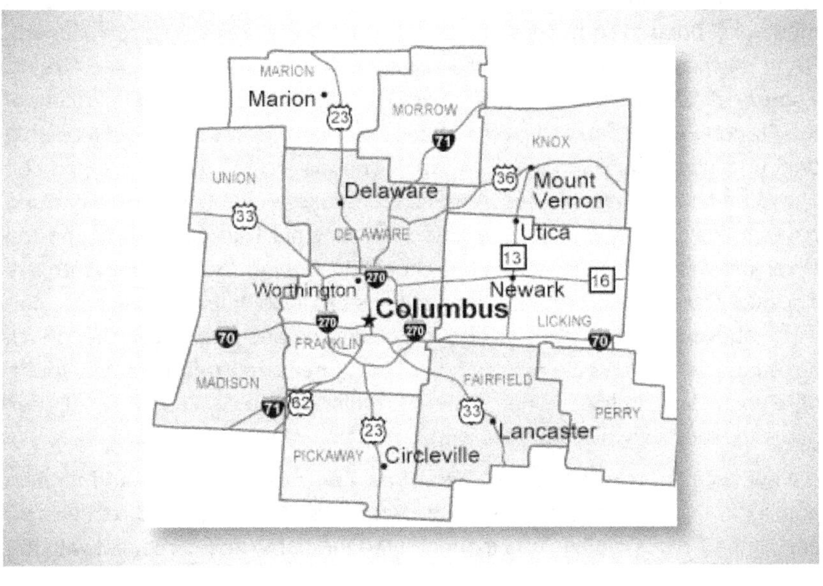

A Quick Tour of our Hand-Picked Favorites Around...

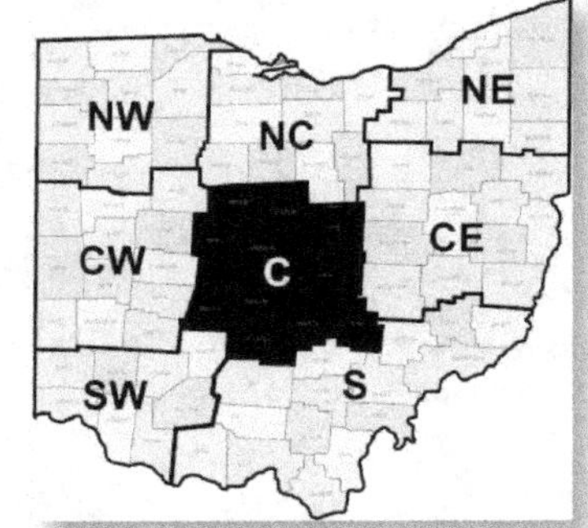

Central Ohio

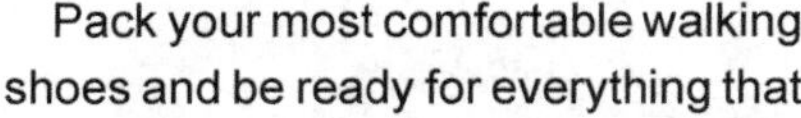

Pack your most comfortable walking shoes and be ready for everything that central Ohio has to offer. An early morning hike on the trails at the Columbus Metro Parks will prepare you for an afternoon at **COSI Science Center** (voted the #1 Science Museum in the nation). All of that walking works up an appetite, so plan to don your scarlet and gray to watch the Buckeyes at The **Ohio State University**. Go Bucks!

How about a visit to the snack food capital of Ohio! What do ducks, a mill and ice cream have in common? Ye Olde Mill at **Velvet Ice Cream**. Learn some history, watch it being made, try some and then feed what's left of your cone to the ducks! On the north end of Columbus sits a small factory and retail store home to the Popcorn Outlet and **Al's Delicious Popcorn**. Meet the Popcorn people while watching a video tour of large poppers spilling out mounds of popped corn. Try some bubble gum flavor or savory pizza popcorn. Right down the street is another ice cream factory. - **Graeter's Ice Cream Factory**! Arrange a tour or just show up and take your own self-guided tour of the French Pot method of the creamisest ice cream. How do they get those big dark chocolate chunks in there anyway? There's an ice cream store and soft play area on the premises, too. And, I know you're probably full from snacking on samples already, but you have to see the giant Buckeye candy and the silver foil wrapped pipes of molten chocolate flowing through the **Anthony Thomas Candy Company Factory** (west side of Columbus). Walk the "cat-walk" above a giant chemistry cooking lesson below. And, even though it's not a food, what kid could resist a tour of the **American Whistle** factory (north of town in Worthington). They make the whistles that coaches and referees use – the loudest whistles in the world!

Now, weave in a visit to the **Columbus Zoo and Aquarium** and its new additions, the polar bears, Alaskan brown bears, Arctic Fox and reindeer as part of the Polar Frontier. To experience the fun of the zoo combined with the thrill of an outdoor waterpark, visit **Zoombezi Bay** Water Park (on the same campus), with six waterslides, a wave pool, kiddie areas and more. And as part of the waterpark admission, entrance to the zoo is free (seasonally).

Finally, head out of town a little ways to the quaint town of Newark. Here you'll find an indoor waterpark, a science museum and even Indian mounds. The **Great Circle Earthworks** are fun to get outside and run around but the small museum that explains the culture of natives who lived there during biblical times gives this place a spiritual tone to just how ancient it is.

Sites and attractions are listed in order by City, Zip Code, and Name. Symbols indicated represent: Restaurants Lodging

SLATE RUN HISTORICAL FARM

Ashville - ***1375 SR 674 North (in Slate Run Park on SR 674, off US 33 east) 43103. http://www.metroparks.net/parks-and-trails/slate-run/. Phone: (614) 329-1392. Hours: Tuesday, Wednesday, Thursday 9:00am-4:00pm, Friday and Saturday 9:00am-6:00pm, Sunday 11:00am-6:00pm (June-August). Closes earlier rest of year. Wednesday – Saturday 9:00 am – 4:00pm, Sunday 11:00am – 4:00pm (September – May). Admission: FREE to browse around. Small admission for special programs - mostly held on weekends. Tours: Available by appointment (special prices). Metro Park open 6:30am-dusk.***

This historic farm depicts life on a working family farm of the 1880's. Visitors may join in with the barnyard and household chores. All the work is done using equipment and methods of the time (some horse-powered machinery). Some of the specially scheduled programs may be: maple syrup demonstrations and production, toy making, fishing, ice cream socials, making root beer, rope making and pretend old-fashioned school. Kids love getting involved and doing chores at Slate Run. They offer nature trails, picnic grounds, and children's play facilities at the adjoining Slate Run Metro Park. On 14-acre Buzzard's Roost Lake, the park offers fishing for children 15 and younger. Lake is stocked with blue gill and large-mouth bass. The lake has an observation deck with a spotting scope for watching wildlife.

BUCKEYE LAKE STATE PARK

Buckeye Lake - ***2905 Liebs Island Road (9 miles South of Newark off State Route 13) Millersport, 43046. Phone: (740) 467-2690. http://parks.ohiodnr.gov/buckeyelake***

Buckeye Lake, constructed as a canal feeder lake in 1826, is Ohio's oldest state park. The park has long been a popular vacation spot and today offers endless water-related recreational opportunities including swimming, skiing, boating (unlimited hp) and fishing. Public swimming areas with parking facilities, change booths and latrines are located at Fairfield Beach and at Brooks Park on the south side of the lake. Permanent & rental properties are available around the lake.

In the 1930's, as many as 1,000 boats a day were crappie fishing on the lake.

CRANBERRY BOG ANNUAL OPEN HOUSE

Buckeye Lake - Cranberry Bog State Nature Preserve. https://naturepreserves.ohiodnr.gov/cranberrybog Take a tour of the island's rare and fascinating plants by pontoon boat. Admission. Permit lottery only. (last Saturday in June)

A.W. MARION STATE PARK

Circleville - *(5 miles East of Circleville off SR 23 to SR 22) 43113. Phone: (740) 869-3124. http://parks.ohiodnr.gov/awmarion*

454 acres of camping, hiking trails, boating and rentals, fishing, and winter sports. Electric motors only are permitted. The nearby floodplains of the Scioto River are adorned with a variety of wildflowers. The Hargus Lake Trail offers five miles of scenic pleasure, providing access to the entire shoreline of the lake. Wildlife indigenous to the area includes fox squirrel, ring-necked pheasant, a variety of songbirds, red fox and white-tailed deer.

CIRCLEVILLE PUMPKIN SHOW

Circleville - Downtown. www.pumpkinshow.com. (740) 474-7000. Ohio's largest and oldest harvest celebration has seven parades, lots of pumpkin, squash and gourds, pumpkin foods (cotton candy, burgers, chips and ice cream), rides and entertainment. See some of the largest pumpkins and the world's largest pumpkin pie (approximately 350 lbs. and 5 feet in diameter). Contests galore like hog calling, egg toss, pie eating and carved pumpkins. FREE. (mid-October, Wednesday-Saturday)

Columbus

COLUMBUS SPORTS

COLUMBUS BLUE JACKETS HOCKEY - (614) 246-PUCK or (800) NHL-

COLS or www.bluejackets.com. Nationwide Arena. NHL Hockey in Ohio. Look for their mascot, Stinger here and at special events. Season runs October-early April. Tickets range from $20-$185.

COLUMBUS CLIPPERS BASEBALL - www.clippersbaseball.com or (614) 462-5250. Huntington Park (Arena District). Semi-professional AAA farm team for the Cleveland Indians. LouSeal is the official mascot for the Columbus Clippers. Krash is the crazy parrot who has taken the position as LouSeal's First Mate. Many post game concerts and occasional fireworks. Play areas for kids south end of ballfield. Tickets: $7.00-$22.00. (April – Labor Day weekend)

COLUMBUS CREW SOCCER - Major League Soccer (Mid April – Late September). (614) 221-CREW or www.thecrew.com. Crew stadium (near Ohio State Fairgrounds). Prices start as low as $10.

OHIO STATE UNIVERSITY BUCKEYES - www.ohiostatebuckeyes.com. (614) 292-2524. Big 10 College sports: Football, Basketball (Men's & Women's), Hockey, OSU Ice Skating, Golf, Swimming, Tennis & Volleyball.

OHIO STATE UNIVERSITY MUSEUMS

Columbus - *Woody Hayes Dr. & High Street (most facilities between High St. & Olentangy River - off SR 315) 43201. Phone: (614) 292-3030. https://campusvisit.osu.edu/WalkingTour.pdf & https://campusvisit.osu.edu/fourways.pdf*

The Student Visitors Center (Room 132 Enarson Hall) provides a packet to chaperones. The self-guided tour (with tour brochure for kids) includes information about ten specific locations on campus, is interactive and suggests activities that the kids can do as they move through campus. It asks questions at each stop geared towards kids in order to get them more acquainted with the university. A completed tour should take about 1 - 1½ hours.

Many other "add-on" Tour Options are available:

ATHLETIC FACILITY TOURS – Schottenstein Center, Monday - Friday on non-event days between 9:00am-3:30pm. 60 minutes. (614) 292-3231. Ohio Stadium, Monday-Friday between 8:00am-5:00pm. (614) 292-9748. Athletic Facility Tours are for groups of students ages 12+.

JACK NICKLAUS MUSEUM - 2355 Olentangy River Road. Tuesday-Saturday 9:00am-5:00pm. www.nicklausmuseum.org. Admission: $5.00-$10.00. Shows the long history of the game, Mr. Nicklaus' place in that history, famous OSU golfers and a prototype of the Nicklaus family's den with personal stories narrated by his wife.

WEXNER CENTER FOR THE ARTS – Family days and guided tours. (614) 292-3535 or www.wexarts.org/ctr/gen/overview.shtml.

CARTOON LIBRARY & MUSEUM– http://cartoons.osu.edu. Located in Sullivant Hall, 1813 N. High Street, The Billy Ireland Cartoon Library & Museum houses the world's largest collection of comic strip tear sheets and clippings.

BIOLOGICAL SCIENCES GREENHOUSE FACILITY – Insectary, a quarantine facility, two research labs, a growth chamber area and prep room. https://bioscigreenhouse.osu.edu/visiting. Must be with group or join group tour. No self-guided. Monday - Friday 8:30am-4:30pm, except holidays.

FOOD SCIENCE BUILDING – tours of miniature pilot plant, OSU Dairy Store (ice cream treats, breakfast, lunch items), Parker Building, 2015 Fyffe Road (off Woody Hayes Dr) (614) 292-6281.

ORTON GEOLOGICAL MUSEUM – skeleton of a giant sloth, fossils, fluorescent minerals, and rocks. The museum is also home to fossil skeleton of a 7-foot-tall giant ground sloth, Megalonyx Jeffersonian. 9:00am-5:00pm. On the oval, free to the public. http://library.osu.edu/sites/geology/museum/index.php.

HISTORIC COSTUME & TEXTILES COLLECTION – (614) 292-3090. Historic textiles from the 15th century to 20th century in costume pieces including men's, women's, and children's garments and accessories. http://costume.osu.edu/visit-us/ 175 Campbell Hall.

OHIO STATEHOUSE

Columbus - *1 Capitol Square, Broad and High Streets (10 acre square in downtown) 43201. Phone: (614) 728-6350 or (888) OHIO-123. www.ohiostatehouse.org/visit/public-tours. Hours: Weekdays 8am-5pm, Weekends 11am-4pm. Admission: FREE. Tours: For groups fewer than 10, free guided tours offered Monday through Friday on the hour from 10am until 3pm, and on Saturdays & Sundays from noon until 3pm. Self-Guided Tours. Visitors may wander on their own anytime during Statehouse hours with a self-guided tour brochure to follow at your own pace. Self guided tour brochures are available at the 3rd Street Information Desk. Note: Museum shop has clever & unique Ohio gifts and souvenirs. Educators: activities and presentations about govt: www.ohiostatehouse.org/visit/school-and-group-tours/teacher-resources*

Learn about Ohio's Statehouse history, its architecture and the legislative process. Visit the place where Abraham Lincoln made speeches in 1859 and 1861. Inside you'll see the rotunda with the state seal and historic paintings and documents. The sweeping grand staircase of the Senate Building was modeled after the Paris Opera House. Restored to its original grandeur in 1996, the Statehouse is filled with priceless historic art, including a marble bust of Abraham Lincoln – the only one the President posed for during his lifetime. Even the Statehouse's expansive grounds have a history, as Civil War Union soldiers frequently camped there. If the Ohio House or Senate is in session, you'll be able to listen to the debates. Educational displays and touch-screen kiosks (ex. Pass through all 88 counties in the Map Room) along with a great Museum shop are found in the basement. The basement is all white painted brick and stone. Why are the formal walls painted light shades of pink or peach? The Atrium used to be called Pigeon Alley - why?

OHIO STATEHOUSE MUSEUM: Interactive, hands-on exhibits challenge visitors' knowledge about Ohio history and the workings of state government and equip them to more fully participate as citizens. Historical artifacts and images tell the stories of those who designed and built the Statehouse and those who have come here to serve. Audiovisual media and theatrical effects will transport visitors to historical events and invite them to imagine themselves governor, legislator or judge.

HOLIDAY TOURS ON CAPITOL SQUARE

Columbus - Ohio Statehouse. Step back in time with a guided tour of the 1861 Statehouse and see holiday decorations as they were in Victorian times. Holiday concerts and occasional activities for kids. sale at store. (monthlong Dec)

COLUMBUS CHILDREN'S THEATRE

Columbus - *512 Park Street (1/2 block north of North Market) 43203. http://colschildrenstheatre.org. Phone: (614) 224-6672.*

Theatre activities for youth of all ages, backgrounds and cultures. Do you remember your first magical theatrical moment? That moment when your heart flew into your mouth, you caught your breath and you were transferred to a new magical world? One of the greatest joys of theatre is witnessing a child's Wide-Eyed-Wonder when they really connect to a play. Many lessons to be learned watching plays like Oliver, Emperors New Clothes or the annual Christmas show. Tickets run $15-$25.00 per person, per show. Children's theatre classes are held at different campuses (downtown, Grove City, Gahanna, Westerville, Dublin and Pickerington). (July-May)

FRANKLIN PARK CONSERVATORY AND BOTANICAL GARDENS

Columbus - *1777 East Broad Street (off I-71) 43203. Phone: (614) 645-TREE or (800) 214-PARK. www.fpconservatory.org. Hours: Daily 10:00am-5:00pm. Admission: $19 adult, $16 senior/student, $12 child (3-17). Note: Café and gift shop. Hot Shop - watch local gaffers demonstrate the art of glass blowing. Family activities each season including Blooms & Butterflies, Holidays, and Orchid Forest.*

A place where you can learn where coffee comes from or watch the careful pruning of Bonsai trees. The kid-friendly ants, iguanas, and lories are becoming enhancements to the conservatory. The large 1895 glass structure resembles the style of London's Crystal Palace. The Conservatory is the only public botanical garden in the world to own a signature collection of Chihuly's artworks, which represents more than 3,000 pieces of glass. Flowers and mushrooms and vines - all made from glass - this color and art really engages the imagination. Chihuly's work is modern art but never "out there" and even more special when presented amongst greenery and natural light. Walk through a simulated tropical rain forest, a desert, a tree fern forest, a Pacific Island water garden and then on to the Himalayan Mountains. Outside is a sculpture garden.

OHIO HISTORY CENTER

Columbus - *1982 Velma Avenue (I-71 to 17th Avenue Exit) 43211. Phone: (614) 297-2300. www.ohiohistory.org/visit/ohio-history-center. Hours: Wednesday-Sunday 10:00am-5:00pm. Closed Christmastime, Thanksgiving. Admission: $13.00 adult, $11.00 senior (60+) & college students,$7.00 student (4-12). Includes Ohio Village entrance (if open). Tours: Blast from the Past and Discovery Days bring out the hands-on fun. Educators: www.ohiohistoryteachers.org is the OHS website with state history lesson plans and activities. Pick up Educational Resource scavenger hunt game flyers near many area entrances. Note: Gift Shop, food and picnic tables. The adjacent Ohio Village is now open summers & for signature events. Ohio Village is designed to recreate the appearance of a typical county-seat town in Ohio during the mid 19th century, about the time of the Civil War.*

There are exhibits and artifacts covering the history of Ohio from archaeology to natural history and the history of Ohio. There are many historical collections from early fossils and Indian tribes (large dioramas and artifact study of prehistoric Indians), original accounts from early explorers, and papers from political leaders such as General Meigs and Thomas Worthington. Other highlights of this history gallery are 1920s children's activities, including a log cabin and pioneer kitchen, where young people can try on pioneer clothes, operate a spinning wheel and "cook" pioneer food. The Center's permanent natural history exhibit features Ohio's plants, animals, geology, geography, and climate and weather.

"The Nature of Ohio" exhibit is guarded by a huge mastodon found in a swamp in Clark County. See the quirky 2-headed calf and Egyptian mummy, too. Continuous early 1900s newsreels, an operating 1880s carriage shop, vintage automobiles, Adena Pipe and Hopewell mica cutouts are here, too. Unique spots highlight the history of White Castle fast food started in Columbus and a space called "What is it?" with objects that make us scratch our heads.

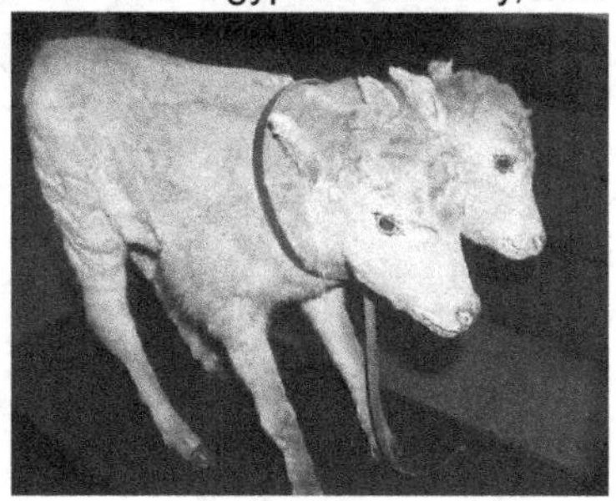

BALLETMET

Columbus - ***322 Mt. Vernon Ave. 43215. www.balletmet.org. Phone: (614) 229-4860. Educators: Fun and Games, links to sample lessons, etc.: http://www.balletmet.org/education-materials/***

Classic to contemporary ballet including the famous Nutcracker. Sneak Peeks - spend time with dancers or Morning at the Ballet (mini programs like Cinderella) seem to engage the younger kids the most.

CENTRAL OHIO FIRE MUSEUM&LEARNING CTR

Columbus - ***260 N. 4th Street, No. 16 Engine House 43215. Phone: (614) 464-4099. www.centralohiofiremuseum.com. Hours: Tuesday-Saturday, 10:00am-4:00pm. Group tours by appointment only. Admission: $6.00 adult, $5.00 senior, $4.00 student, Under 6 FREE.***

Visually, the hand-drawn, horse-drawn, & motorized fire vehicles will initially interest the kids. Curiosity will have them asking firefighters about the day-to-day lives in an engine house. Then, kids can climb on board a fire engine, slide down a fire pole, and video drive through a smoke-filled bedroom. Walk through a kitchen to see what dangers may lurk. A child paramedic can sit in the back of an ambulance, access a patient and listen to the radio calls coming in. On a group tour? Look for Boots the Fire Mouse as your escort.

COLUMBUS MUSEUM OF ART

Columbus - ***480 East Broad Street (four blocks east of the Capitol) 43215. Phone: (614) 221-4848 info line. www.columbusmuseum.org. Hours: Tuesday-Sunday 10:00am-5:00pm. Thursday until 9pm. Admission: $18.00 adult, $9.00 senior and student (age 4-17). Military FREE. FREE for all on Sunday. Parking is free. New Cafe ($5 Kids Menu) and Gift Shop (w/ large children's area).***

American and European art from 1850-1950. Also the new wing is full of contemporary works. See the life-size horse of welded steel or the works of Columbus realist George Bellows and folk artist Elijah Pierce. Doodles and First Saturdays are weekly programs for families. Ask the front desk for My Museum Gallery/Sculpture Guide. Art Speaks audio tour $3.00 - is where art talks. Family Adventures offers art-interactive docent-led creative, colorful weekdays where kids learn how works of art are created and preserved. The Center for Creativity is a family-friendly experience, complete with hands-on activities, such as sculpture making, a Creativity Challenge, and an interactive Wonder Room, where visitors interact with art as well as create art.

COLUMBUS SYMPHONY ORCHESTRA

Columbus - ***55 East State Street (most performances at Ohio Theatre) 43215. Phone: (614) 228-8600. www.columbussymphony.com***

Enjoy several family performances with pre-concert activities. Tickets start at $10.

COSI

Columbus - ***333 West Broad Street (I-71 exit Broad or Front St. or I-70 exit Broad or Fourth St. to downtown riverfront) 43215. Phone: (614) 228-COSI or (888) 819-COSI. www.cosi.org. Hours: Wednesday-Sunday 10:00am-5:00pm, Fridays til 9pm. Open holiday Mondays. Closed most major winter holidays and first two weeks of September. Admission: $25 adult, $20child (2-12). Special exhibits and movies add on $6.00+. Note: Science 2 Go Store, AtomiCafé.***

Explore hands-on exhibits focusing on science, technology, health and history. Take your preschool-aged children to Kid-Space. They pretend they are a doctor or nurse, paint their faces, do a puppet show, water play, ride in a boat, and just have a good active time there. Other favorite areas are Big Science Park (outdoor), where older kids conquer their fears and ride the high wire cycle. Ocean Learning World features a simulated shipwreck with dive tanks and a yellow submarine you can climb inside. Progress is where you travel through time and interact with people in a small Midwestern town. Gadgets is a giant "erector set".

The Life area has an Echo Free room, Hot/Cold Coils and Rat Basketball (plus some mature displays that make this area PG). In Space, you get dizzy in a tunnel and see a great space 3D movie. The idea of "learning worlds" really makes visitors feel like they are someplace else.

THURBER HOUSE

Columbus - ***77 Jefferson Avenue (Downtown) (I-71 exit Broad Street, head west one block and turn north on Jefferson) 43215. www.thurberhouse.org. Phone: (614) 464-1032. Hours: Tuesday, Thursday, Saturday, Sunday 1:00-4:00pm except major holidays. Tours: Self-guided tours are free. Visitors have the option of taking a guided tour (on Sundays) for a small fee of $4.00 for adults and $2.00 for students and seniors. Group tours by reservation.***

James Thurber, the well-known humorist and cartoonist, grew up in Columbus. The restored home is where James lived during his college years. Thurber House is a living museum. They allow visitors to experience Thurber's life by becoming a guest of the Thurber family. While in the house museum, visitors are invited to sit on the chairs, play a tune on the downstairs piano, or, touch the typewriter that was Thurber's while he was at the New Yorker. The house is featured in several of Thurber's stories. (Stories about the time Thurber lived in this house are included in his My Life and Hard Times and The Thurber Carnival.) Be sure to read some of Thurber's works before you visit or purchase some of his books at the bookstore in Thurber House.

TOPIARY GARDEN

Columbus - ***480 East Town Street (Old Deaf School Park, NW corner of E. Town & Washington, downtown, east of the Main Library) 43215. Phone: (614) 645-0197. www.topiarygarden.org. Hours: Visitor Center open Tuesday, Thursday, Saturday, 11:00am-3:00pm and Sunday Noon-4pm (April-December). Educators: http://www.topiarypark.org/activities.html***

The topiary (greenery shaped like people, boats, animals, etc.) garden and pond depicts the theme "A Sunday Afternoon on the Island of La Grande Jaffe". FREE (open daily dawn to dusk).

AL'S DELICIOUS POPCORN(THE POPCORN OUTLET)

Fun Fact: How high can popcorn kernels pop? Up to 3 feet in the air.

Columbus - *1500 Bethel Road (SR 315 to Bethel Road exit west) 43220. Phone: (614) 279-3964. www.popcornstorecolumbus.com. Hours: Monday-Saturday 11:00am-7:00pm. Admission: FREE. Tours: By Appointment, Approximately 20-30 minutes. Tours are limited to 25 people.*

This wonderfully enthusiastic staff will answer every question you've ever had about popcorn. Kids love watching the 2-minute video tour of the large poppers and closely watch the popped corn flow out. They have a tremendous assortment of 60 spicy and sweet flavors to coat the popcorn. They have a challenge presented with the Bubble Gum flavor: If you can blow a bubble from it (it tastes that real!), you get free popcorn. You won't leave without trying lots of favorite flavors like Pizza, Buckeye Mix or Jelly Bean. Kids and parents will want to bring their allowance to spend on these treats! Their huge selection of colorful tins will fill many of your gift needs. A great "quick stop" as part of a day trip.

GRAETER'S ICE CREAM PLAYLAND

Columbus - *2136 Bethel Road (near intersection of Sawmill Road) 43220. Phone: (614) 442-7622. www.graeters.com. Hours: Daily 10am-10pm.*

You'll enjoy informative videos and see their unique French Pot process that makes only two gallons of ice cream at a time (old-fashioned, no air whipped in as in modern, commercial brands). Try a dip of the signature chocolate-chipped flavors. Specially made liquid chocolate is poured into the ice cream, frozen and then broken by paddles, creating planks of dark chocolate within the ice cream. The Lil Pints Soft Play Area may be just the place (indoors) to let the kids expend some of their sugar energy.

ANTHONY THOMAS CANDY COMPANY

Columbus - ***1777 Arlingate Lane (I-270W to Roberts Road Exit) 43228. Phone: (614) 274-8405 or (877)Candy-21. www.anthony-thomas.com. Admission: $1-$2.00 (age 3+). Admission fee may be used towards a purchase. Tours: Tuesdays and Thursdays from 9am to 3pm. Also Wednesdays each summer. You don't need to make an appointment and there is no size limit on the group. Free sample at end of tours. Approximately 60 minutes. Factory Candy Shop Note: Gift shop open during tour times. You finish your tour in the retail store.***

Have you seen "Willy Wonka's Chocolate Factory?" This tour will remind you of that movie, especially when you first see the clean, bright white equipment, near spotless floors and dozens of silver insulated pipes running to several production lines. View chocolate and fillings being prepared and molded in rooms remaining at a constant 90 degrees F. with 0% humidity (so workers and chocolate don't sweat!) Walk along the comfortable, glass-enclosed suspended "Cat-Walk" and observe eight lines producing 25,000 pounds of chocolates per shift. A couple of wrapping machines are exclusively for fundraisers and airline chocolates, but most of the production line packers can be seen hand packing chocolates for stores. A giant physics and chemistry cooking lesson!

LEGOLAND DISCOVERY CENTER

Columbus - ***157 Easton Town Center (I-70 exit 107) 43219. www.fortrapids.com. Hours: Daily 10am-7pm. Open until 8pm Saturdays. Admission: Day Pass $24 per person (age 2+); Online discounts.***

LEGOLAND Discovery Center Columbus is a 36,000-square-foot, two-story, indoor attraction that features: Two interactive rides: Kingdom Quest and Merlin's Apprentice. A 4D Cinema where you can enjoy your favorite LEGO movies with additional wind, rain and snow effects. 10 LEGO play zones including an area where you can build and test your own race cars and a LEGO DUPLO area for younger children. MINILAND Ohio which includes iconic landmarks from Columbus, Cleveland, Cincinnati made out of over 1.5 million LEGO bricks.

"We are all about families having fun together through playful learning," said management. "We provide two to three hours of interactive and educational entertainment for families, no matter the weather! We want children and their parents to be inspired to build anything, anywhere inside the attraction."

RED, WHITE AND BOOM

Columbus - Downtown. www.redwhiteandboom.org. Full day of parades, rides, entertainment and the largest fireworks display synchronized to music and lights in the Midwest. (July 3rd)

OHIO STATE FAIR

Columbus - Ohio Expo Center, I-71 & 17th Avenue. www.ohiostatefair.com. Includes the largest junior fair in the nation, puppet shows, petting zoo, rodeo, tractor pulls, horse shows, fishing and lumberjack shows, exhibitors from agriculture to the arts, rides and big name entertainment. Favorite family areas include: the Natural Resources area (live wildlife, log cabin, butterfly house); the Nursery; and the Butter Cow sculpture and ice cream. Admission. Family Value Day on Monday. (twelve days beginning end of July thru the first week of Aug)

GREEK FESTIVAL

Columbus - Greek Orthodox Cathedral, Short North Area, 555 N. High Street. Gyros, baklava, music, dance, tours of the church, cooking demos and videos about Greece. Admission. (Labor Day wkend) www.columbusgreekfestival.com

FIRST NIGHT COLUMBUS

Columbus - Ohio Statehouse Square & downtown locations. A family oriented non-alcoholic event with indoor and outdoor activities such as kid's/parent's food, entertainment and crafts, and a countdown to midnight. www.firstnightcolumbus.com. Admission. (New Years Eve)

IRISH FESTIVAL

Columbus (Dublin) - Coffman Park, 6665 Coffman Road. www.dublinirishfestival.org. A weekend of all things Irish, from entertainment, dance competitions and sports demos to the very best in Irish foods. Kids fun includes: Ferry Teas, Pirates Parties, Caber Toss, Braemer Stone throw, Irish Dancing, Storytelling, crafts, playland with inflatables. Admission. (first weekend of Aug)

MOTTS MILITARY MUSEUM

Columbus (Groveport) - *5075 South Hamilton Road (I-270 exit Rte 33/SR 317) 43125. Phone: (614) 836-1500. www.mottsmilitarymuseum.org. Hours: Tuesday-Saturday 9:00am-5:00pm, Sunday 1:00-5:00pm. Admission: $10.00 adult, $8.00 senior, $5.00 student.*

Its purpose is to bring military history into perspective by collecting and preserving memorabilia. Secondly, it educates the public on the importance of past, present and new military events that impact our lives (good way to "tie-in" current events). Best on a group tour with a specific theme in mind.

FRANKLIN COUNTY FAIR

Columbus (Hilliard) - Franklin County Fairgrounds. www.fcfair.org. Open during the fair is Northwest Village including the church, 1850's log cabin, outhouse, caboose, train station, granary, barn and museum with vintage household equipment. Admission. (mid-July for 7 days)

MOTORCYCLE HALL OF FAME MUSEUM

Columbus (Pickerington) - *13515 Yarmouth Drive (I-70 east exit 112A, left on SR 204) 43147. Phone: (614) 856-2222. www.motorcyclemuseum.org. Hours: Daily 9:00am-5:00pm. Closed winter holidays. Admission: $10.00 adult, $5.00 AMA members, $8.00 senior, $3.00 student (12-17). FREE child (under 12).*

The Museum is more than just a wide range of motorcycles on display. Its goal is to tell the stories and history of motorcycling. A self-guided tour features a wall mural, the history of motorcycles, and the Glory Days. Themed "sets" (some permanent - some traveling) add to the presentation. Be sure to visit their website for current exhibits. If you're a custom bike lover, this exhibit is for you; lots of chrome, lots of heavy metal, and exotic paint schemes. Kids are most attracted to the 50 motorcycles on display. Motocross, BMW, and Harley abound here.

PHOENIX BATS FACTORY

Columbus (Plain City) - *7801 Corporate Blvd, Suite E (I-270 exit Rte 33/SR 317) 43064. Phone: (614) 873-7776. www.phoenixbats.com. Hours: Weekdays 9:00am-5:00pm. Tours: Open tours are available Mondays and Fridays at 1:30pm. No reservation required - just show up. Includes a custom engraved mini bat to commemorate your visit. $10/person.*

The Phoenix Bat Company is a specialized wooden-bat creator and manufacturer. The company produces premium rock maple and northern white ash baseball and softball bats. Combining premium grade woods with the most advanced, state of the art lathe in the bat manufacturing industry.

During the one hour tour you'll learn about how the business got started with vintage baseball players and a man who liked to make wood spindles. Next, they highlight which MLB pros use the bats and show samples of their specially ordered bats. Names like Ordonez, Carerra and Ramirez perked the boys' ears. Next move into the computer corner to see how the bat is generated on a graphics program first, then sent into the factory to be produced.

The computer generated model is now fed into the humongous Italian lathe that takes a large dowel of wood and in one slow back and forth motion forms and sands the baseball bat into shape!

The finishing process is messy. Lots of dipping (and dripping stations) abound in a separate temperature controlled room. Finally, you watch the engraver embed a special logo or message into each bat. That same engraver is used to specialize your personal mini-bat tour souvenir.

COLUMBUS ZOO AND AQUARIUM

Columbus (Powell) - *4850 Powell Road (Route 257, I-270 to Sawmill Road exit, follow signs) 43065. Phone: (614) 645-3400. www.columbuszoo.org. Hours: Daily 9:00am-7:00pm (Summer), Daily 10:00am-4:00pm (September-May). Closed only Thanksgiving & Christmas. Admission: $21.99 adult, $16.99 senior (60+) and child (3-9). Discounts for Franklin county residents. Discount combo ticket w/Zoombezi Bay available. Tuesday is Senior Day and Mon-Weds is half off admission for Franklin County residents. Half price admission in Jan & Feb. $10.00 Parking fee. Note: Gift Shops and Concessions. Food Court. Pony, Camel, boat, train and carousel rides ($1-$4 each or all ride wristband). Jungle Jacks Landing (all ride wristband $10). Play gym. Picnic facilities.*

The famous Director Emeritus of the zoo, Jack Hanna, is a regular on national talk shows. Highlights of the naturally landscaped zoo include cheetahs, black rhinos, lowland gorillas, Habitat Hollow (what makes human/animal habitats home- play & pet area), and North American eagles. A 100,000-gallon coral reef exhibit, Stingray Bay touchtank (extra fee), and one of the largest reptile collections in the United States are also featured. The habitat "Manatee Coast" is modeled after the famous Island Refuge in Florida with a 190,000 gallon pool and floor to ceiling

glass viewing walls! The expanded African Forest exhibit offers a walk-through rainforest-themed area with incredible interaction with monkeys.

Other exhibits include the Islands of Southeast Asia (primitive ruins, Indonesian buildings and music, komodo dragons, orangutans and otters) and an Australia area. A waterway allows narrated boat rides through the exhibit to give visitors a different view while still providing more room for the animals to roam freely. Polar Frontier is home to polar bears, brown bears, arctic foxes, reindeer and mountain goats in a 13-acre exhibit space.

Old-fashioned amusement rides are found at Adventure Cove. Try splashing down a log flume, the sea dragon coaster, bumber cars, scrambler, tea cups, etc. It just keeps getting better!

EGGS, PAWS & CLAWS

Columbus (Powell) - Columbus Zoo and Aquarium. Ages 2-12. Admission. Easter Bunny appearance, treat stations, egg hunts, and kids' entertainment and crafts. (Usually held the Friday/Saturday before Easter).

WILDLIGHTS

Columbus (Powell) - Columbus Zoo and Aquarium. Something for everyone, millions of lights, zoo animals of all kinds, and when we visited we even saw an underwater "Santa in a diving suit" - What fun! Great hot chocolate, too! Ice skating, carolers, delicious treats and wagon/train rides. Walk-thru. Daily, evenings. Admission. (Thanksgiving - January 1)

ZOOMBEZI BAY

Columbus (Powell) ***- 10101 Riverside Drive (Route 257, I-270 to Sawmill Road exit, follow signs) 43065. Phone: (614) 645-3550. www.zoombezibay.columbuszoo.org Hours: Typically 11:00am-6:00pm. (Memorial Day weekend thru Labor Day). Extended summer break hours. Adm: $27-$35 per person. Online discounts.***

The park right next to the Columbus Zoo has 15 contemporary water slides with names such as Cyclone, Sea Snakes and Tahitian Twister. Wave pool fanatics like us love the 4 foot waves created in Wild Tides, while Baboon Lagoon provides safe water fun for younger kids with 12 marine animal play structures and another giant pool that is only about a foot deep. Families can "base" from ample chairs and tables available at central locations by the wave pool or the kiddie lagoon.

We also liked their menu selection and pricing. Fried food, modest entrees and even a dozen healthy (and yummy, try the grilled caesar chicken salad wrap) choices are offered at fair prices with generous portions.

TOMATO FESTIVAL

Columbus (Reynoldsburg) - Civic Park, 6800 Daugherty Drive. (614) 866-2861. www.reynoldsburgtomatofestival.org. Ohio's tomato harvest is celebrated with things like free tomato juice, fried green tomatoes, tomato pies, tomato fudge, tomato cakes & cookies, Tiny Tim Tomatoland, crafts, parade and The Largest Tomato Contest ($100 per pound). Fee for parking. (September - Weds-Sun)

HANBY HOUSE

Columbus (Westerville) - *160 West Main Street (across from Otterbein College, between SR 3 & Cleveland Ave.) 43081. www.hanbyhouse.orge Phone: (614) 891-6289. Hours: Saturday and Sunday 1:00-4:00pm (May-September). Groups by appointment. Admission: $1.00 - $3.00 per person.*

"Up on the Housetop reindeer pause, Out Jumps dear ol' Santa Claus. " Hanby played many roles in his life; student, abolitionist, father, teacher, minister. But it was as a composer that we remember him. Benjamin Hanby was the composer of over 80 folk songs and hymns including "Sweet Nelly Gray" and "Up On the Housetop". Children will enjoy seeing Ben's original instruments and musical scores. This home was part of the Underground Railroad. Be sure to notice and ask about the roses in a vase by the front window. The tour also includes viewing a short introduction movie.

OHIO RAILWAY MUSEUM

Columbus (Worthington) - *990 Proprietors Road (Off State Route 161, just past railroad tracks, head north) 43085. www.ohiorailwaymuseum.org/. Phone: (614) 885-7345. Hours: Sunday Noon-4:00 pm (May-September). Admission: $7.00-$9.00 (age 4+).*

They have displayed approximately 30 pieces of Ohio Railway History dating from 1897 – 1950. The guide explains that steam engines have their own personality. Get close to one under steam and hear it talk! Try a hand truck or catch a one mile trolley. Special seasonal train excursions take you on a steam train day-trip. See website for details. Small admission for museum.

ORANGE JOHNSON HOUSE

Columbus (Worthington) - *956 High Street (just north of State Route 161) 43085. Phone: (614) 846-1676. www.worthingtonhistory.org. Hours: (Open House) Sunday 2:00-5:00pm (April-December). Closed holidays. Admission: $3.00-$5.00 which includes a tour.*

This place is best known by locals for cooking and combs! The Orange Johnson House is a restored early 1800's home. This property offers a unique view of both the pioneer and antebellum periods in Worthington. Part of it is Federal style, the back part is pioneer. There are many authentic objects and toys that children can pick up and pretend to use. In 1816 Orange Johnson, a hornsmith, who specialized in comb-making bought the property. Visitors learn about the comb making trade and see a collection of 19th century women's hair combs. The guide will describe chores children were given in those days (your own children will think they have it made!). A good time to visit is when they have cooking demonstrations. The smell in the air engages everyone to explore early settler's kitchen tools and techniques. The Old Rectory in downtown Worthington has a doll museum with changing exhibits.

CHRISTMAS OPEN HOUSE

Columbus (Worthington) - Orange Johnson House. You are invited to stroll through the beautifully decorated 19th century house, sample holiday treats in front of the keeping room fireplace and listen to traditional music in the drawing room. Open house is free. Programs have fee. (first and third Sunday in December)

AMERICAN WHISTLE CORPORATION

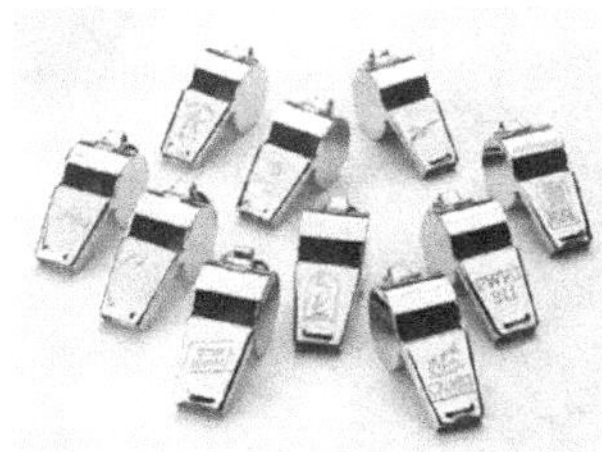

Columbus (Worthington) - *6540 Huntley Road (I-71 to Route 161 west, turn right on Huntley-look for small sign) 43229. www.americanwhistle.com. Phone: (800) 876-2918. Admission: $5.00 per person. Tours: Monday-Friday 9:00am-5:00pm. One hour long, 15-40 people, appointment necessary. Don't have at least 15 people? They can add your group onto an already existing tour. Note: Gift shop where you'll want to buy a lanyard to go with your new whistle or a gold plated whistle! Educators: the Ohio Grade 4 curriculum includes learning what is involved in the factors of production include land, labor, capital and entrepreneurship...all covered at the factory tour.*

Do you know what a lanyard is? Do you know what makes a whistle louder? See and hear the only metal whistle manufactured in the United States (used by police, referees, coaches, etc.). These "American Classics" are the loudest whistles in the world - 4 decibels higher pitch than the competitors! You'll learn everything you ever wanted to know about whistles and really get to see a small manufacturing operation up close. See mechanical engineering at work - in one-of-a-kind machines designed to perform specific tasks. Learn how a whistle works - and how sciences like aerodynamics and chemistry contribute. Learn how a whistle can be an effective safety tool for people of all ages. These people know how to give great tours!

Delaware

ALUM CREEK STATE PARK

Delaware - *3615 South Old State Road (7 miles Southeast of Delaware off State Route 36/37, 1 mile West of I-71) 43015. http://parks.ohiodnr.gov/alumcreek. Phone: (740) 548-4631.*

8,600 acres with a great sandy beach! Food service is available at the marina. Camping (tent, RV, and cabin rentals), hiking trails, lots of good boating, boaters swimming holes, boat rentals, fishing, a Nature Center and winter sports. Over forty miles of trail wind along the lakeshore through mature beech-maple forests and across deep ravines. The forest is home to the fox squirrel, woodchuck, rabbit, white-tail deer and many other species of wildlife. And, they have a great Dog Park and Beach area just for dogs of all sizes (separate areas) to play by the water, too. Snowshoes, our beagle, loves this place best. Because they're so close to metro Columbus, they host many well-attended seasonal events on and off the water (ex. Fall Fest, Fishing Tournaments).

ALUM CREEK HOLIDAY FANTASY OF LIGHTS

Delaware - Alum Creek State Park. Hundreds of thousands of lights and holiday/ storybook characters. Entrance is at Campgrounds. Drive thru. Free cookies and cocoa with Santa.Daily, evenings (unless noted). Adm. (Thanksgiving - Jan 1)

DELAWARE STATE PARK

Delaware - *(6 miles North of Delaware on US 23) 43015. Phone: (740) 369-2761. http://parks.ohiodnr.gov/delaware.*

Dense woodlands, expansive meadows and a reservoir blend to create Delaware State Park. Once home to the Delaware Indians, this recreational area offers 3,145 acres of camping, hiking trails, boating and rentals, fishing, swimming, and winter sports. The trails connect the lakeshore with each of the four camping areas, transecting meadows, woodlands and wetlands. Eat at the nearby Hamburger Inn, (740) 369-3850, 16 N. Sandusky St, 50's theme.

OLENTANGY INDIAN CAVERNS

Delaware - *1779 Home Road (US 23 North to Home Road, follow signs, 6 miles north of I-270) 43015. Phone: (740) 548-7917. www.olentangyindiancaverns.com. Hours: Daily 9:30am-5:00pm (April-October). Admission: $9.95 adult, $6.95 child (7-16). Note: Large picnic facilities. Frontierland with gem mining, maze, and*

mini-golf $5.00 extra. Gift shop. The caverns not wheelchair or stroller accessible. Guided tours (summers). Otherwise you can tour on your own.

Wyandot Indians used these underground caves until 1810 for protection from the weather and their enemies. The caves were formed by an underground river that flows to the Olentangy River hundreds of feet below the surface. The caves were originally discovered during a search for oxen that broke loose from a wagon train. The tour lasts 30 minutes and takes you through winding passages and coves underground. Then, you visit the museum where Indian artifacts found in the caves are displayed. If you're still in an adventurous mood, play some outdoor games.

PERKINS OBSERVATORY

Delaware - *3199 Columbus Pike (2 miles south of Delaware, 1 miles south of US 23/SR 315) 43015. Phone: (740) 363-1257. http://perkins.owu.edu/ Hours: Friday nights. Admission: $10.00 general. Recommended order in advance, by phone.*

Gaze at the galaxies, count the craters on the moon, and enjoy an entertaining astronomy lesson along with a historical tour of this unique observatory built in 1923. Children who have studied astronomy will especially enjoy this. The stars naturally fascinate them at night so this is a real treat to see them this close. The program includes a tour of the observatory, an amusing talk on astronomy, and then telescope observation if it is a clear night (otherwise, maybe a planetarium show). There's also Mind & Space games in the Kids Zone area. Occasional lawn telescope observation and rocket launches.

MAPLE SYRUP FESTIVAL

Delaware - Camp Lazarus. 4422 Columbus Pike. www.camplazarus.org. (740) 548-5502. Syrup making demos. Pancake dinners/breakfasts. Sugarbush tours by foot or by wagon or by train. Admission. (weekends in March)

HARVEST FAIR, STRATFORD ECOLOGICAL

Delaware - Stratford Ecological Center. 3083 Liberty Road. 43015 www.stratfordecologicalcenter.org. Entertainers & storytellers take over the main stage. Big kids are occupied as the pasture becomes "Kid's World" with kites, stilts, face painting, and a giant earth ball. Little tykes are kept active in the hay bale toddler area with farm toys. Kids of all ages can climb on a tractor, make apple cider, ride on a horse-drawn wagon, make paper, grind grain, etc.Stratford sells home-grown food for lunch and volunteers provide baked goods for sale. The Center is also open to the public wkdays plus programs on wkends. Admission. (third Saturday in September)

LITTLE BROWN JUG & ALL HORSE PARADE

Delaware - Delaware County Fairgrounds, 236 Pennsylvania Avenue. (800) 335-3247 or www.littlebrownjug.com. The most coveted horse race for three-year old pacers held on the fastest half-mile track in the world. Kick off parade with the largest all-horse, mule and donkey parade east of the Mississippi. Admission. (mid-September - Saturdays only)

FLINT RIDGE

Glenford - 15300 Flint Ridge Rd. (SR 16 east to SR 668 south) 43739. Phone: (740) 787-2476 or (800) 283-8707. www.flintridgeohio.org. Hours: Saturday & Sunday 10am-5:00pm (May-October). Admission: $3-$5.00. Note: Flint Preserve open year-round, 9:30am to Dusk.

Because of flint's features, it has been respected throughout the ages and used in the making of tools, weapons, ceremonial objects of native cultures, and in modern times in the production of jewelry. Indians came to see this stretch of hills for flint stone (official gemstone of the State of Ohio). Displays show how flint is formed from silica and what objects can be made today with flint (like sparks that start flames when flint is rubbed against steel). Outdoors you can explore the trails past ancient quarry pits. There are several hiking trails and a paved nature trail with Braille and regular text for visitors looking for a beautiful hiking area. How else can we use flint?

FALL FUN DAYS

Grove City - Circle S Farms. 9015 London Groveport Rd. www.circlesfarm.com. Pumpkin Patches/ Hayrides/ Corn Mazes/ Fall Playland - Admission. 2 mazes, entertainment on weekends, snack bar & autumn treats. Plan on at least two hours playtime. Open weekends, some weekdays (by appointment) and weeknights. (late September - late October).

GREAT CIRCLE EARTHWORKS

Heath - *455 Hebron Road (I-70 to SR 79 north, follow signs to Convention & Visitors Bureau) 43056. www.ohiohistory.org/visit/museum-and-site-locator/newark-earthworks Phone: (800) 589-8224. Hours: Park open daylight hours all year. Museum open Summers Wednesdays&Thursdays too. Friday-Sunday Noon-4:00pm. Note: The Great Circle Museum is also the new home of the Licking County Convention and Visitors Bureau.*

The Moundbuilders is a circular mound 1200 feet in diameter with walls 8 to 14 feet high. The Hopewell Indians were believed to exist between 100BC and 500AD - around the same time as the New Testament. A small museum and county visitors center orient you by touch screen options and large screen video to this ancient people and the mysterious giant circular mound (the largest ever!). As you walk outside, you walk right into the mouth opening of a circular mound. Once inside, just imagine the Hopewell Indian ceremonies that occurred many years ago. Research has concluded that the central Eagle shaped mound was the site of a grand ceremonial site. Octagon Earthworks and Wright Earthworks are both additional local sites that preserve other features of prehistoric Ohio. Admission is free, donations accepted.

PUMPKIN MAZE PLAYLAND

Hebron - 4413 National Road SW, Pigeon Roost Farm, 43025(I-70 exit 122 to Rte. 40). Pumpkin Patches / Hayrides / Corn Mazes / Fall Playland - Admission (average $7.00). Plan on at least two hours playtime. Open Tuesday-Sunday 10am-7pm. www.pigeonroostfarm.com. (mid September - late October).

Lancaster

AHA! A HANDS-ON ADVENTURE CHILDREN'S MUSEUM

Lancaster - *1708 River Valley Circle South 43130. Phone: (740) 653-1010. www.aha4kids.org. Hours: Wednesday-Monday 10am-4pm, Winter Sundays 12pm-4pm. Admission: $8.00 per person. Note: Outdoor picnic tables.*

AHA! the liveliest, convenient, and educational, place for children (especially those age 0-7) in town. There's Lego Play, Sand Play, Train Play, Water Play, Craft areas, Pretend Theater, Market, Pizza Shop, Vet Office and Garden areas…even music play with flowers.

SHERMAN HOUSE MUSEUM

Lancaster - *137 East Main Street 43130. Phone: (740) 654-9923. Hours: Tuesday-Sunday Noon-4:00pm (April - mid-December). Guided tours last 45 minutes for each home. www.shermanhouse.org Admission: $6.00 adult, $2.00 students under 18 (includes guided tour). FREEBIES: Activity sheets - www.fairfieldheritage.com/sherman/sherman_just_for_kids.htm*

The Sherman House Museum was the birthplace of General William Tecumseh Sherman and his brother, U.S. Senator John Sherman, and home to the remarkable Sherman Family. One upstairs bedroom houses family memorabilia, and another offers a re-creation of General Sherman's Civil War field tent including several items he used during the war, and a sound and light presentation depicting his passion for the Union.

The last room houses an excellent exhibit, "Sherman at War," explaining his war story with artifacts, paintings, maps, weapons, and GAR memorabilia. Imagine how life must have been in the "Little Brown House on the Hill," the Sherman House, with eleven children and four adults as you visit the wooden structure in which one of the most infamous Civil War Generals was born.

WAHKEENA NATURE PRESERVE

Lancaster (Sugar Grove) - *2200 Pump Station Road (US 33 to County Road 86 west, follow signs) 43155. www.ohiohistory.org/places/. Phone: (740) 746-8695 or (800) 297-1883. Hours: Wednesday-Sunday 8:00am-4:30pm (mid March- mid November). Admission: FREE.*

Wahkeena, named with an Indian word meaning "most beautiful" is a located on the edge of the Hocking Hills. Trees, ferns, mountain laurels, wildflowers, orchids, and sandstone cliffs. All that beauty plus 70 species of birds and 15 species of mammals including woodpeckers and deer. At the lodge, tour groups may view nature study exhibits. Two trails available for hiking.

WAGNALLS MEMORIAL LIBRARY

Lithopolis - *150 East Columbus Street 43136. www.wagnallslibrary.org. Phone: (614) 837-7003. Hours: Monday-Thursday, Saturday 10am-8pm.*

(Adam Wagnall was the co-founder of the Funk and Wagnalls Publishing Co.). The series programs and workshops have included light and serious drama, dance groups, mime, a puppeteer and a wide variety of musical events ranging from the classical to bluegrass. Tickets $8.00-$12.00. Tours of the library are available by appointment and include a description of the unusual architectural features and history of the Wagnalls family.

MADISON LAKE STATE PARK

London - *(3 miles East of London off State Route 665) 43140. Phone: (740) 869-3124. http://parks.ohiodnr.gov/madisonlake*

One of the best examples of existing prairie in Ohio is within the Darby Plains of Madison County. Bigelow Cemetery State Nature Preserve near Chuckery contains prairie plants including big bluestem, Indian grass and purple coneflower. Smith Cemetery Prairie contains stiff goldenrod, gray willow and wild petunia. The 106-acre lake is ideal for sailboats, row boats and canoes. A 300-foot sand beach provides enjoyment for swimmers and sunbathers. Changing booths and latrines are provided. A scenic ½-mile hiking trail takes visitors through woodlands and along the lakeshore.

Marion

HARDING HOME

Marion - ***380 Mount Vernon Avenue (2 miles west of State Route 23 on State Route 95) 43302. www.hardinghome.org Phone: (740) 387-9630. Hours: Wednesday-Saturday 10am-5pm, Sunday and Holidays Noon-5:00pm. Admission: $7.00 adult, $3.00-$4.00 student (all ages). Educators: Bio online. www.ohiohistoryteachers.org has several themed lesson plans online. Note: Memorial is a circular monument (with columns of white marble) containing the tombs of Mr. and Mrs. Harding on Delaware Avenue.***

REOPENED SEPTEMBER 2020 A great way to learn Presidential history without a fuss from the kids. Do you know what the fancy pot is in the guestroom - the one lying on the floor? They have displayed a podium used at Harding's inauguration in 1920 as our 29th President. See the porch where Harding campaigned what was later called the "Front Porch Campaign", speaking to over 600,000 people overall. A special small house was built behind the main house for the press associates visiting the area to cover the campaign. Look for the ornate collar worn by their dog "Laddie Boy".

MYSTERIOUS REVOLVING BALL

Marion - ***Marion Cemetery 43302. Hours: Dawn-Dusk.***

Can you scientifically solve the "Marion Unsolved Mystery"? Here's the scoop! The ball is a grave monument for the Merchant family (located in the northeast corner of the cemetery) erected in 1896. The 5200-pound granite ball turns mysteriously with continuous movement. There has been no scientific explanation for this revolution and the phenomenon is featured in many newspapers including "Ripley's Believe It or Not"!

WYANDOT POPCORN MUSEUM

Marion - ***169 East Church Street (Heritage Hall – Marion County Museum of History) 43302. www.wyandotpopcornmus.com. Phone: (740) 387-HALL Hours: Wednesday-Sunday 1:00-4:00pm (May-October). Weekends Only (November-April). Closed most holidays. Admission: $3.00-$6.00 (age 6+).***

Before you enter the Popcorn Museum, see the hand-made miniature, working carousel and Prince Imperial (a stuffed 25 year old horse from France). As you enter the large, colorful tent, you'll be enchanted by the antique popcorn poppers and concession wagons. See the first automated popper and the first all electric popper – all in pristine condition. It's the only museum like it in the world. Free popcorn is served daily.

POPCORN FESTIVAL

Marion - Downtown. www.popcornfestival.com. Highlights include a parade, tours of the Popcorn Museum, popcorn sculptures and nationally known entertainment nightly. Free. (weekend after Labor Day)

MARION COUNTY FAIR

Marion - Marion County Fairgrounds, 220 E. Fairground Street. (740) 382-2558. Huber Machinery Museum open (steam & gas tractors, threshers and road-building equipment, plus Marion steam shovel #6). (first week of July)

APPLE FESTIVAL

Marion - Lawrence Orchards. 2634 Smeltzer Road. Apples & cider. Apple pie eating & peeling contests. Candy apples. Wagon/hayrides. Apple Dumplings, Fritters, Donuts, butter, etc. Pioneer crafts. Petting Zoo. www.lawrenceorchards.com. (September weekend)

CHRISTMAS BY CANDLELIGHT

Marion - Marion County Fairgrounds, 220 E. Fairground St. www.marioncounty.com. Hundreds of thousands of lights & holiday / storybook characters. Daily, evenings. Drive thru. Admission. (Thanksgiving - January 1)

THE MAIZE AT LITTLE DARBY CREEK

Milford Center - Little Darby Creek, 8657 Axe Handle Rd. Pumpkin Patches / Hayrides / Corn Mazes / Fall Playland - Admission (average $6.00). Plan on at least two hours playtime. Open weekends, some weekdays (by appointment) and weeknights. Cow train, rubber duck races, corn cannon. www.mazeandberries.com. (late September - late October).

MT. GILEAD STATE PARK

Mt. Gilead - *4119 State Route 95 (1 mile East of Mt. Gilead on State Route 95) 43338. Phone: (419) 946-1961. http://parks.ohiodnr.gov/mountgilead*

Picnicking, fishing and hiking can be enjoyed year-round. Six and a half miles of trails, including a two-mile multipurpose trail for hikers and horseback riders, traverse Mt. Gilead State Park. 172 acres of camping, hiking trails, boating, fishing & some winter sports.

DEER CREEK STATE PARK RESORT

Mt. Sterling - ***20635 Waterloo Road (I-71 to SR 56 to SR 207, 7 miles south of town) 43143. Phone: (740) 869-3124 Park or (740) 869-2020 Lodge. www.deercreekstateparklodge.com Admission: FREE.***

This resort park features a modern lodge, cottages, campground, golf course, swimming beach and boating for outdoor enthusiasts. Nature Programs, bike rentals, hiking trails, boating and rentals, fishing, golf, and winter sports are available throughout park.

The Resort has over 100 guest rooms (some with bunk beds, some with lofts), 25 fully furnished two-bedroom cottages (screened porch, many with gas fireplaces, fire ring and grills), indoor/outdoor pools, whirlpool/sauna, gamerooms, sport courts, fitness center, full service restaurant and plenty of activities. Great to plan a group/family get-together here as there are things to do and places everywhere to gather for games (cards, board games) or crafts (Shrinky Dink, buttons, sand art, etc) or evening family videos or hayrides or campfires. They have short hiking trails that are "kid-friendly" (we loved "tracking" the paw prints on the trails early morning) and their Holiday or Theme Weekends are well-planned with entertainment and special guests (i.e. astronauts). Be careful, this place could be habit forming!

Newark

KNOX COUNTY HISTORICAL MUSEUM

Newark - 875 Harcourt Road 43050. (740) 393-5247 www.knoxhistory.org Hours: Generally open March through November each year, except major holidays, Wednesday evenings from 6pm to 8pm, and Thursday through Sundays from 2pm to 4pm. Admission: $3.00 adult (age 12+)

They have displays that are kid-friendly, and time-tested by the 350 third-graders who visit and tour the Museum each Spring.They especially like Paul Lynde's nifty 1964 Ford Thunderbird, our large steam-engine collection, and (surprisingly) the extensive early telephone collection.

CHERRY VALLEY LODGE

Newark - ***2299 Cherry Valley Road (Cherry Valley Lodge, I-70 exit 126. OH37 NE to OH16 E.) 43055. www.cherryvalleylodge.com. Phone: (740) 788-1200***

Guest rooms are perfectly designed to bring the kids. The L-shaped layout with two queen beds features an armoire that separates the two sleeping areas. The Lodge also has indoor and outdoor pools, disc golf, volleyball and horseshoe courts plus a toddler play area. When you want to wander outside a little, they have 14 miles of scenic bike paths to try or, you can feed the ducks in the courtyard botanical garden. A fitness center is also available for those wishing to exercise during their visit. Restaurants and snack bars located throughout the property. All rooms feature refrigerators.

DAWES ARBORETUM

Newark - ***7770 Jacksontown Road (SR 13, I-70 exit 132) 43056. Phone: (740) 323-2355 or (800) 44-DAWES. www.dawesarb.org. Hours: Grounds open daily dawn to dusk. Visitors Center open: Monday-Friday 1-3pm, weekends Noon-3pm (May-Oct). Closed Thanksgiving, Christmas and New Years. Admission: FREE.***

The Dawes Arboretum features plants tolerant of central Ohio's climate. Azaleas, crab apples, hollies, oaks and conifers are a few of the collections accessible from the 4.5 mile Auto Tour and more than 8 miles of hiking trails. There's also meadows, woods, gardens, cypress swamp, holly, and a Bird-Watching garden. Try a free visit each season to see the new colors.

THE WORKS - OHIO CENTER OF HISTORY, ART & TECHNOLOGY

Newark - ***55 South First Street (I-70 to SR 13 north to between 1st & 2nd streets) 43055. Phone: (740) 349-9277. www.attheworks.org. Hours: Tuesday-Saturday 9:00am-5:00pm. Some Labs only open when staffed from 11:00am-2:00pm. Admission: $12.00 adult, $10.00 senior (55+), $8.00 child (3-17).***

"The Works" is a reoccurring theme. The art gallery and studio have the name, "Art Works." Pottery and ceramics are the central theme of the studio; you decide how you want to experience them, whether creating your own Bisque Studio (fired pottery), or throwing on the wheel in the mud room. In "Glass Works" watch workshop glass blowers demonstrate their craft as they create artistic pieces of glassware including bowls, paperweights and seasonal items. Also found in the complex is the Digital Works (web design and TV studio).

The original 1880s machine shop complex houses The Works and traces the development of industry in central Ohio from prehistoric Indians to the 21st century. Learn methods of transportation thru the years or which products were made here (ex. Mason jars and engines for farm machines). In one long afternoon, our kids made their own race cars, then played Wii fitness, found where they have the most body heat, created funky electrical circuits, and then sat mesmerized watching a glassblower work his craft...

PUMPKIN MAZE PLAYLAND - LEEDS FARM

Ostrander - Leeds Farm, 8738 Marysville Road. Pumpkin Patches / Hayrides / Corn Mazes / Fall Playland - Admission ($10-$12). Plan on at least two hours playtime. Pedal carts. Zip line. Pig races. Mountain slides. Open weekends, some weekdays (by appointment) & weeknights. www.leedsfarm.com. (late Sept - late Oct).

PUMPKIN MAZE PLAYLAND - SHARP FARMS

Sugar Grove - Sharp Farms, (off US 33). Pumpkin Patches / Hayrides / Corn Mazes / Fall Playland - Admission (average $6.00). Plan on at least two hours playtime. Open weekends, some weekdays (by appointment) and weeknights. www.sharpfarm.com. (late September - late October).

HARTMAN AVIARY

Sunbury - *9000 Cheshire Road (I-71 Sunbury exit - Rtes. 36.37 east. Right on Golf Course Rd. towards Sunbury Golf Course) 43074. http://hartmanaviary.com. Phone: (740) 965-9464. Hours: From mid-April until mid-October Hartman Aviary opens it outside facilities to the public on Saturdays, Noon to 4pm.*

The owner has painstakingly committed to breeding high quality and well-socialized parrots for private sale. During open house, visitors are able to see hundreds of parrots in large outdoor flights. Visitors are able to get inches away from the smaller conjures and lories to the largest hyacinth macaws. In most cases you can hand-feed fruit, nuts and seeds to birds. There is no cost, as it is a service to the aviary to help socialize the young birds. Be sure to learn about their inovative products (leach, flight line, yard perch) that allow your pet birds to enjoy the outdoors without "flying off". You don't have to purchase anything – unless you want a baby parrot to take home and love.

NUTCRACKER FAMILY RESTAURANT

Pataskala - 63 E Broad St. Phone: 740-964–0056. www.nutcrackerpataskala.com A neon sign at the Nutcracker Family Restaurant in Pataskala reads "Step back to the '50s." You'll find scratch-made items such as bacon-wrapped meatloaf, corned beef hash and country-fried steak, as well as comfort classics such as macaroni and cheese, and applesauce made with apples from nearby Lynd Fruit Farm.

Breakfast is served all day, and daily dinner specials include all-you-can-eat spaghetti and all-you-can-eat ocean perch on select days. Sweet treats include freshly baked pies, frosted-mug root beer and hand-dipped ice cream for old-fashioned root beer floats and pie à la mode. Every nutcracker that you see now in the building was donated by people in the community. Playing in the background is music from the 1950s. There are two jukeboxes, one from the 1950s that patrons can crank up for a dime a song. Bring a quarter to give your children a ride on the antique horse — a perfect photo op. Take another photo beside the side view of a model 1956 Chevrolet Bel Air car that's affixed to the wall.

VELVET ICE CREAM: YE OLDE MILL ICE CREAM MUSEUM

Utica - *Velvet Ice Cream (State Route 13) 43080. Phone: (740) 892-3921 or (800) 589-5000. www.velveticecream.com. Hours: Daily 11:00am-7:00pm (May-October). Extended evening summer hours. Weekend entertainment summers. Admission: FREE. Tours: 30 minute Public Tours Monday - Friday 11:00am-3:00pm only. Please Note: The manufacturing facility does not produce ice cream on certain holidays & weekends. On these days, a video of the production line is shown in its place.*

Did you know that the ice cream cone originated by mistake at the St. Louis World's Fair when a waffle vendor rolled waffles into cones for an ice cream vendor who ran out of serving cups? Learn all sorts of ice cream trivia at the

Ice Cream Museum located in the restored 1817 mill and water wheel which is surrounded by 20 acres of wooded parklands with ducks and picnic areas. While you are at the mill, stop by the NEW viewing gallery to watch ice cream being made and packaged and learn what it takes to produce more than 6 million gallons of velvety smooth ice cream every year. Then, come into the 18th century ice cream counter and try Velvet's newest creations such as Raspberry Fudge Cordial or an old favorite like Mint Chocolate Chip.

ICE CREAM FESTIVAL

Utica - Velvet Ice Cream hosts a tribute to our national dessert, ice cream, with family entertainment and lots of food made from ice cream. Kids can watch sheep herding with border collies, catch the kiddie tractor pull and wheelbarrow races, or watch the parade or magic circus. Admission. (Memorial Day Weekend)

HARVEST FESTIVAL

Utica - Velvet Ice Cream hosts Hay rides, petting zoo, pumpkins, live entertainment. (every Sunday afternoon in October)

Chapter 2 *Central East Ohio*

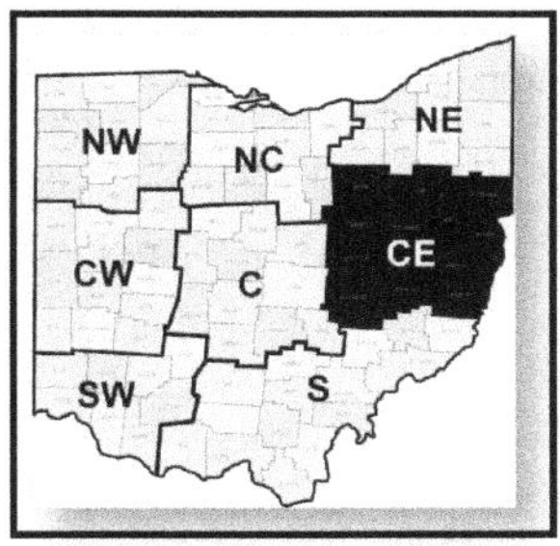

Barnesville

- Barnesville Pumpkin Festival
- Dickson Cattle Company

Bellaire

- Toy & Plastic Brick Museum

Belmont

- Barkcamp State Park

Berlin

- Behalt, Amish & Mennonite Ctr.
- Christmas In Berlin
- Schrock's Amish Farm & Village
- Wendell August Forge Gift Tour

Blue Rock

- Blue Rock State Forest
- Muskingum River State Park

Bolivar

- Fort Laurens

Cambridge

- Living Word Passion Play
- Mosser Glass
- Salt Fork State Park
- Salt Fork State Park Resort

Canal Fulton

- St Helena Iii Canal Boat
- Yankee Peddler Festival

Canton

- Canton Classic Car MuSeum
- Canton Symphony Orchestra
- Hoover Historical Center
- Italian American Festival
- Mckinley Museum & Discover World
- Players Guild Theatre
- Pro Football Hall Of Fame
- Sippo Lake Park

Canton, North

- Harry London Chocolate Factory
- Maps Air Museum

Carrollton

- Bluebird Farm Toy Museum And Restaurant
- McCook House

Columbiana

- Pumpkin Maze Playland

Coshocton

- Hot Air Balloon Festival
- Roscoe Village

Cumberland

- The Wilds

Dellroy

- Atwood Lake Resort

Dennison

- Dennison Railroad Depot Museum

Dover

- Broad Run CheeseHouse
- Victorian Home Open House, J.E. Reeves
- Warther Carvings

East Liverpool

- Beaver Creek State Park
- Museum Of Ceramics
- Tri-State Pottery Festival

Frazeysburg

- Longaberger Museum And Factory Tour

Gnadenhutten

- Gnadenhutten

Hartville

- Pumpkin Maze Playland
- Quail Hollow State Park

Kidron

- Lehman's Hardware

Lisbon

- Guilford Lake State Park

Magnolia

- Elson Flouring Mill

Millersburg

- Guggisberg Cheese Factory
- Holidays At The Mansion
- Yoder's Amish Home

Nashport

- Dillon State Park

New Concord

- John & Annie Glenn Historic Site

New Philadelphia

- Muskingum Watershed Lakes
- Shoenbrunn
- Trumpet In The Land
- Tuscora Park

Norwich

- Nat'l Road / Zane Grey Museum

Orrville

- Jumpin Pumpkin Special
- Smuckers Company Store & Café

Shreve

- Apple Festivals

Steubenville

- Fort Steuben, Historic
- Jefferson Lake State Park

Sugarcreek

- Alpine Hills Museum
- Ohio Swiss Festival

Walnut Creek

- Coblentz Chocolate Company

Wilmot

- Amish Door Dinner Theatre

Wooster

- Cat's Meow Village
- Hartzler Family Dairy
- Melvins
- Ohio Agricultural R & D Center
- Pumpkin Maze Playland
- Wayne County Historical Museum

Zanesville

- Apple Festival
- Lorena Sternwheeler
- Stars & Stripes on the River

Zoar

- Zoar Village

A Quick Tour of our Hand-Picked Favorites Around...

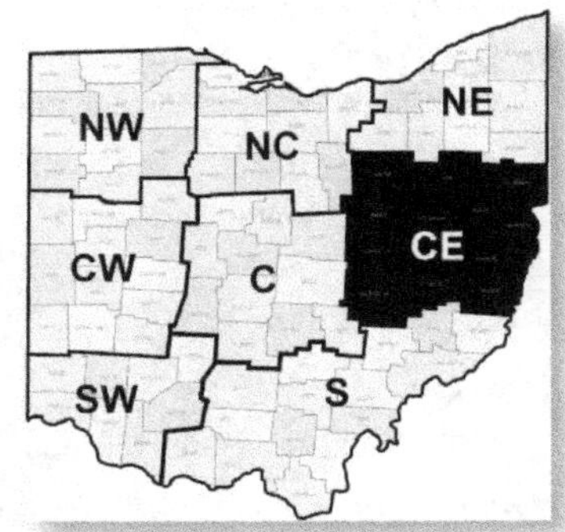

Central East Ohio

If you're longing to experience a back-to-the-basics lifestyle, a trip to Ohio's Amish country is the place! The world's largest Amish community exists in Ohio. Look for attractions in Amish communities like: Berlin, Millersburg, Walnut Creek, Dover, Wilmot, and Sugarcreek. A good first stop for a crash course in the history of the Amish is the Amish and Mennonite Heritage Center near Berlin. This is where "**Behalt**", a giant cyclorama, depicts the people of this area. Kids are curious how the artist "scratched" paint to create the mural. Enjoy beautiful scenery, visit an **Amish Farm,** savor homemade foods and listen for the clip-clop of a buggy. Say Cheese! Cause there's lots of **Cheese Factories** to view and sample around here.

At **Warther Carvings**, the Warther Family guides visitors through the life of Ernest "Mooney" Warther, declared the "World's Master Carver" for his ingenious interpretation of the history of trains. If any place is labeled "seeing is believing," this is it! (hint: have the kids sit in front for the demo portion of the tour and they might win something).

How about mixing chocolate and football together for a day trip? Within just a few exits of each other are **Harry London Chocolate Factory** (try a melt in your-mouth London mint or buckeye!) AND the **Pro Football Hall of Fame** (take their scavenger hunt and then throw some passes) in North Canton.

Want to mix old-fashioned craft into a modern or a historical setting? Some **Glass Factory Tours** are "heated" places to visit in Cambridge. We'd recommend overnighting nearby at **Salt Fork State Park Resort** which has accommodations for every style. Or, try your hand at pounding a hammer on metal to see if you can create art. The folks at **Wendell August Forge** can – with hammering you can watch art being created. Then, go to an authentic canal town at **Roscoe Village** in Coshocton. You might even get roped into doing some chores or crafts! After midday lunch, take a lesson in a one-room schoolhouse - but beware of the dunce cap!

Sites and attractions are listed in order by City, Zip Code, and Name. Symbols indicated represent: Restaurants Lodging

DICKINSON CATTLE COMPANY

Barnesville *- 35000 Muskrat Road (I-70 exit 202 south, then west) 43713. Phone: (740) 758-5050. www.texaslonghorn.com. Hours (Store): Monday-Saturday 10:00am-5:00pm, Sunday 1:00-6:00pm (April-October). Tours: 75 minutes. Group Tours for adults are $10.00 with special rates for youth $4.00 (4-12). Small family groups can join larger booked tours. Note: Cattle, steaks, smoked longhorn jerky & sticks and longhorn related products available at the Head to Tail Store.*

With the largest herd of registered quality Texas Longhorn Cattle east of San Francisco this large, family-owned ranch offers narrated tours on an adorable purple with white polka-dotted cow bus. See up to 1000 Texas Longhorns grazing the fields, hand-feed the cattle and clear water fish. Close up views of BueLingo, Texas Longhorn, and African Watusi cattle herds. Gizmo is an International Champion Sire that is on the tour route. What shape do they use for branding?

BARNESVILLE PUMPKIN FESTIVAL

Barnesville - Downtown. www.barnesvillepumpkinfestival.com. All kinds of pumpkin contests (largest pumpkin, pumpkin rolling and pie eating), parade, foods, fiddle contest, rides, crafts and entertainment. Free. (Thursday – Sunday - last full weekend of September)

TOY & PLASTIC BRICK MUSEUM

Bellaire *- 4597 Noble Street (I-70 to Rte. 7 south to Noble Street exit) 43906. Phone: (740) 671-8890. www.brickmuseum.net. Hours: Tuesday-Sunday 10:00am-5:00pm (May-August). Admission: $8.00 adult, $6.00 senior and student (5+).*

This museum is housed in a former school and the rooms are full of over 4 million bricks, over 500 lifesize statues, over 1000 Lego creations, some animatronics and some robotics. Look for themes like Space, TV cartoons and animals. Want a preview? Take a look thru website pictures of over 300 creations, then write down which ones you want to search for when you visit.

BARKCAMP STATE PARK

Belmont - *65330 Barkcamp Park Road (I-70 exit 208, off SR 149) 43718. Phone: (740) 484-4064. http://parks.ohiodnr.gov/barkcamp*

Belmont County's rugged hills provide the backdrop for picturesque Barkcamp State Park. The Lakeview Trail, Woodchuck Nature Trail, Hawthorn Trail and Hawk Trail provide opportunities for nature study, bird watching and wildlife observation. Barkcamp's bridle trail meanders along the entire lakeshore. A special paved trail winds through the pioneer village, enters the adjoining mature woodlands and provides access to the Antique Barn. Interpretive signs are placed along the route explaining the cultural and natural history of the park. 1,232 acres of camping, hiking trails through rolling hills and woodlands, boating, fishing, swimming and winter sports.

Berlin

BEHALT, AMISH & MENNONITE HERITAGE CENTER

Berlin - *5798 County Road 77 (north of State Route 39, follow signs) 44610. Phone: (330) 893-3192. www.behalt.com. Hours: Monday-Saturday 9:00am-5:00pm. Shorter hours in winter. Admission: $9.00 adult, $4.50 child (6-12). Note: Pioneer Barn houses an original Conestoga Wagon that brought early settlers to Holmes County. Restored one-room school, dating from 1856 used to tell story of Amish education.*

Behalt means "to keep or remember". Besides a free 15-minute video presentation, visitors may take a 30-minute interpretive tour (paid admission) of a colorful, stunning 265-ft x 10-ft original oil painting depicting Amish and Mennonite history. This 10' x 265' cyclorama mural by artist Heinz Gaugel clearly explains the heritage of Amish and Mennonite people from the beginnings of their faith to the present day. The circular mural took four years to paint using superimposing layers of oil paint to create a sense of many events occurring in a small space and time. This makes the mural almost 3D when viewing. The exterior of the building is painted with an old technique called "sgraffito" which means scratched. Mr. Gaugel applied five layers of plaster to the wall (green, dark red, dark yellow, white and black). The artist starts scratching through the layers to expose the colors he wants. The tour is narrated with stories so vivid that you feel as if you are a part of the scene.

SCHROCK'S AMISH FARM AND VILLAGE

Berlin - ***4363 State Route 39 (1 mile East of Downtown) 44610. Phone: (330) 893-3232. http://amishfarmvillage.com/. Hours: Monday-Saturday 10:00am-4:30pm (May-October). Tours and Admission: $4.00-7.00. Note: Gifts shops (many).***

We stopped at the farm to pet animals, watched a slide show about Amish lifestyles, and received a tour through the home. Kids, even adults, were surprised to see that all appliances were gas fueled including the lamps (the gas generated light source was hidden in the table under the lamp). We learned why there are no faces on Amish dolls and why only pins and occasional buttons are used in clothing.

WENDELL AUGUST FORGE GIFT TOUR

Berlin - ***7007 Dutch Country Lane (3 miles West of Berlin - Route 62) 44610. Phone: (330) 893-3713 or (866) 354-5192. www.wendellaugust.com/ohio-amish-country-store/#. Admission: FREE. Tours: Monday-Saturday 9:00am-5:00pm.***

Free tour of the workshop where they have set up a simulation space as metal giftware is taken through a fascinating eleven step process. The gift metal is hammered over a pre-designed template with random hand, or machine

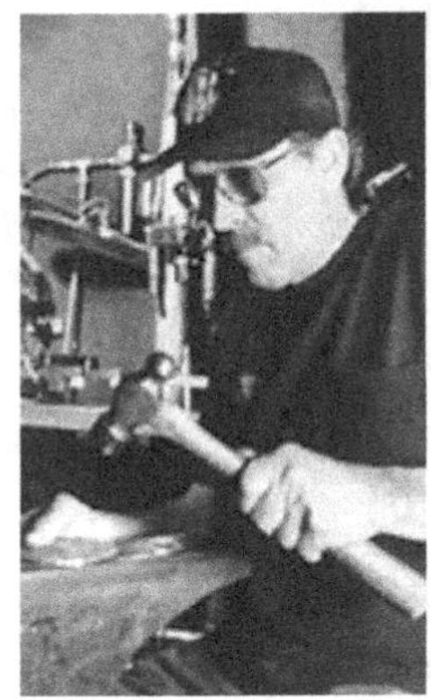

operated hammer motions. It was interesting to think someone close to the craft had to design the machine operated hammer for this specific purpose – probably a craftsman who's hands got tired! The impression is now set in one side and the signature hammer marks will stay on the other side. The artist stamps his seal and then the item is forged (put in a log fire) to get smoke marks that bring out the detail of the design. After the item cools, it is cleaned to remove most of the dark smoke color and the metal object is then thinned by hand hammering. The facility also features a video highlighting the company's history. Now try your hand at being a craftsperson yourself in the interactive hand hammering room and take home a treasure made by you ($2.00 fee).

CHRISTMAS IN BERLIN

Berlin - Downtown & Schrocks Amish Farm, (330) 893-3467. Sleigh rides, buggy rides, hayrides and crafts. Live Nativity Parade. Luminaries, shopping. The live nativity parade and candle-lighting ceremony occurs on the town square. Live animals like sheep, donkey and even camels are paraded by shepherds. Actors as Mary, Joseph, too. FREE (Friday after Thanksgiving in November)

BLUE ROCK STATE FOREST

Blue Rock - *6665 Cutler Lake Road (located 12 miles southeast of Zanesville off SR 60) 43720. Phone: (740) 674-4035. http://forestry.ohiodnr.gov/bluerock Hours: Daily 6:00am - 11:00pm.*

4,579 acres in Muskinghum County. 26 miles of bridle trails and fishing are offered. Former fire lookout tower. Blue Rock State Park is adjacent. A public beach is located on the north end of the lake. Several miles of hiking trails begin near the campground and picnic areas of the park. Additional hiking trails are in the adjacent forest lands. Horsemen can enjoy more than 26 miles of bridle trails through the Forest. No overnight facilities are available.

MUSKINGUM RIVER STATE PARK

Blue Rock - *(120 acres along 80 miles of the Muskingum River extending from Devola to Ellis Locks) 43720. Phone: (740) 452-3820. http://parks.ohiodnr.gov/muskingumriver*

The Muskingum River is formed by the confluence of the Walhonding and Tuscarawas rivers in Coshocton flowing south through Zanesville where it joins the Licking River. The river travels 112 miles in all and its 10 locks are still hand-operated in the same manner as 150 years ago. A trip on the Muskingum River Parkway is not complete without going through one of the ten locks. These manually-operated locks are similar to those built before the turn of the century and are now recognized as one of America's great engineering accomplishments. Visitors are offered camping, hiking trails, boating, and fishing.

FORT LAURENS

Bolivar - *11067 Fort Laurens Rd. NW (I-77 and State Route 212 - Follow Signs) 44612. http://fortlaurens.org/. Phone: (330) 874-2059. Hours: Wednesday-Saturday 11am-4:00pm, Sunday and Holidays Noon-4:00pm (summer). Only open weekends in the spring and fall. Admission to museum: $3.00-$5.00 per student or adult.*

Visit the site of the only U.S. Military fort in Ohio during the American Revolution. This fort was built in 1778 in an ill-fated campaign to attack the British at Detroit. Supplying this wilderness outpost was its downfall, as its starving garrison survived on boiled moccasins and withstood a month-long siege by British-led Indians. The fort was abandoned in 1779. Today, only the outline of the fort remains, but a small museum commemorates the frontier soldier, housing a video giving the fort's history and audiovisual displays from the fort's excavation. Re-enactment weekends are the best time to visit.

SIEGE OF FORT LAURENS LANTERN TOUR

Bolivar - Fort Laurens - Experience the Siege at Fort Laurens in this interactive lantern tour where your guide helps you escape the fort under siege. You are guided through the woods by lantern light to safety at the nearby military camp. Guests enjoy warm drinks and snacks as they participate in campfire stories told by reenactor soldiers. Not recommended for those with mobility problems or for the very young. Pre-paid reservations required. Admission. (third Sat in Oct)

Cambridge

NATIONAL MUSEUM CAMBRIDGE GLASS

Cambridge - *136 S 9th Street (7 miles Northeast of Cambridge on US 22) 43725. www.cambridgeglassmuseum.org Phone: (740) 432-4245. Hours: Wednesday-Saturday 9am-4pm, Sunday Noon-4pm (April-October). Closed Easter & July 4th. Admission: $5.00 general (age 12+), $4.00 senior.*

View a short vintage film that explains the handmade glassmaking process used by the Cambridge Glass Company (1902-1958). Dress up holding tools used many years ago and then see over 8,000 pieces of colorful Cambridge Glass. In the Education Center feel the quality of the crystal, play with glass marbles, and do a pencil rubbing from an authentic etching plate.

GUERNSEY COUNTY HISTORY MUSEUM

Cambridge - *218 N Eighth Street, downtown 43725. Phone: (740) 439-5884. theosrestaurant.us. www.facebook.com/GuersneyHistory. Hours: Tuesday, Thursday & Saturday Noon-3pm (May-October). Extended hours November & December. Admission: $5.00 adult, $3.00 child.*

This 188 year old, restored 16 room home, contains antique furnishings, products and personal items from Guersney County. Included for kids: a display of an authentic one-room school house and a life like replica of a coal mine from the 1890's.

THEO'S RESTAURANT

Cambridge - *632 Wheeling Avenue, downtown 43755. Phone: (740) 432-3878. theosrestaurant.us. Hours: Monday-Saturday 10am-9pm.*

Tons of good sandwiches and specials of the day. Famous for their Coney Dogs & Mile High Pie (tall lemon meringue)...and their good service!

NOTHING BUT CHOCOLATE

Cambridge - ***731 Wheeling Avenue, downtown 43755. Phone: (740) 439-5754. www.nothingbutchocolate.com.*** Handcrafted chocolates and specialty items made in small batches. She has "roll&dip parties" (dip treats in chocolate) and her Buckeye candies are winning state competitions. They are that good!

LIVING WORD PASSION PLAY

Cambridge - ***6010 College Hill Road (2 miles west of State Route 209) 43725. Phone: (740) 439-2761. www.livingworddrama.org. Hours: Friday – Saturday 7:30pm (Mid-June – late September). Admission: $18.00 adult, $16.00 senior (60+), $6.00 child (4-12). Free Set Tours 7pm. Note: Concessions, Gift Shop, Rain Checks, Free Parking.***

Bible stories come to life before your eyes. Experience an evening back in the Holy Land, in 30 AD with an authentic representation of Old Jerusalem. Beginning with the Sermon on the Mount, The Living Word reflects on the last three years of the life of Christ, with dramatic depictions of Palm Sunday, the last supper, Gethsemane, Pilate's court, the crucifixion and the resurrection. Live animals are also used in the play, including a white donkey and an authentic horse-drawn Roman chariot. Even though most know the story, this presentation is moving...

MOSSER GLASS

Cambridge - ***9279 Cadiz Road (I-77 exit 47. US 22 West) 43725. Phone: (740) 439-1827. www.mosserglass.com. Tours: Monday-Friday 8:45am-9:45am and 11:00am - 2:00pm. No tours first 2 weeks in July and last 2 weeks in December. Best not to tour if it's hot outside as the plant is not air conditioned. FREE.***

Mosser is a glass manufacturer that's been around for 30+ years. Mosser makes glass pitchers, goblets, lamps, figurines, auto parts (headlights),

and paper weights. Your guide starts the tour explaining the glassmaking process from the beginning when glass powder (sand and cullet-broken glass) are heated to 2000 degrees F. in a furnace. Once melted, the molten glass is pulled on a stick and then iron molded or pressed, fire glazed and finally cooled in a Lehr which uniformly reduces the temperature of the object to prevent shattering. We saw them make old Ford car headlight covers and red heart shaped paperweights. They add selenium to make red glass.

SALT FORK STATE PARK

Cambridge - ***14755 Cadiz Road (7 miles Northeast of Cambridge on US 22) 43755. http://parks.ohiodnr.gov/saltfork Phone: (740) 439-3521 park or (800) 282-7275 reservations. Admission: FREE.***

As Ohio's largest state park, Salt Fork boasts recreational facilities to suit nearly every taste. Everyone seems to spend at least a couple of hours each day at the Lodge area with overnight rooms, gift shops, indoor and outdoor pools & spa, fitness center, volleyball, basketball and tennis. The dining room serves breakfast, lunch and dinner in a rustic overlook setting (also, seasonal snack bars are available). The gameroom, with multiple ping-pong and air hockey tables, is downstairs. Fun family activities are planned seasonally (i.e. crafts, pool games, kid's bingo, family movies, bonfires, plus Parent's Night Out (once or twice a week). The Nature Center is open with planned activities (seasonally, Wednesday-Sunday) and explorations.

Bring your own boat to this beautiful lake (or rent one at Sugartree Marina 740-439-5833 - Kids love the pontoon or speed/ski boats). Another option, if you didn't bring your own boat, is the Salt Fork Activity Center which operates pontoon tours. The tours include the Stone House or cane pole fishing with snacks and picture for only $5.00/person. Lots of camping, fishing, golfing, and well- marked hiking trails too. A great place to kick back and create family memories!

SALT FORK STATE PARK RESORT LODGE

Cambridge - ***14755 Cadiz Road (7 miles Northeast of Cambridge on US 22) 43755. www.saltforkstateparklodge.com Phone: (740) 439-2751 lodge or (800) 282-7275 reservations.***

This massive pine beam and stone lodge captures the atmosphere and flavor of the grand park lodges built at the turn of the century. The lush wooded surroundings contain miles of hiking and horseback riding trails, large and healthy populations of deer (you'll see them around most every turn), turkey, flowers, song and water birds. Salt Fork State Park Resort has created the "Family Fun Package" These packages typically include one night of lodging in a hillside cottage, free weekend golf for children at Salt Fork Golf Course, complimentary geocaching for two hours, s'mores for a family of four, a hiker welcome pack including a kid's compass and a park map with a listing of hiking trails. Also included is a value coupon book for discounted prices on a selection of items and activities in the Lodge. Other packages include movies and treats.

Bunk Rooms - These cozy, newly freshened rooms, which are great for families, include two double beds and one set of bunk beds. This room also features a refrigerator, small table and chairs, cable television, and Bunkrooms adjoin to king rooms. Views include either the woods or pool areas. We were extremely impressed with the staff and the amount of activities offered: bonfires, make your own t-shirt, paint ball, sports, etc. Staying for a few days? Complete nature and family activities around the park and win prizes. It's a clever way to bring back goal-oriented fun with parents AND children together. ____

Canal Fulton

ST HELENA III CANAL BOAT

Canal Fulton - *125 Tuscarawas St (Canalway Center) (I-77 to Exit 111 Portage Street West, follow signs) 44614. www.discovercanalfulton.com/heritage_society/st_helena_iii.html. Phone: (330) 854-6835. Admission: $5.00-$9.00 (age 5+). Tours: Daily 1:00pm & 2:30pm (Summer, except Mondays when closed). Weekends only (May)*

The St. Helena III docks and departs from the Canal Fulton Canalway Center and can carry up to sixty passengers down an original section of the Ohio-Erie Canal. The canal trip is an one-hour horse drawn canal boat freighter ride with a narrative history of the canal system and the local area. Appearing as it did in the 1800's, the view also includes Lock IV, one of the few remaining working locks on old canal routes. Included in the tour is a Canal Museum with pictorial stories of colorful local history and canal memorabilia including tools used to build and repair canal boats.

OLDE CANAL DAYS

Canal Fulton - St. Helena III Canal Boat. (330) 854-6295. Along the Ohio/Erie canal see a water float parade, fireworks, music contests, saw carving and concerts. (last weekend in August)

YANKEE PEDDLER FESTIVAL

Canal Fulton - Clay's Park Resort. www.yankeepeddlerfestival.com. 13190 Patterson St. NW. Step back in time 200 years and visit pioneer America. See master artists and crafters setting up rustic shops along streams and amid lovely wooded dales, with foods and snacks cooked over open fires, and with non-stop entertainment across the 75-acre grounds. Keep up to the hour and follow events with the Town Criers, visit with the militia and mountain men, or learn drills with hands-on instruction. Visit with the master crafters and artists while they demonstrate the way they transform nature into something unique for you and yours. Admission. (three weekends in September)

Canton

CANTON CLASSIC CAR MUSEUM

Canton - *Market Avenue at 6th Street entrance 44702. Phone: (330) 455-3603. www.cantonclassiccar.org. Hours: Daily 10:00am-5:00pm. Admission: $5.00-$7.50 (age 6+), $3.00 child (4&under).*

Housed in Ohio's earliest Ford-Lincoln dealership, this museum offers over 45 antique, classic and special interest cars displayed in the motif of flapper era Roaring 20's. Favorite exhibits are the Rolls Royce, the Bullet Proof Police Car, the Amphicar (car and boat) and famous movie cars or Amelia Earhart's 1916 Pierce Arrow.

CANTON SYMPHONY ORCHESTRA

Canton - *2323 17th Street NW 44702. www.cantonsymphony.org. Phone: (330) 452-2094.*

Presents classical, holiday, pops, family and youth concerts/symphony. Especially for the younger set: Kinder Concerts, mini-operas and Symphonyland (only $5). Online Teacher's Guides are available each season.

PLAYERS GUILD THEATRE

Canton - *1001 North Market Avenue 44702. www.playersguildtheatre.com. Phone: (330) 453-7619.*

Family series presents plays based on award winning children's stories like The Hobbit and a Christmas Carol. Performances Thursday-Sunday. Tickets run $12.00-$15.00 per seat.

MCKINLEY MUSEUM & DISCOVER WORLD

Canton - *800 McKinley Monument Drive, NW (I-77 south exit 106, I-77 north exit 105, follow signs) 44708. Phone: (330) 455-7043. www.mckinleymuseum.org. Hours: Monday-Saturday 9:00am-4:00pm, Sunday Noon-4:00 pm. Closed major holidays. Admission: $10.00 adult, $9.00 senior (60+), $8.00 child (3-18). Note: Planetarium. Museum Shop.*

After you park, take the 108 steps leading up to the bronze doors of the stunning McKinley Memorial where President William McKinley and his wife and children were laid to rest. A few steps away is the McKinley Museum where you can visit McKinley Hall,

Historical Hall and the Street of Shops. Walk along the 19th Century Street of homes, general store, print shop, and doctor's office. Kid's eyes sparkle at the model trains and pioneer toys such as paper dolls and or mini cast-iron kitchen appliances. Last, but even more exciting for kids, is Discover World. A large dinosaur robot named "Alice" greets you and a real Stark County mastodon Bondo Betty is around the corner. Find hidden fossil drawers, make a fossil, look for the queen bee in a living beehive, touch a chinchilla, play a tune on tone pipes, visit Space Station Earth or be a weather forecaster – All in one afternoon!

PRO FOOTBALL HALL OF FAME

Canton - ***2121 George Halas Drive NW (I-77 and US 62) 44708. Phone: (330) 456-8207. www.profootballhof.com. Hours: Daily 9:00am-8:00pm (Memorial Day-Labor Day). Daily 9:00am-5:00pm (Rest of Year). Closed Christmas Only. Admission: $28.00 adult , $24.00 senior (62+), $21.00 youth (6-12). Parking $10.00 Look for Packages or Discounts online. Note: Tailgating Snack Bar – over the counter / vending. FREEBIES: Be sure to ask for their Investigative Reporter Scavenger Hunt. Kids pretend they are sports reporters looking for "the scoop" story about pro football history. Educators: Activity Guides online: www.profootballhof.com/hall/teacheractivityguide.aspx***

If you're an NFL Football Fan, the anticipation builds as you enter the grounds of the sprawling Hall of Fame. At the top of the curving ramp upstairs you view the first 100 years of football with Pro Football's Birth Certificate and the oldest football (1895) available for display. Then, hit some Astroturf and browse through Pro Football today and Photo Art Gallery (award winning, some amazing, photographs of football heroes in action). Older children look forward to the Enshrinement Galleries and Super Bowl Room. Game Day Stadium's 100-Yard film is shown in a two-sided rotating theater. Start at the Locker Room Show. Then the entire seating area rotates 180 degrees to the Stadium Show where you become part of a NFL game with a 2 story Cinemascope presentation. You see, hear and almost make contact with the players! What a rush! The Hall of Fame's newest galleries, Moments, Memories &

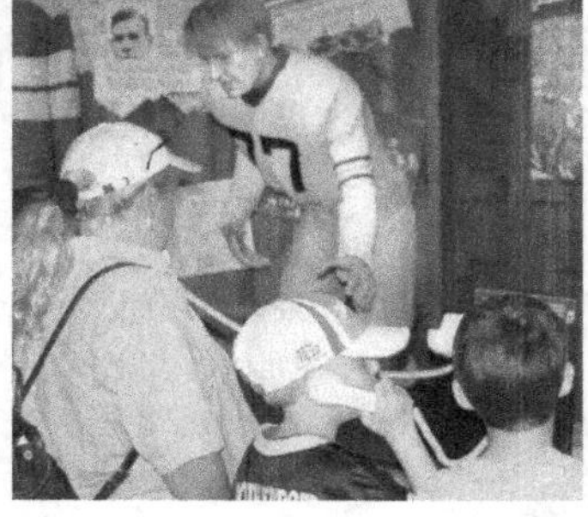

Mementos Gallery and the Pro Football Today Gallery feature new and old artifacts in the collection. This place is full of shoes and jerseys galore from famous players old and new. What did the first helmet look like? Who's your favorite team? What are their stats? By the way, there are action activity stations around every corner and especially downstairs where you can throw, catch and commentate on football. What fun!

ENSHRINEMENT FESTIVAL

Canton - (800) 533-4302. www.profootballhoffestival.com. Check out the 9 days of celebrating football greats including a parade, hot air balloon show, enshrinement ceremony and a televised professional game. Some fees. (first week of August)

SIPPO LAKE PARK

Canton - *5712 12th Street NW (I-77 exit 106 west) 44708. https://starkparks.com/parks/sippo-lake-park/ Phone: (330) 477-3552. Hours: Daily 7am-11pm.*

Sippo Lake Park features an enclosed Clubhouse and open picnic shelters for rent. Other on-site amenities include boat rentals, fishing, nature programming, and short hiking trails. Motor boats, row boats and paddle boats available for rental or bring your own boat (10 hp limit). Nearby marina offers food and beverages for sale as well as bait, fishing tackle, and fishing licenses. A large Canalway Adventure Center with 11 interactive exhibits, and FeLeap's Lily Pad Gift Shop are available to peruse. (open weekdays 8:30am-4:30pm and Saturday 10:00am-4:00pm or Sunday 1:00-5:00pm). Admission: FREE

HOOVER HISTORICAL CENTER

Canton - *1875 Easton Street NW (I-77 Portage Street/North Canton Exit to Walsh University campus) 44720. www.facebook.com/HooverHistoricalCenter. Phone: (330) 499-0287. Tours: Thursday-Saturday at 1:00, 2:00, 3:00 and 4:00pm (March-October). Closed holidays. Admission: Free. Note: Only known vacuum cleaner museum in the world.*

See the Hoover Industry beginnings as a leather tannery. When automobiles came on the scene, W. H. Hoover searched for a new product. He bought the rights to inventor Murray Spangler's upright vacuum cleaner and introduced it in 1908 - The Hoover Suction Sweeper Model O (On display). A short video details the history of the company.

Guided tours of the farmhouse include a display of antique vacuums. A favorite is the Kotten Suction Cleaner (1910) that requires a person to rock a bellows with their feet to create suction. An early 1900's electric vacuum weighed 100 pounds (and they advertised it as a portable!).

ITALIAN AMERICAN FESTIVAL

Canton - Stark County Fairgrounds, 305 Wertz Avenue. www.cantonitalianfesta.org. Italy in Ohio with entertainment, foods, dancing, exhibits, rides and a bocce tournament. Thursday - Sunday. Admission. (long weekend late June)

Canton, North

HARRY LONDON CHOCOLATE FACTORY

Canton, North ***- 5353 Lauby Road (I-77 Exit 113 Airport) 44720. Phone: (330) 494-0833 or (800) 321-0444. www.harrylondon.com. Tours: Monday-Thursday 10:00am-4:00pm. Admission: FREE. Tour: 45 minutes. Reservations required. Tours leave every hour on the hour. Note: Chocolate Hall of Fame, Largest Chocolate Store in the Midwest. They may not be as pretty, but BooBoos candies are discounted at the store.***

London's has produced quality gourmet chocolates since 1922 using original family recipes. Live the fantasy of making, molding, wrapping, and boxing chocolate candy, fudge, and butterscotch. Oh, it smells so good here! Did you know cacao beans were once used as money and medicine? Learn this and more as you view a video and then walk near warm tanks full of chocolate (80,000 lbs. of chocolate inside each tank). Upstairs, along the mezzanine, watch as fillings are enrobed in chocolate – all over. Workers here can't wear jewelry or perfume but they get free samples all work day! Be sure to try a Mint Meltaway or Pixies. Note: London is now owned by Fannie May.

MAPS AIR MUSEUM

Canton, North ***- 2260 International Parkway, Akron-Canton Airport (I-77 to Exit 113) 44720. Phone: (330) 896-6332. www.mapsairmuseum.org. Hours: Tuesday-Saturday 9:00am-4:30pm. Sundays 11:30am-4:00pm. Admission: $6.00-$10.00.***

The staff here are pilots, mechanics, officers, and crew who desire to preserve the legacy of America's aviation heritage. Their slogan "Rebuilding History – One Rivet At a Time" really describes their dedication to acquire and renovate some of the world's greatest military aircraft. MAPS offers not just displays of mint condition aircraft, but also a "hands on" view of the restoration of some of the world's greatest aircraft by people who may have flown them years ago.

Carrollton

BLUEBIRD FARM PARK

***Carrollton** - 190 Alamo Road (at the bottom of the Square, take 332 south for two blocks, turn left on 3rd Street S.E.) 44615. www.ccparkdistrict.org/bluebirdfarmpark.html Phone: (330) 627-7980. Hours: Monday-Friday 11am-3pm. Admission: Museum $2.00 adult, FREE child. Note: Reasonable gift ideas in the gift shop barn. Christmastime magical here. Restaurant lunch and dinner.*

A century old farmhouse restaurant featuring a fresh, daily menu of family-priced, old-fashioned dishes like ham loaf, Swiss steak, and chicken casserole cooked only as Grandma could. Walk off your homemade dessert on the nature trail. The Toy Museum features playthings available to American children from the 1800's to the present (brightly, cleverly displayed). Look for some popular dolls like Raggedy Ann and Andy, Shirley Temple, Mickey and Minnie Mouse, and the beloved Teddy Bear…many made abroad. Ask for the scavenger hunt pages to play a game in the museum. This entire property is a wonderful haven for families…don't miss it when in Amish / Swiss area of Ohio!

MCCOOK HOUSE

***Carrollton** - 15 South Lisbon St, Downtown Square (west side of square) 44615. Phone: (330) 627-3345 www.ohiohistory.org/visit/museum-and-site-locator/mccook-house. Hours: Friday-Saturday 10:00am - 5:00pm, Sunday 1:00 - 5:00pm (Summers); Weekends only (Labor Day to mid- October). Admission: $3.00 adults, $1.00 child (6-12). Note: History of Carroll County lifestyles and industry portrayed upstairs - the clothing will appeal to girls.*

The family earned the name of "Fighting McCooks" due to their extensive military service in the Civil War. Daniel McCook built this home and his family lived here until 1853. During the Civil War, Daniel's family contributed nine soldiers to the Union cause including 5 generals. Four of Daniel's family including Daniel himself died in the conflict. You're greeted by the painting in the front room. Each son and their father are portrayed. What's unique about the one son, John James I? In the hallway, you'll find an 1838 large map of Ohio. Can you find your home town or was it even around then? Look for the real tree trunk with cannon balls stuck in it from the Civil War.

PUMPKIN MAZE PLAYLAND

Columbiana - *Detwiler Farm. 4520 Renkenberger Road. www.detwilerfarm.com. Pumpkin Patches / Hayrides / Corn Mazes / Fall Playland/indoor straw maze / petting zoo - Admission (average $6.00). Plan on at least two hours playtime. Open weekends, some weekdays (by appointment) and weeknights. (late September - late October).*

Coshocton

Learning the art of making a broom

ROSCOE VILLAGE

Coshocton - *100 N Whitewoman (State Route 16 and 83, near US 36 - I-77 exit 65) 43812. Phone: (740) 622-9310. www.roscoevillage.com. Hours: Most village shops open at 10:00am. Special events May-December. Visitor Center daily 10:00am-4:00pm. Shops and Center closed major winter holidays. Admission: "Living History Tour" $5.00-$10.95 (ages 5+). Visitors Center craft: $2.50. Just Browsing FREE! Tours: Guided 10:30am and 1:30pm. Note: Monticello III Canal Boat-A horse drawn replica of a 1800's canal boat, offers narrated trips on the 1 1/2 mile restored section of the original Ohio-Erie Canal. $6-$8.00 for canal boat ride. 1:00pm-4:00pm daily from Memorial Day - Labor Day. Weekends only Labor Day to mid-October.*

Historic buildings offer a glimpse into the daily life of these craftsmen and their families. Maybe take a lesson in the one-room school or see the trappings of the 1800's daily life in the doctor's house. Watch craftsmen practice their trades of broom making, weaving, pottery, printing and more. Spend gobs of time in the General Store where you can play with and buy old-fashioned toys like harmonicas, paper dolls and wooden toys. Plan to have the kids bring their allowance because you won't be able to resist! The Johnson-Humrickhouse Museum is full of prehistoric American Indian tools and pottery, an Ohio Pioneer house and Oriental decorative arts (Samurai swords). During the summer, visit the Hillside where demonstrations of brick-making and woodworking take place. Grab baked goods or a light lunch at the Sweet Shop. The Warehouse is a wonderful sit-down dining option.

Visitors Center: Kids can try their hand at candle dipping, tin punching or rope making in the Hands-On facility. They can "discover" the sights and sounds of the canal era with games, puzzles, music and activities in the Discovery Room. Look over the realistic dioramas and working lock models.

APPLE BUTTER STIRRIN FESTIVAL

Coshocton - Roscoe Village. Over 100 crafters. Smell the fresh apple butter simmering over an open fire as you stroll through the street to the tunes of bluegrass and old-time music. Watch cooking demonstrations, participate in a craft auction, a hog-calling contest or sign up for a quilt raffle. Events throughout the weekend include living history tours, canal boat rides, musical entertainment and children's activities. Admission. (mid-October weekend)

CHRISTMAS CANDLELIGHTINGS

Coshocton - Roscoe Village. Shop for holiday gifts in a 19th century holiday setting and then stay for the candlelighting ceremony each night at 6:00pm. Strolling carolers, visits w/ Santa, live arctic reindeer, chestnuts roasting over open fire, hot-mulled cider & cookies, and carriage rides. Also see display of decorated trees and gingerbread houses on Main Street. Parking fee. (first 3 Saturdays in Dec)

HOT AIR BALLOON FESTIVAL

Coshocton - County Fairgrounds, 707 Kenilworth Avenue. (740) 622-5411. Balloon launches at dawn and dusk, Nightglow (Saturday), entertainment and rides. FREE. (second weekend in June). www.coshoctonhotairballoonfestival.com

THE WILDS

Cumberland - *14000 International Road (I-70 exit 155, Zanesville or exit 169, SR 83 - follow signs) 43732. Phone: (740) 638-5030. www.thewilds.org. Hours: Daily 10am-4pm (May-September). Weekends only in October. Admission: $30.00 per guest. Parking $6.00. Tours: Safari Transports depart from the Visitor Center every 30 minutes on open days beginning at 10am. Tour is 2.5 hrs long. The last Safari Transport departs at 4pm. Safari Transport vehicles feature large windows & are air conditioned. Strollers & coolers are not allowed on Transport vehicles. Online Reservations suggested. Note: You can visit the Wilds Gift Market, Overlook Cafe, Butterfly Habitat, and Birding Station without admission.*

Once a strip mine (donated by American Electric Power) it is now home to the International Center for the preservation of wild animals. Conservation is key at the Wilds where over 9000 acres of forest and grassland with 150 lakes is home to animals in a protected open range habitat (no pens, stables, and cages) designed to create an environment for reproduction. Check out the Mid-Sized Carnivore Conservation Center, where highly social animals such as cheetahs and African wild dogs wander. Take a bus to view the other animals as they roam free in this preserve. You'll see many animals you don't see in zoos like African gazelles, reticulated giraffes, mountain zebras, tundra swans and red wolves in herds.

With lots of "tender loving care" and adaptation exercises, injured animals may now roam free. You might also see real wild horses that look like a rhinoceros and a horse. They are very strong and tough (yet beautiful to watch). Other opportunities available to visitors include an education center where you can learn from interactive computer kiosks and various displays that focus on the relationship between humans and their environment.

ZIPLINE SAFARI

Enjoy the Wilds from an aerial perspective! Led by two professionally trained guides, this 2 ½ hour zipline safari tour consists of 10 ziplines and a rappel built on a series of observation platforms overlooking various exotic animal species that are home to the Wilds. You'll zip along a network of cables, through the trees, over the animal watering holes, lakes, and pastures, finally landing among the amazing giraffes. Participants: $84. Kid's Special - Each child between age 10-15 are half off per each regular priced adult (18 and older) on weekdays only. Open daily (May - October).

DENNISON RAILROAD DEPOT MUSEUM

Dennison - *400 Center Street (off SR 250 or SR 36, Dennison exit to Second St.- turn right along tracks) 44621. www.dennisondepot.org. Phone: (740) 922-6776. Hours: Tuesday-Friday 10:00am-5:00pm, Saturday 11:00am-4:00pm, Sunday 11:00am-3:00pm. Admission: $8.00 adult, $6.00 senior, $4.00 child (7-17). Note: Special train rides depart each season.*

During WW II the Dennison Depot was located on the National Railway Defense Route. It was the main stopping point on the route because it was the exact mid-point between Columbus and Pittsburgh. One evening, a town's lady noticed the servicemen seemed sad, so she organized a few other friends to start a GI canteen. The community became so popular among the soldiers that it was called Dreamsville, USA. The canteen for WW II servicemen is now used as a museum of local history, a gift shop, an old fashioned candy counter and a theme restaurant. Lunch is served at the Over the Rail Diner, a unique 1940s family restaurant offering Victory Garden Salads and Dreamsville Desserts (groups: ask about the "hobo lunch" served in a souvenir bandana). Admission to the museum includes kids being able to ring a steam locomotive bell, swing a lantern, climb a caboose and watch trains run on the model train layout.

POLAR EXPRESS

Dennison – Dennison Railroad Depot Museum. Train trip in decorated coaches with Santa. Songs and treats. Dress warmly. Weekends only. Admission.

Dover

BROAD RUN CHEESEHOUSE

Dover - *6011 County Road 139 NW (4 miles west of I-77, old SR 39) 44622. Phone: (330) 343-4108 or (800) 332-3358. www.broadruncheese.com. Admission: $1.50 per person (age 5+). Tours: Monday – Saturday (Mornings), by reservation usually. 20 minutes long with samples. Gift Shop with novelties, cheese and sausage. Note: keep in mind cheese-making is a morning process and is usually completed by 11am.*

Catch a window of Swiss, Baby Swiss, Brick, and Muenster productions. They make 640,000 pounds of cheese from 8,000,000 pounds (yes, pounds!) of milk each year. After your view you can sample cheese. What happens to the cream that is separated off from the cheese? (hint: it's made into another tasty product). Ever seen thick, warm milk cut into cubes? (forms "curds" and "whey"). What makes the holes?

WARTHER CARVINGS

Dover - *331 Karl Avenue (I-77 to exit 83 to State Route 211 east) 44622. Phone: (330) 343-7513. https://thewarthermuseum.com/. Hours: Daily 9am-5pm. Admission: $15 adult, $5-$7.00 student (4-17). Tours: Last tour begins one hour before closing. Note: Tree of Pliers – 500 interconnecting pairs of working pliers carved out of 1 piece of walnut wood! Mrs. Warther's Button Collection – Over 70,000 in museum! Gift Shop & garden trails. Short videos throughout the tour keep it interesting.*

A must see tour of the visions of a master craftsman! Mr. Warther started carving at age 5 with a pocketknife while milking cows and later during breaks working at a mill. Before your tour begins, take a peek into the original 1912 workshop or at the display of wood carved postcards. A favorite carving of ours was the steel mill (3 x 5 feet) with moving parts depicting the foreman raising a sandwich to eat, and another worker sleeping on the job. The Abraham Lincoln Funeral Train has thousands of mechanized movements powered by a sewing machine motor.

Hundreds of tiny moving parts...
all carved by hand...amazing!

See models of steam locomotives and trains using mostly walnut, ivory, and arguto (oily wood) for moving parts which still run without repairs for over 60 years! The late Mr. Warther loved entertaining children with his carvings and he would carve a pair of working pliers with just a few cuts in a piece of wood in only a few seconds! Now, one of the family members carves pliers for each child visiting (if you pay attention and sit in the front row). This is "Where enthusiasm is caught, not taught." Truly amazing!

CHRISTMAS OPEN HOUSE, J.E. REEVES

Dover - 325 East Iron Avenue. Buildings decorated for holidays, Santa visit, entertainment & refreshments served. Great way to expose younger ones to historical homes that might be boring otherwise. Admission. www.doverhistory.org. (begins thanksgiving weekend for one month)

East Liverpool

BEAVER CREEK STATE PARK

East Liverpool - *12021 Echo Dell Road (8 miles North of East Liverpool off State Route 7) 43920. Phone: (330) 385-3091. www.beavercreekwildlife.org.*

3,038 acres of camping, hiking trails, fishing and winter sports. Approximately sixteen miles of hiking trails take the visitor to historic canal locks and through a steep walled gorge. Hikers will find several beautiful waterfalls by exploring the many tributary streams. A short trail from the campground to Oak Tree Point gives an excellent panorama of the scenic valley. The rich history of the area invites visitors to explore Gaston's Mill, pioneer village and abandoned canal locks. The Education Center has live turtles as well as several live native snakes for visitors to see. They also have over 300 mounted mammals including deer, bears, beaver, fox, coyote, badger, bobcat, mountain lion and a gray as well as both bald and golden eagles and many song birds that can be found in and around Columbiana County (Center only open weekends 1 to 5 pm from May thru early October).

MUSEUM OF CERAMICS

East Liverpool - *400 East 5th Street (corner of Broadway) 43920. Phone: (330) 386-6001 or (800) 600-7880. www.themuseumofceramics.com. Hours: Tuesday-Friday 9:30am-3:30pm (April-December). Closed most major holidays Admission: $6.00 adult, $3.00 student (all ages).*

The exhibits in the museum depict the growth and development of East Liverpool and its ceramic industry from 1840 to 1930, the period when the city's potteries produced over 50% of the ceramics manufactured in the United States. Displays cover good and bad times of the ceramic industry and the effects on its people. Life- sized dioramas of kiln, jigger and decorating shops with a collection of old and new ceramics make the museum easy to follow.

TRI-STATE POTTERY FESTIVAL

East Liverpool - (330) 385-0845. Celebration of pottery heritage featuring pottery Olympics, industry displays, potters at work, ceramic museum, international doorknob tossing championships, factory tours (local companies like Hall China or Pioneer Pottery), art show, rose show, window displays, amusement rides and daily entertainment. (third weekend in June)

GNADENHUTTEN

Gnadenhutten - *352 South Cherry Street (I-77 to SR 36 east) 44629. Phone: (740) 254-4143. www.facebook.com/Gnadenhutten-Museum-and-Historical-Site-189932091031372З/. Hours: Tuesday-Friday 1pm-5:00pm, Saturday 10:00am-5:00pm (June-August). Weekends only (May, September-October). Admission: $1.00 donation. Note: A 'friendly' cemetery tour on the premises. Look at the graves tombstone hands- why are they turned in different directions-what does it mean?*

Gnadenhutten (Huts of Grace) was settled five months after Schoenbrunn on October 9, 1772. Joshua, a Moravian Mohican Elder, brought a large group of Christian Mohican Indians from Pennsylvania to this location. This settlement grew rapidly and the group worked hard and prospered. All went well until the Revolutionary War began and the English at Detroit wanted all Indians to fight against the Americans. The local Indians refused. When they would not leave, in September 1781, troops and Indian warriors rounded up all the Indians living in New Schoenbrunn, Gnadenhutten, and Salem and took them to Captives town. During the winter in the captive town many died of diseases. Permission to go home was granted to 150. They arrived back home in February 1782 and were gathering food and belongings, when Pennsylvania Militiamen under Colonel Williamson surrounded them. After a night of prayer and hymn singing, ninety men, women and children were massacred, then all cabins were set afire on March 8, 1782. Two boys escaped to warn others and to tell the story.

See the sites of the two buildings where the Indians spent the night before their death. Those buildings, the Mission House and Cooper Shop (the actual basement foundation where one boy hid - it will take your breath away!), have been restored and are located on their original sites. The story of the massacre is told in the outdoor drama "Trumpet in the Land".

PIONEER DAYS

Gnadenhutten - Historical Park & Museum. An 1840's pioneer encampment, entertainment, parade, arts and crafts. FREE. (first weekend in August)

QUAIL HOLLOW STATE PARK

Hartville - *13480 Congress Lake Road (2 miles North of Hartville) 44632. Phone: (330) 877-6652. http://parks.ohiodnr.gov/quailhollow*

Quail Hollow is a landscape of rolling meadows, marshes, pine and woodland trails surrounding a 40-room manor. Now called the Natural History Study Center, the former Stewart family home is primarily used for educational, nature-oriented and community activities. The home is open on weekends 1:00-5:00 pm. Quail Hollow has over 19 miles of trails ideal for hiking, jogging, nature study or cross-country skiing. Eight interpretive nature trails explore the unique natural habitats for which each is named. There is also a five-mile, day-use bridle trail and four-mile mountain bike trail. The Nature For All trail is a 2000 ft. paved interpretive trail for those visitors with a physical challenge.

LEHMAN'S HARDWARE

Kidron - *4779 Kidron Road (Rte. 30 east, exit Kidron Road, head south) 44636. Phone: (330) 857-5757. www.lehmans.com/. Hours: Monday - Saturday 9:00am-5:00pm, Closed Sunday.*

Heading from Ohio Amish country west, you may be surprised to find some old-fashioned goodness in Wayne County. Try to plan a visit to Kidron on a Thursday - it's auction day. Next door, visit the famous Lehman's Hardware, where you'll find all the non-electrical appliances and equipment used by the Amish. Lehman's was founded by Jay Lehman in 1955 to serve the Amish who believe in simple living without electricity or other modern innovations. From his Amish customers, Jay learned that non-electric products often give us the ability to complete a task faster and more efficiently than commonly accepted modern methods. In a twist of irony, the company's key customers (once the Amish) are now a key vendor. Don't forget to bring your toy and kitchen tools wish list. Look for

You can browse here for hours for all kinds of unique items...

the giant copper kettles and cast iron pots and plenty of toy wagons and farm games. Around every corner is a museum-quality artifact with a description.

Visit http://countrylife.lehmans.com/about/ online for free tips on how to live simply

GUILFORD LAKE STATE PARK

Lisbon - ***6835 East Lake Road (6 miles Northwest of Lisbon off State Route 172) 44432. Phone: (330) 222-1712. http://parks.ohiodnr.gov/guilfordlake***

Guilford Lake State Park is a quiet fishing lake located in northeastern Ohio on the west fork of the Little Beaver Creek. A half-mile hiking trail skirts the scenic lakeshore and provides opportunities for exercise and wildlife observation. 488 acres of camping, boating, fishing, swimming and winter sports.

ELSON FLOURING MILL

Magnolia - ***261 North Main Street (SR 183, southwest edge of town) 44643. Phone: (330) 866-3353. www.elsonmill.freeservers.com. Tours: Every Thursday at 10:00am and 2:00pm, April through November. Only by Appointment. Admission is $2.00 per person. The working mill conducts business 8:00am - 5:00pm weekdays and 8:00am - noon Saturdays.***

Visit this picturesque red mill in the center of a canal village. Founded in 1834 by the great-great grandfather of the present owners, it gives a glimpse of industry in the 1800's. Built of virgin timber cleared from the land on which the mill stands, it has been in continuous operation by the Elson Family. Corn meal has been made at the mill since 1834 and can be purchased still today.

GUGGISBERG CHEESE FACTORY

Millersburg - ***5060 State Route 557 (Off State Route 39, I-77 exit 83) 44654. Phone: (330) 893-2500. www.guggisberg.com. Hours: Monday-Saturday 8:00am – 6:00pm, Sunday 11:00 am – 4:00pm) (April – December). Monday-Saturday 8:00am – 5:00pm (December – March)***

Home of the original Baby Swiss – you can watch through a window as cheese is being made (best time to view is 8:00 am – Noon weekdays). We learned milk is brought in the early mornings from neighboring Amish farms. Cultures and enzymes are added to form curd. Curd is pressed into molds and brine salted. Each cheese is aged at least a month for flavor. A short video is always playing that details this process if you can't view it personally.

YODER'S AMISH HOME

Millersburg - ***6050 State Route 515 (between Trail and Walnut Creek) 44654. Phone: (330) 893-2541. www.yodersamishhome.com. Hours: Monday-Saturday 10:00am-5:00pm (mid-April thru October). Admission: Tours $8.25 Adult, $4.75 Children (2-12). Buggy Rides $4.75 Adult, $3.75 Children. Add about $3.00-$4.00 each for the tour of the school. Combo (all three tours) saves $3-$4.00.***

Step back to a simple time and way of life. This home was built in 1866 and shows authentic furnishings from that period. Local, knowledgeable guides take you on a 30-40 minute tour through both homes on the property and the barn. Your guide will explain a great deal about the history and lifestyle of the Amish people. Learn what a "hoodle stup" is. Then step into an 1885 barn with animals to pet. Most popular tends to be the turkeys – (Yes, you can try to pet turkeys!). Buggy rides are given by retired real Amish farmers who tell stories during the ride.

OLD FASHIONED APPLE BUTTER STIRRING

Millersburg – Yoder's Amish Home. 30 gallon copper kettle on the fire in the morning and begin the process of apple butter. Do you know how many apples go in a 30-gallon batch? When you visit, you can take a turn stirring and try a sample too! They stir all day and fill up jars to be sold. (first three Saturdays in Oct)

HOLIDAYS AT THE MANSION

Millersburg - 484 Wooster Road. www.victorianhouse.org. Holidays at the Mansion is a very special time to see the Victorian House in all its grandeur. Buildings decorated for holidays, Santa visit, entertainment and light refreshments served. Great way to expose younger ones to historical homes that might be boring otherwise. Admission. (mid-November thru December weekends)

DILLON STATE PARK

Nashport - ***5265 Dillon Hills Drive (8 miles west of Zanesville off State Route 146) 43830. Phone: (740) 453-4377. http://parks.ohiodnr.gov/dillon***

The wooded hills and valleys of the area offer outdoor adventure with 7690 acres of camping, hiking trails, boating and rentals, fishing, swimming (sandy beaches), and winter sports. The Ruffed Grouse Nature Trail is approximately 3/4-mile long and introduces the hiker to the varied habitats of

the area. This trail is a branch of the 6-mile long Licking Bend Trail which skirts the lakeshore. Three other fascinating trails--Blackberry Ridge Trail (1 mile), King Ridge Loop (1.1 miles) and Hickory Grove Loop (1.5 miles) are located very near the camping and cottage area. Family deluxe cottages with A/C and cable. Nearby, in the Blackhand Gorge, carved by the Licking River, a sandstone cliff bore a soot blackened (Black Hand Sandstone) engraving of a human hand. This mysterious petroglyph is thought to have served as a guide marker for Indians searching for Flint Ridge.

JOHN & ANNIE GLENN HISTORIC SITE

New Concord ***- 72 West Main Street (I-70 to New Concord exit, across from library) 43762. Phone: (740) 826-3305. www.johnglennhome.org. Hours: Wednesday-Saturday 10:00am-4:00pm, Sunday 1:00-4:00pm. (May thru September). Closed major holidays. Admission: $7.00 adult, $6.00 senior, $3.00 student. Educators: Bios of the Glenns and US history study guides are online.***

John Glenn, astronaut and politician, spent his boyhood in this home that has been moved and restored to its late 1930's appearance as a museum dedicated to telling 20th century American history through the lives of John and Annie Glenn. It enlightens visitors about life in 1937 during the Great Depression, in 1944 during WWII, and in 1962 when John Glenn orbited Earth. Kid-friendly areas include: "talk" to Astronaut Glenn in space (wasn't his capsule small?); look for his triclycle & train set; and his radio he bought and shared with Annie when they were young. Great way to inspire kids if they work hard and stay out of trouble, they could be famous some day.

ATWOOD LAKE PARK

Mineral City ***- 9500 Lakeview Rd NE (off SR 212 to SR 542 or off SR 39 entrance) 44656. Phone: (330) 735-2211. https://atwoodpark.mwcd.org/***

Camping, hiking trails, boating & rentals, fishing, swimming, visitor center and winter sports. Beach with paddle boat rentals & food service. Comfortable, spacious 4 bedroom cabins with trails! Bring along the extended family and plan a mini-reunion. Because the cabins are spacious and have separate bedrooms, everyone can have their "space", yet convene in the center gathering area for games, conversation or television. Summertime kids activities, too.

New Philadelphia

MUSKINGUM WATERSHED CONSERVANCY DISTRICT LAKES

New Philadelphia - ***44663. www.mwcd.org. Phone: (877) 363-8500.***

All of the MWCD parks feature camping all year long, so a getaway for a day or weekend is easy. Stays in family vacation cabins also are available for a few weeks at Pleasant Hill and Seneca parks, several months at Tappan Lake Park and all year at Atwood Lake Park. Contact the park of your choice for details. Hiking trails, boating and rentals, fishing, swimming, visitor center, lodge or cabins and food service. Nature programs.

SHOENBRUNN

New Philadelphia - ***State Route 259, East High Avenue (4 miles East of I-77 exit 81) 44663. www.ohiohistory.org/visit/museum-and-site-locator/schoenbrunn-village Phone: (330) 339-3636. Hours: Tuesday-Saturday 9:30am-5:00pm; Sunday Noon-5:00pm (Summer). Weekends only (September-October). Admission: $7.00 adult, $4.00 student (7-17). Note: Museum. Video orientation. Gift Shop. Picnic facilities. A special, interactive event is usually held one Saturday each month. Tape recorded tours available at no extra cost.***

Take a self-guided tour of the reconstructed log building village founded by a Moravian missionary in 1772. The Moravian church founded Schoenbrunn ("beautiful spring") as a mission to the Delaware Indians. Being the first settlement in Ohio, Schoenbrunn claims the first civil code, the first church (learn about the love feast still occasionally held here, especially near Christmas), and the first school. Problems associated with the American Revolution prompted Schoenbrunn's closing in 1777. Today the reconstructed village includes seventeen log buildings and gardens...many occupied by costumed interpreters demonstrating period crafts and customs.

First settlement church

TRUMPET IN THE LAND

New Philadelphia - ***Shoenbrunn Amphitheatre (-77 to Exit 81) 44663. Phone: (330) 339-1132. www.trumpetintheland.com. Hours: Several performances per week (except Sunday) 8:30 pm (mid-June to late August) Admission: $20.00 adult, $18.00 senior, $10.00 child (3-12). Backstage tours a few dollars extra. Note: See listing for Gnanenhutten to review a more detailed history of this saga before you go. Other productions are either historical or contemporary.***

In an Ohio Frontier setting (the first settlement at Schoenbrunn), meet historical characters like David Zeisgerber (missionary converting Indians), Simon Girtz (renegade), Captain Pipe (young warrior who hated white men) and John Heikewelder (explorer)...all vital historical figures in the founding of Ohio. The Revolutionary War breaks out and Moravian Indian Christians would not take sides. Feel their stress and desires to try to remain neutral in a hostile environment.

TUSCORA PARK

New Philadelphia - ***South Broadway Street (I-77 to US 250 east) 44663. Phone: (800) 527-3387. www.newphilaoh.com/tuscora_park Summer Ride Hours: Monday-Thursday 4:30-8:00pm. Weekends Noon-8pm.***

The central feature is the antique big carousel or the summer showcase concert series or swimming pool. What draws little ones and families is also the Ferris wheel, 6-8 kiddie rides (including a train ride and mini roller coaster), batting cages and putt-putt - all at low prices. Most rides and activities are around $1.00. Great alternative to higher priced amusement "vacations" in summer.

NATIONAL ROAD / ZANE GREY MUSEUM

Norwich - ***8850 East Pike (U.S. 40 / I-70 Norwich Exit) 43767. Phone: (740) 872-3143 or (800) 752-2602. www.ohiohistory.org/visit/museum-and-site-locator/national-road-and-zane-grey-museum Hours: Wednesday-Saturday 10:00am-4:00pm, Sunday & Holidays 1:00-4:00pm (May-October). Admission: $7.00 adult, $3.00 student (all ages).***

"Head West Young Man" in a Conestoga wagon as you explore the history of US-40 National Road. Built based on a concept of George Washington, it stretches between western territories in Illinois to the eastern state of Maryland. It was vital to the development of the frontier heading west and later called "America's Main Street". Play a game where children locate all the different types of bridges on this route (examples: the "Y" and "S" Bridge). The facility also commemorates author Zane Grey and his western novels and the area's ceramic heritage.

SMUCKERS COMPANY STORE AND CAFÉ

Orrville - *333 Wadsworth Road (Rt. 57, 1/4 mile north of Rt. 30) 44667. Phone: (330) 684-1500. www.jmsmucker.com/smucker-cafe-store. Hours: Monday-Saturday 9:00am-6:00pm. Closed Sunday. Note: Café offers delicious recipes made with ingredients from their brands. Enjoy a wood-fired pizza.*

You'll see the Simply Smuckers store brimming with your favorite jams and relishes - plus Pillsbury Dough Boys and Jif products. Walk through the on-site museum to learn about The Company's heritage and journey - spanning over 100 years. There are always delicious products to sample - usually something sweet and something savory - all in a beautiful timber frame barn.

JUMPIN PUMPKIN SPECIAL

Orrville - 145 South Depot Street. Orrville Railroad. www.orrvillerailroad.com. Phone: (330) 683-2426. The Jumpin' Pumpkin Jamboree features food, games, parade, pumpkin decorating contest, etc. Trains rides depart on the hour beginning at Noon with the last ride at 5:00pm. The train will be leaving from and returning to the McGill St. Siding. Small Admission. (mid-October Saturday)

APPLE DUMPLING FESTIVAL

Shreve - Whispering Hills RV Park. Apples & cider. Apple pie eating contests. Apple peeling contests. Apple butter. Candy apples. Wagon/hayrides. Apple Dumplings, Fritters, Donuts, etc. Parades. Pioneer crafts. Petting Zoo. www. whisperinghillsrvpark.com. (first weekend in October)

Steubenville

JEFFERSON LAKE STATE PARK

Steubenville - *501 Twsp Rd 261A (16 miles Northwest of Steubenville on State Route 43) 43944. Phone: (740) 765-4459. http://parks.ohiodnr.gov/jeffersonlake*

In the sandstone bedrock can be found layers of coal which were formed by decaying swamp vegetation. 933 acres of camping, rough hiking trails, boating, fishing, swimming and winter sports.

FORT STEUBEN, HISTORIC

Steubenville - *120 South Third Street 43952. www.oldfortsteuben.com. Phone: (740) 283-1787. Hours: Monday-Saturday 10:00am-4:00pm, Sunday 11am-4:00pm (May-October). Visitor Center open weekdays year-round. Admission: $9.00 adult, $5.00 youth (6-12). Note: Pick up a map at the CVB office here for the Steubenville City of Murals: During a self-guided tour (free) you can see 25 giant full color*

(almost 3D) murals with the theme "Preserving a Piece of America" on the sides of downtown buildings – many "jump" right off the wall and appear almost like a photograph.

Historic Fort Steuben is a reconstructed 18th century fort built on the original site overlooking the Ohio River that opened the Northwest Territory to expansion and settlement. The 150 soldiers garrisoned in the fort protected the surveyors from hostile tribes as they laid out the first Seven Ranges of the Northwest Territory. Exhibits depict military life in 1787. An active archaeological dig is part of the tour. Buildings housing exhibits include the hospital, the Officers' Quarters, the Enlisted Men's Quarters, the Blacksmith, the Quartermaster's, and the newly opened Commissary. This is a nicely restored fort complex that kids can explore easily.

FORT STEUBEN FESTIVAL

Steubenville - This first American Regiment was built to protect government surveyors from hostile Indians. Next to the fort site is the first Federal Land Office built in the U.S. in 1801. Watch mountain men reenactment groups, storytellers and craftspeople. Admission. (third weekend in June)

Sugarcreek

ALPINE HILLS MUSEUM

Sugarcreek - *106 West Main Street 44681. www.facebook.com/alpinehillsmuseum Phone: (888) 609-7592. Hours: Daily 9:00am-4:30pm, except Sundays (April - November). Extended summer hours. Admission: FREE*

Three floors of Swiss, German and Amish heritage. Many audio-visuals & push buttons "spotlight" parts of well-explained dioramas of an Amish kitchen, Swiss cheesehouse and a woodshop & printshop. Nearby, the best Swiss steak & mashed potatoes in town are at the ***Swiss Hat restaurant***.

OHIO SWISS FESTIVAL

Sugarcreek - Downtown. (888) 609-7592. Experience the best of Switzerland from Polka bands, dancing, tons of Swiss cheese, Steinstossen (stone throwing) and Schwingfest (Swiss wrestling). FREE (last Friday & Saturday of September)

COBLENTZ CHOCOLATE COMPANY

Walnut Creek - ***4917 State Route 515 and State Route 39 (I-77 exit 83 Dover to Rte. 39 west) 44687. www.coblentzchocolates.com. Phone: (800) 338-9341. Hours: Monday – Saturday 9:00am – 6:00pm (July – October). Close at 5:00pm (November-May). Best viewing is from 9:00am-3:00pm.***

Watch through the kitchen windows as chocolate is stirred in large vats with automatic paddle stirs. They have a window going 65 feet along the side of the kitchen so you can see candy being made, from cooling to pouring onto tables to wrapping. Caramels, fruits, and nuts are hand dipped and layered on large trays to cool and dry. Also, see molds for chocolate forms used to create bars of barks and holiday shapes. Savor the sweet smell of fresh milk and dark chocolate as you decide which treats to buy. Our favorite are the chocolate covered Dutch pretzels with sprinkles or nuts on top.

AMISH DOOR DINNER THEATRE

Wilmot - ***1210 Winesburg Street, US 62 44689. www.amishdoor.com. Phone: (800) 891-6142. Hours: Doors open at 6:15pm. Shows generally begin around 7:00pm.***

Come celebrate the joy of dinner and a show at the Amish Door. Through original plays, classic stories and festive songs, you'll experience light-hearted, fun biblical "twists" of classic themes and musicals. Tickets are around $40 and include a bountiful, all inclusive meal featuring all the Amish Door favorites

Wooster

CAT'S MEOW VILLAGE

Wooster - ***2163 Great Trails Drive (just off E LincolnWay, near Rte. 30) 44691. Phone: (330) 264-1377. www.catsmeow.com. Hours: Monday-Friday 9am-3pm.***

Just a few miles outside of downtown toward Wooster on SR 30, you'll find The Cat's Meow Village, maker of the two-dimensional wooden buildings found in gift shops around the country. Hang out with the production team. Some kids may like the "Mewseum" where you can make your own piece or play some guessing games with Casper, the mascot. Did you know Casper is hidden on every Cat's Meow memory piece?

HARTZLER FAMILY DAIRY

Wooster - ***5454 Cleveland Road (rte 3) 44691. www.hartzlerfamilydairy.com. Phone: (330) 345-8190. Tours: are by appointment. Mostly weekdays, some Saturdays. Tours (min 15 people) $3.75 per person. (includes single dip cone).***

A true "family affair" with oodles of generations of kids working all about. Get the "scoops" from Mom Hartzler at the Ice Cream Shoppe. Tour the processing plant that is adjacent to the ice cream shoppe. Walk through the family farms and processing plant where you'll see milk bottling, butter churning and ice cream making. Guided by a Hartzler Family Member, you'll determine the secrets about why their milk looks and tastes different than most.

Cows drink 25-50 gallons of water each day--nearly a bathtub full!

TJS RESTAURANT

Wooster - 359 West Liberty Street 44691. Phone: (330) 264-6263. www.tjsrestaurants.com Hours: Tuesday-Saturday 4 - 9pm. Downtown Wooster: Looking for some new kitchen accessories or Little Tykes playstuff, stop in to the Everything Rubbermaid Store. Several little boutiques, The Wooster Book Company (nice kids section) and unique bakeries or cafes are in the square, too. After you've shopped, enjoy a delicious hot meal at TJs. The brick oven smell will lure you in and their friendly wait staff and reasonable gourmet pricing (average dinner entree around $12) will please your appetite and they have a Kids Menu.

OHIO AGRICULTURAL RESEARCH AND DEVELOPMENT CENTER

Wooster - *1680 Madison Avenue (off I-71 exit SR 83 or US 30 west to Madison Ave. exit) 44691. Phone: (330) 202-3507. http://oardc.osu.edu/. Hours: Monday-Friday 8:00am-5:00pm. Admission: FREE. Tours: Guided tours for groups of 10+ by appointment. Weekdays 9:00am-4:00pm. Self guided maps at visitor center. Note: You can also visit the 88 acre Secrest Arboretum which has many walking trails and a children's play area. Enter off Madison at the main entrance to OARDC and drive through SECREST ARBORETUM. Get out and walk if it's blooming.*

This center is the foremost, nationally known agricultural research Ohio State University facility with inventions to their credit such as crop dusting and adding vitamin D to milk. Many experiments on insects, honeybees and composting are going on. See how animals are raised, how the right wheat is important for bread making, how laser beams detect the size of water droplets in pesticide applications, and how a jellyfish gene can help soybean scientists.

Stop in to the Visitors Center and take a picture with a cow or play with some food ideas. Also in the complex is the Bug Zoo. If you dare, hold a millipede or sample bug "treats" at special programs conducted every so often in Cafe Insecta. Why are bugs like tools? Be sure to sign up for other popular programs for families or groups where you might be able to pull out DNA or plant soybeans in plaster! Most importantly, they teach you how agriculture impacts everyone-everyday. If self-guided tours are your option, you can see the Center which contains some activities for children such as a microscope and computer display as well as the bug zoo. This might spark the future scientist within your child.

WAYNE COUNTY HISTORICAL SOCIETY MUSEUM

***Wooster** - 546 East Bowman St. 44691. www.waynehistoricalohio.org. Phone: (330) 264-8856. Hours: Friday-Saturday 1:30-4:30pm (March - October). Tours by appointment only November, December and January. Closed holidays. Admission: $5.00 adults; children under 14 free.*

From magnificent model ships to the weird seven-legged pig or the amusing squirrel Orchestra, the staff and volunteers here are so passionate about their artifacts and research stories. Here's some other sites to look at: Log Cabin (early settlers home life), Schoolhouse (McGuffy Readers, dunce cap and stool, and potbelly stove, it accurately recreates the atmosphere of a late 1800's learning center), Indians, Women's Vintage Dress Shop, and Outdoor Bake Oven (typical of the massive outdoor ovens which were once found on virtually all German farms in the area during the 19th century).

PUMPKIN MAZE PLAYLAND - RAMSEYER FARMS

Wooster - Ramseyer Farms. 3488 Akron Road. Pumpkin Patches / Hayrides / Corn Mazes / Fall Playland. Admission (average $6.00). Plan on at least two hours playtime. Open weekends, some weekdays (by appointment) and weeknights. www.ramseyerfarms.com. (late September - late October, closed Sunday/Monday).

LORENA STERNWHEELER

***Zanesville** - Moored at Zane's Landing Park (West End of Market Street – I-70 to Downtown Zanesville Exit – Follow signs) 43701. Phone: (740) 455-8883. www.facebook.com/LorenaSternwheeler Hours: Wednesday and Saturdays (June – August). Weekends Only (September to mid-October). Admission: Public Rides: $10.00 adult, $9.00 senior, $6.00 child (2-12). $15-$35 lunch or dinner cruises.*

There was a mythical sweetheart of the Civil War named Lorena who inspired a song written by the famous Zanesvillian, Rev. Henry Webster. The 104' long, 59-ton boat was christened "Lorena" after that popular song. A one-hour cruise on the Muskingum River at a very reasonable rates (afternoon/twilight).

STARS & STRIPES ON THE RIVER

Zanesville - Zanes Landing Park, Downtown Riverfront. (740) 453-7889. www.zanesvillejaycees.org/StarsStripes.asp A full day of parades, rides, entertainment and fireworks. (July 4th).

PUMPKIN MAZE PLAYLAND & APPLE FESTIVAL

Zanesville - McDonald's Greenhouse, 3220 Adamsville Rd. (740) 4452-4858. www.facebook.com/mcdonaldsgreenhouseltd/ Five acre corn maze, pick your own pumpkin, hay ride, petting zoo, Enchanted Forest, giant slides, corn box & agricultural displays. Apples & cider, butter. Apple pie eating & Apple peeling contests. Candy apples. Wagon/hayrides. Apple Dumplings, Fritters, Donuts, etc. Parades. Pioneer crafts. Petting Zoo. Giant sand box, pumpkin painting. Admission (wkends mid-Sept thru Oct)

ZOAR VILLAGE

***Zoar** - 198 Main Street (State Route 212 – I-77 to Exit 93) 44697. Phone: (800) 262-6195 or (330) 874-3011. http://historiczoarvillage.com/ Hours: Wednesday-Saturday 9:30am-5:00pm, Sunday, Holidays Noon-5:00 pm (Summer). Weekends Only (April, May, September, October). Restricted hours for FREE Museum. Admission: $8.00 adult, $4.00 child (6-12). Note: Video presentation first explains Zoar history. Probably best to tour with an emphasis on early Ohio home and community life (w/German-American heritage) theme vs. a focus on their political and religious practices (cult-like aspects).*

The 12 block district of 1800's homes and shops include a dairy, bakery, museum, gardens, storehouse, tin shops, wagon shops, and blacksmith. They are actual original buildings in a real town of 75 families. Some buildings are staffed, others open by guided tour. Volunteers give craft demonstrations during the many yearly special events like the Harvest Fest (Oct) & Christmas.

Chapter 3
Central West Ohio

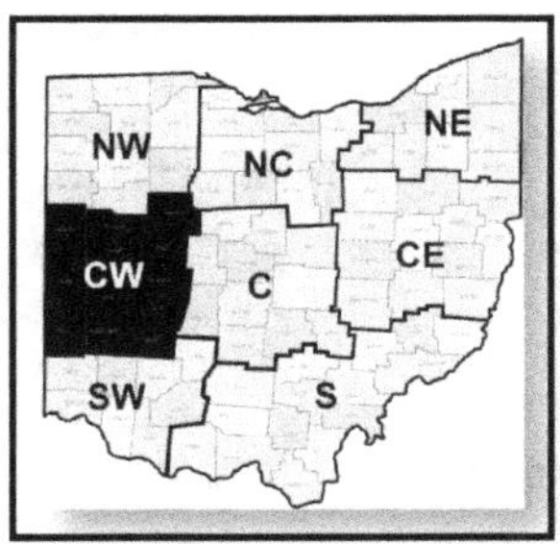

Arcanum
- Kinda Kooky Korn Maze

Bellefontaine
- Zane Shawnee Caverns

Clifton
- Clifton Mill

Dayton
- Aullwood Audubon Center And Farm
- Boonshoft Museum Of Discovery
- Carillon Historical Park, Dayton History
- Citizens Motorcar Packard Museum
- Cox Arboretum
- Dayton Art Institute
- Dayton Philharmonic Orchestra
- Dayton Sports
- Dunbar House
- Family New Year's Eve Celebration
- Learning Tree Farm
- Riverscape
- Sunwatch
- Wright Cycle Company Complex

Dayton (Fairborn)
- National Museum Of The USAF

Dayton (Huber Heights)
- Carriage Hill Farm And Museum

Dayton (Miamisburg)
- Miamisburg Mound
- Wright B. Flyer

Dayton (Vandalia)
- Dayton Air Show

Fort Recovery
- Fort Recovery

Greenville
- Annie Oakley Days
- Bear's Mill
- Garst Museum, Annie Oakley Center
- Kitchenaid Experience & Factory Tours

Jackson Center
- Airstream Factory Tour

Lakeview
- Indian Lake State Park

Lockington
- Lockington Locks

Ludlow Falls
- Lights At Ludlow Falls

Minster
- Lake Loramie State Park

New Bremen
- Bicycle Museum Of America

New Carlisle
- Pumpkin Maze Playland

Piqua
- Piqua Historical Area Tour

Springfield
- Buck Creek State Park
- Fair At New Boston

St. Mary's
- Grand Lake St. Mary's State Park

St. Paris
- Kiser Lake State Park

Trotwood

- Sycamore State Park

Troy

- Brukner Nature Center
- Idle Hour Ranch
- Troy Strawberry Festival

Urbana

- Cedar Bog
- Freshwater Farms Of Ohio

Wapakoneta

- Armstrong Air And Space Museum

West Liberty

- Mad River Theater Works
- Ohio Caverns
- Piatt Castles (Mac-O-Chee And Mac-A-Cheek)

Wilberforce

- National Afro-American Museum And Cultural Center

Xenia

- Blue Jacket
- Greene County Historical Society Museum

Yellow Springs

- John Bryan State Park
- Young's Jersey Dairy Farm

Zanesfield

- Marmon Valley Farm

A Quick Tour of our Hand-Picked Favorites Around...

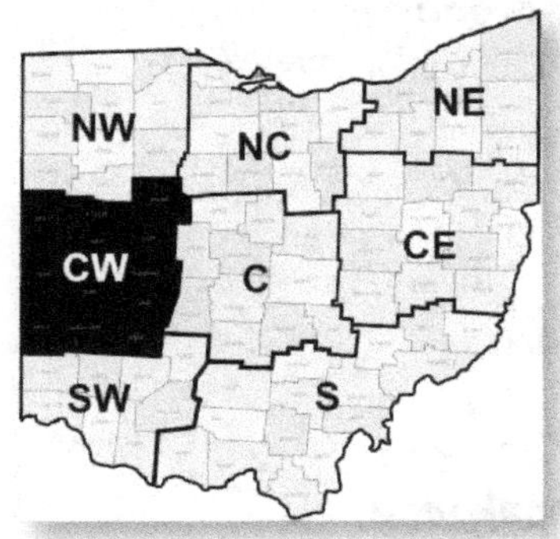

Central West Ohio

Meet the inventors of flight and the pilots of space in this area. The dream of flight was imagined by many, but achieved by Orville and Wilbur Wright, two brothers from Dayton who built and flew the first mechanically powered airplane. Their **Wright Cycle Company** and **Carillon Park** are probably the most kid-friendly sites to catch a glimpse of their genius. Walk on the same workshop floors of these famous folks who wouldn't stop at a "no" until they had a "yes". The **National Museum of the U.S. Air Force**, located just east of Dayton, also tells the story of the 100-plus years of flight, from its beginning to today's stealth age. ..and it's a FREE attraction. The world's only B-2 stealth bomber on public display is here, too. North of Dayton in Wapakoneta is the **Armstrong Air & Space Museum** where you'll see another form of aviation. Astronaut Neil Armstrong has permitted display of many space artifacts and a wonderful interactive area that immerses kids into "space."

Canals, not planes, are the hot topic at **Piqua Historical Area**. Ever tried to churn butter by hand? What about trying some ice cream or butter freshly made by costumed 1800s-period folks? Later, take a "slow ride" on the canal with mules leading the way.

Dayton is host to some other great sites like the **Boonshoft Museum of Discovery** where interactive techno exhibits combined with a zoo and planetarium make for more than a day's worth of fun. Their sister location nearby is **Sunwatch** – an ancient Indian village recreated from actual archeological digs in the area. What did they find and where did the Indians go?

Ever pow-wowed with famous Indians like **Tecumseh**? Xenia is the place. Pioneers and Indians, oh my! At the local county museum you'll find a log cabin tucked away in a complex of buildings. This is the home of Rebecca Galloway – a white girl who was adored by Shawnee chief, Tecumseh. Actually view the chair he sat in while waiting for his date.

Finally, head out into the quaint countryside for a "meet-n-greet" with some farm animals of very different sorts. Visit Ohio's largest indoor fish hatchery and retail fish farm market – **Freshwater Farms**, in Urbana. Start your tour by petting a sturgeon fish. Why can you touch them, but not catfish? Next, stop for yummy ice cream and visit with the cows that made it famous at **Young's Jersey Dairy** in the picturesque town of Yellow Springs, near Springfield. The cutest cows in the world make the sweetest milk for creamy ice cream. Plan an entire day here as there's petting areas, pre-arranged group tours, putt-putt, eateries, and some of the best seasonal festivals anywhere.

Sites and attractions are listed in order by City, Zip Code, and Name. Symbols indicated represent: Restaurants Lodging

KINDA KOOKY KORN MAZE - BRUMBAUGH FRUIT FARM

Arcanum - Brumbaugh Fruit Farm, 6420 Hollansburg-Arcanum Road. Pumpkin Patches/ Hayrides/ Corn Mazes/ Fall Playland - Admission (average $8.00). Plan on at least two hours playtime. Open weekends, some weekdays (by appointment) and weeknights. www.brumbaughfruitfarm.com. (early September - late October).

Bellefontaine

ZANE SHAWNEE CAVERNS

Bellefontaine - *7092 State Route 540 (5 miles east of town) 43311. Phone: (937) 592-9592. www.zaneshawneecaverns.com Hours: Thursday-Sunday 11:30am-5:00pm. Admission: Caverns $16.00 adult, $7.00 child (5-12). Museum $9.00 adult, $4.00 child. Pioneer Village $2.00-$6.00. Cavern & Museum pkg. Rate. Note: There are a lot of extras like hayrides, gift shop, snack bar, and camping. Remember to dress appropriately as the temperature in the caverns is a constant 48-50 degrees.*

See crystals in objects formed like straws, draperies, and popcorn. They boast the only "cave pearls" found in Ohio. This property is now owned and operated by the Shawnee People. The Museum has artifacts from actual tribe members and some from prehistoric Indian digs (Hopewell, Ancient). Separate display cases give a special look to other Native American cultural areas including: Great Lakes Tribes, Northern Iroquois, Southwestern Tribes, Great plains, Southeastern Tribes and the Eskimo People. Also on display is the evolution of corn - Zea Maize to modern corn and Native American weapons along with several dioramas. Probably the best time to visit are Pow Wow weekends.

CLIFTON MILL

Clifton - *75 Water Street (I-70 West to SR 72 South) 45316. Phone: (937) 767-5501. www.cliftonmill.com. Hours: Monday-Friday 9:00am-4:00pm, Saturday-Sunday 8:00am-5:00pm. Note: Restaurant and store. Walk off your meal by parking down the road at Clifton Gorge Nature Preserve and "hiking" the small sand/gravel walkway past bridges and on platforms that give you a "crows nest" view of the gorge - beautiful.*

A surprise treat tucked away in a small town where Woody Hayes grew up. Built in 1802 on the Little Miami River, it is the largest operating water powered gristmill in the nation. Before or after a yummy breakfast or lunch overlooking the river, take a self-guided tour for a small fee (spring or summer Monday-Friday 10am-2pm, $3.00). There are 5 floors to view. The 3rd floor (main operations) is where you see how everything on the other floors above and below come together. The turbine takes the flowing water's energy to move a system of belts to the grindstones. As the stones rotate, raw grain is poured into the hopper, through a chute and into a space between the stones which grind it. The most interesting part of the tour is the belt to bucket elevators that are the "life of the mill" transporting grain and flour up and down 5 levels.

Restaurant seating with a view of a waterwheel, river and covered bridge. Pancakes, mush, grits and bread are made from product produced at the mill. Best pork barbecue sandwich ever! Breakfast and lunch only except dinners on Friday/Saturday. Restaurant serves kids meals around $3-5.00. Adult meals are double. Be sure to buy some pancake mix to take home!

CLIFTON MILL LEGENDARY LIGHT DISPLAY

Clifton - Clifton Mill. Miniature village, Santa's workshop and 1802 log cabin. 3.2 million lights. Promptly lit at 6:00pm. (month of December)

Dayton

DAYTON DRAGONS BASEBALL

Dayton - Fifth Third Field. I-75 to First Street Exit 53. (937) 228-BATS or www.daytondragons.com. Class A team for Cincinnati Reds. Check out the new FunZone: Pop-a-Shot (challenge a friend and winners can take home bragging rights); Speed pitch (unleash your fastball) and Inflatable Bounce house (features a slide). Tickets are $9 - $19.

DUNBAR HOUSE

Dayton - *219 North Paul Lawrence Dunbar Street (2 blocks north of 3rd Street, east of US35) 45401. www.ohiohistory.org/visit/museum-and-site-locator/paul-laurence-dunbar-house. Phone: (937) 224-7061. Tours: Friday-Sunday 10am-4pm. Admission: FREE.*

The restored home of the first African American to achieve acclaim in American literature. From a young poet at age 6 to a nationally known figure (until his death at age 33 of tuberculosis), the guide helps you understand his inspiration especially from his mother and her stories of slavery. Personal belongings, like his bicycle built by the Wright Brothers and a sword presented to him by President Roosevelt, are noted as the guide leads you to his bedroom where he wrote 100 novels, poems and short stories.

"We smile, but, O great Christ, our cries
To thee from tortured souls arise.
We sing, but oh the clay is vile
Beneath our feet, and long the mile;
But let the world dream otherwise,
We wear the mask!"

-Paul Laurence Dunbar, from the poem, "We Wear the Mask"

CITIZENS MOTORCAR PACKARD MUSEUM

Dayton - *420 South Ludlow Street - Downtown (I-75 to US 35 exit, head east a few blocks) 45402. Phone: (937) 226-1917. www.americaspackardmuseum.org. Hours: Monday-Friday Noon-5:00pm, Saturday and Sunday 1:00-5:00pm. Open Every Day except major holidays. Admission: $6.00 adult, $5.00 student.*

See the world's largest collection of Packard automobiles in an authentic showroom. The art deco Packard dealership interior exhibits are spread through 6 settings, including the service area and period decorated salesman's office.

DAYTON PHILHARMONIC ORCHESTRA

Dayton - *125 East First Street (many performances at the Schuster Center for the Performing Arts) 45402. Phone: (937) 224-9000. www.daytonphilharmonic.com.*

Plays classical, pops, and Summer outdoor concerts. Young People's Concerts and Magic Carpet Concerts. The Family Concert Series often features Side-by-Side appearances with the Youth Orchestra with themes like Clowns, Bach to the Future or Mozart for the Mind.

RIVERSCAPE

Dayton - *111 E. Monument Avenue (MetroPark's RiverScape, I-75 exit 53B) 45402. Phone: (937) 278-2607. www.riverscape.org.*

Enjoy the RiverScape landscaped gardens, a free summer concert, major community festivals and family walks and bike rides along the river corridor recreation trails. And, don't forget your bathing suit. A popular spot for visitors looking to cool off on hot summer days is the Interactive Fountain where multiple fountain jets shoot water as high as 15 feet into the air choreographed to the sounds of family friendly music. And, the fun isn't over when it gets cold -MetroParks' invites you to come "Skate the Scape" as RiverScape becomes home to the regions only outdoor ice skating rink, festive light displays and other family winter activities. Concessions available.

CITYFOLK FESTIVAL

Dayton – Riverscape. www.cityfolk.org/festival/festival.html. Hundreds of the country's best folk performers and artists entertain you with shows, activities, games, crafts and food. (first weekend in July)

DAYTON ART INSTITUTE

Dayton - *456 Belmonte Park North (I-75 exit 53B or 54B) 45405. Phone: (937) 223-5277 or (800) 296-4426. www.daytonartinstitute.org. Hours: Wednesday-Saturday 11am-5pm, Sunday Noon-5pm. Admission: $15 adult, $10 senior (60+), $5 student (7-17).*

Overlooking the Great Miami River and downtown Dayton, The Dayton Art Institute's Italian Renaissance-style building houses an extensive permanent collection of American, European, Asian and African art. Experiencenter (features 20 hands-on activities) encourages interaction with art and experimentation with artistic elements of line, pattern, color, texture and shape. A gallery bag and an alphabet book are also available at the Entrance Rotunda desk allowing families to further explore featured special exhibits through the use of games and learning activities.

DAYTON AVIATION HERITAGE

WRIGHT CYCLE COMPANY COMPLEX

Dayton - ***16 South Williams Street (I-75 exit 53A, off West 3rd Street) 45407. Phone: (937) 225-7705. www.nps.gov/daav/. Hours: Daily 9:00am-5:00pm except major winter holidays. Admission: Donation. Tours: Join a ranger for a walking tour of the historic Wright-Dunbar Village, the neighborhood of the Wright brothers and Paul Laurence Dunbar. Visitors are advised to carry water on hot days. (offered daily during summer). Educators: curriculum guides - www.nps.gov/daav/forteachers/lessonplansandteacherguides.htm***

This is the neighborhood in which the Wright brothers lived and worked. This is the neighborhood in which they started their printing business, entered into the bicycle business and became involved with the mystery of flight.

The Wright Cycle Company complex consists of the Wright Cycle Company building and the Aviation Trail Visitor Center and Museum. The brothers operated their second print shop here as Wright & Wright, Job Printers. In this location, the Wrights edited and published newspapers for West Side patrons, including the Dayton Tattler, written by Paul Laurence Dunbar.

The bicycle craze in America began in 1887 with the introduction from England of the safety bicycle (two wheels of equal size). It made the freedom of cycling accessible to a much wider market. The Wright brothers' best known pre-aeronautical occupation was bicycle repair and manufacture. This building is the actual site where the Wright Brothers had a bicycle business from 1895-1897 and developed their own brand of bicycles. On this site, they also developed ideas that led to the invention of flight almost 7 years later.

> **Did You Know?**
>
> On September 7, 1904, the Wright brothers use a catapult launching device for the first time at Huffman Prairie Flying Field, Dayton, Ohio.

The dream of flight was imagined by many, but achieved by Orville and Wilbur Wright - just two brothers from Dayton who happened to fly the first mechanically powered airplane. You'll walk on the same floorboards that the brothers did and see actual plans for a flying bicycle!

CARILLON HISTORICAL PARK, DAYTON HISTORY

Dayton - ***1000 Carillon Blvd. (I-75 to Exit 51) 45409. www.carillonpark.org. Phone: (937) 293-2841. Hours: Monday-Saturday 9:30am-5:00pm. Sunday and Holidays Noon - 5:00pm, closed on Thanksgiving, Christmas Eve, Christmas Day, New Year's Eve & New Year's Day. Admission: $8.00 adult, $7.00 senior, $5.00 child (3-17). Note: Museum Store sells period toys, snacks and candy. Wooded park with Ohio's largest bell tower, the Carillon Bell Tower (57 bells), also has many shaded picnic areas. CULP'S CAFE, reminiscent of Culp's Cafeteria located in downtown Dayton in the 1930s and 1940s, serves soup, salads, sandwiches, ice cream and sodas.***

A must see - over 65 acres of historical buildings and outdoor exhibits of history, invention and transportation. Called the "Little Greenfield Village" in Miami Valley and we definitely agree! Inventions like the cash register, innovations like flood control, and industries like Huffy Corporation and General Motors are represented throughout the Park. Many of the oldest buildings from the early 1800's are represented too (tavern, home, school). As you enter buildings, a costumed guide orients you to colorful stories of the famous people who once occupied them. The highlight of the collections is the 1905 Wright Flyer III, the world's first practical airplane. The hands-on area is fun. Our favorites are the Deed's Barn (learn about the Barn Gang and the big companies they started) and the rail cars that you can actually board-the Barney & Smith is ritzy!

AULLWOOD AUDUBON CENTER AND FARM

Dayton - ***1000 Aullwood Road 45414. http://aullwood.center.audubon.org. Phone: (937) 890-7360. Hours: Monday-Saturday 9:00am-5:00pm, Sunday 1:00-5:00pm. Closed holidays. Admission: $7.00 adult, $5.00 child (2-18).***

The Discovery Room has more than 50 hands-on exhibits. Visitors can begin walks on five miles of hiking trails here. Around the building are special plantings of prairie and woodland wildflowers and a butterfly - hummingbird garden. The nearby Farm (9101 Frederick Pike) is the site of many special events. Cows, pigs, horses, chickens, turkeys, sheep, goats and barn swallows can all be found here if you come at the right time. The sugar bush, organic garden, herb garden and access to the trails are here. The glacial erratics are the start of the Geology trail. On it, you can explore the recent erosion of the land and the water cycle, the leavings of the continental glacier, and the old bedrock with its load of Ordovician fossils.

MAPLE SYRUP FESTIVAL

Dayton – Aullwood Audubon Center and Farm. Syrup making demos. Pancake breakfasts. Sugarbush tours by foot or wagon. (weekends late February and/or March)

APPLE FEST

Dayton – Aullwood Audubon Center and Farm. The whistle of Ken Ullery's antique steam engine and the delicious aroma of simmering apple butter beckon one and all to the festivities. Sample pie and everything apple flavored, enjoy live entertainment, visit farm-friendly animals, and hop on a horse drawn wagon. Meet Johnny Appleseed or watch the herding of sheep. (last weekend in September. Enchanted Forest hike is last weekend in October)

BOONSHOFT MUSEUM OF DISCOVERY

Dayton - *2600 DeWeese Parkway (North of downtown I-75 to exit 57B, follow signs) 45414. Phone: (937) 275-7431. www.boonshoftmuseum.org. Hours: Monday-Saturday 9:00am-5:00pm, Sunday Noon-5:00pm. Closed major winter holidays. Admission: $14.50 adult, $12.50 senior, $11.50 child (3-16). $4-$6 more for Space Theater shows. Note: Vending area. Discovery Shop.*

A Children's Museum, a Science Center, Nature Center and Planetarium all in one place! Interactive technology exhibits combined with a zoo make for more than a day's worth of fun. Here's highlights of each space:

A treehouse of discovery...

DISCOVERY CENTER - mastodon bones, desert animals (daytime vs. nighttime creatures using flashlights!), touch tide pool (ever seen a red sea cucumber? Touch one!), rainforest and a treehouse with binoculars for outdoor window views.

DISCOVERY ZOO – An indoor tree house & zoo with small animals in natural surroundings. Visit the den of bobcat Van Cleve or a coyote, river otter, groundhog, fox or turtle. A Falcon nest Web Cam is a popular area - something new is always happening with that family. Both parents will tend to the chicks so keep an eye out for both Mercury and Snowball at the nest.

SCIENCE CENTRAL – Inventions stations (water table w/ sticky water, airfort and force (tubes & funny windbag blower machines), chemistry lab, and a climbing discovery tower (nets, tubes & slide) provide hands-on adventures.

SPLASH - explore the story of water in the Miami Valley...from dams to water treatment.

KIDS' PLAYCE - baby garden, pioneer cabin, dig, slide & little creatures. Dress up spot.

LEARNING TREE FARM

Dayton - ***3376 South Union Road 45417. www.learningtreefarm.org. Phone: (937) 866-8650. Hours: Dawn to Dusk. Best weekdays when most facilities are open or during special programs. Admission: Hands on the Farm: $3.00 general self-guided. Special Programs: guided $7.00 general. $1.00 discount per person for groups (12+). Note: bring a picnic lunch.***

The history of the family which originally owned the farm, from their initial voyage to Ohio to the present day, has been researched and displayed. Visitors may tour the house, visit the farm animals, hike on the farm's land, and participate in hands-on activities like caring for animals, crafts, and sheep shearing. Special programs like "Finding Freedom on the Farm" highlights storytelling, quilts used by escaping slaves, and a clue game played thru nearby land and daily activities of the safe house station.

SUNWATCH

Dayton - ***2301 West River Road (I-75 to Exit 51, west on Edwin C. Moses Blvd., cross South Broadway, turn left) 45418. www.sunwatch.org. Phone: (937) 268-8199. Hours: Tuesday-Saturday 9:00am-5:00pm. Sunday and Holidays Noon – 5:00pm (April-November). Admission: $7.00 adult, $6.00 child (6-17) & senior (60+). Tours: Guided tours daily at 1:30pm. (Summer) Note: Occasional Flute Circle weekends offer music, storytelling and food like Bison burgers, Indian tacos and summer Indian corn. Visitor's are welcome to carry-in their own food. A beverage vending machine is available.***

SunWatch Indian Village/Archaeological Park is a partially reconstructed Fort Ancient period Native American village along the Great Miami River. Here visitors can explore Dayton's first neighborhood, walk in reconstructed houses, hear the intriguing history of the Fort Ancient people, and discover the role the sun played in daily life. Archaeological excavations at a site near the Great Miami River uncovered evidence of an 800-year-old village built by the Fort Ancient Indians. The reconstructed 12th Century Indian Village has self-guided tours of the thatched huts, gardens, and artifacts of the lifestyle of a unique culture. Some activities include story telling, archery, toys and games, harvesting, a multi-media presentation, and best of all, learn to tell time by charting the sun. See how the Indians used flint and bone to create jewelry and tools - then buy some as souvenirs. This is a nice family-friendly introduction to ancient Indian lifestyles - be sure to view the orientation film first.

KEEPING THE TRADITIONS POW WOW

Dayton – Sunwatch. www.tmvcna.org/4powwow.htm. Native American dancing, singing, foods. The event features both men's and women's dances, including the men's grass dance and the women's shawl and jingle dance, performed wearing full regalia. In addition, traditional American Indian food and arts and crafts will be available from vendors. One of the largest Pow Wows in Ohio. Admission (age 13+). (last weekend in June)

17TH CENTURY REENACTMENT

Dayton – Sunwatch. The event features both men's and women's dances, including the men's grass dance and the women's shawl and jingle dance, performed wearing full regalia. In addition, traditional American Indian food and arts and crafts will be available from vendors. Included with regular admission. (Mid-October weekend)

COX ARBORETUM

Dayton - *6733 Springboro Pike (I-75 exit 50B to OH 74 south) 45449. Phone: (937) 434-9005. www.metroparks.org. Hours: Daily 8:00am to dusk. Visitor Center weekdays 8am-5pm and weekends 11:00am-4:00pm.*

Cox Arboretum MetroPark is a hands-on landscaping arboretum. Best family features are: Water Garden & Rock Garden; the Bell Children's Maze; and the Butterfly House and Garden (Butterfly House is a seasonal display). The newest fun space is the Tree Tower. The tower gives visitors a view of the conifer collection from 46 feet up.

170 acres total including the nationally recognized Edible Landscape Garden. Every season has something special to offer, from spring's splashes of bright color to winter's textures. In addition to exploring gardens, hike trails through mature forests and colorful meadows. FREE admission.

NATIONAL MUSEUM OF THE USAF

Dayton (Fairborn) - *Wright Patterson Air Force Base 1100 Spaatz St. (I-75 to State Route 4 East to Harshman Road Exit) 45433. www.nationalmuseum.af.mil/. Phone: (937) 255-3286. Hours: Daily 9:00am-5:00pm. Closed Thanksgiving, Christmas and New Years. Admission: FREE. Tours: The free USAF Heritage Tour begins at 1:30pm Monday through Friday. Saturdays 10:30am & 1:30pm. No reservation required. Educators: Scavenger Hunt - www.nationalmuseum.af.mil/education/educators/index.asp Note: Largest Gift Shop imaginable. Concessions.*

3D THEATER - 6 story with hourly 40 minute space/aviation films - feel like you're flying with the pilots. Fee. (937-253-IMAX. Morphis MovieRide Theater - actually move, tilt and shout. extra fee).

HUFFMAN PRAIRIE FIELD - Rte. 44 (937-257-5535). See where The Wright Brothers first attempted flight.

This museum tells the story of the 100-plus years of flight, from its beginning to today's stealth age. For the best in family entertainment / educational value, this museum is definitely a must see! You'll have a real adventure exploring the world's oldest and largest military aviation museum that features over 50 vintage WWII aircraft (even the huge 6-engine B-36) and 300 other aircraft and rockets. See everything from presidential planes, to Persian Gulf advanced missiles and bombs, the original Wright Brothers wind tunnel, to the original Apollo 15 command module. Look for the observation balloon (easy to find—just look up ever so slightly), Rosie the Rivetor and "Little Vittles" parachuted goodies. Discovery Hangar Five follows a common museum trend and focuses on the interactive learning of why things fly and different parts of airplanes. Continuous films played at stations throughout the complex (with chairs-take a break from all the walking). This attraction houses more than 400 total aircraft and missiles, including the world's only B-2 stealth bomber on public display. National Aviation Hall of Fame is next door.

JULY 4TH CELEBRATIONS

Dayton (Fairborn) – National Museum of the USAF. The day includes parades, rides, entertainment and fireworks. Balloon Festival.

CARRIAGE HILL FARM AND MUSEUM

Dayton (Huber Heights) - ***7860 East Shull Road (I-70 to Exit 38 - State Route 201 north) 45424. Phone: (937) 278-2609. www.metroparks.org/parks/carriagehill/. Hours: Tuesday-Saturday 10:00am-5:00pm, Sunday Noon-5:00pm. Shorter winter hours. Admission: Donation. Note: Picnic area, fishing, horseback riding, cross country skiing, hayrides and bobsled rides. No bikes on trails, though.***

Farm life in the 1880s comes alive at Carriage Hill Farm. Stop at the Visitor Center for exhibits highlighting lifestyles of a century ago, a children's interactive center and the Country Store gift shop. The self-guided tour of an 1880's working farm is a great benefit to the community. The farm includes a summer kitchen, workshop, blacksmith and barns. Household chores and farming are performed as they were 100 years ago and a variety of farm animals fill the barn. They are best to visit when workers are planting or harvesting gardens.

MIAMISBURG MOUND

Dayton (Miamisburg) - ***(I-75 to State Route 725 exit 44, follow signs) 45342. Phone: (937) 866-5632. www.ohiohistory.org. Hours: Daily Dawn to Dusk. Admission: FREE. Note: Park, Picnic tables and playground.***

Take the 116 stairs up a 68-foot high and 1.5 acre wide mound built by American Indians. This is the largest conical burial mound in Ohio. Archaeological investigations of the surrounding area suggest that it was constructed by the prehistoric Adena Indians (800BC - AD100). The mound measures 877 feet in circumference.

WRIGHT B. FLYER

Dayton (Miamisburg) - ***10550 Springboro Pike (I-75 exit 44, State Route 741 – Dayton Wright Airport) 45342. www.destinationdayton.com/wrightb/hanger.html. Phone: (937) 885-2327. Hours: Tuesday, Thursday, and Saturday 9:00am-2:00pm. Admission: There is no charge for the museum or to look at the aircraft. Aircraft ride certificates may be purchased for $150.00. This entitles the certificate bearer to an orientation ride replicating the Wright Brothers' original flight patterns over Huffman Prairie! Otherwise, only donations.***

A group decided to build a flying replica of the first production aircraft ever built - the Wright Brothers B Model Airplane. The result is a fully operational flying aircraft that closely resembles the original Wright B Model that flew over Huffman Prairie in 1911. This hangar houses a flyable replica of the 1911 plane built by Wilbur and Orville Wright. They also have a half scale model of the plane and other aviation exhibits and souvenirs.

DAYTON AIR SHOW

Dayton (Vandalia) - Dayton Int'l Airport. (I-75 exit 64). www.daytonairshow.com. This is the leading event of its kind highlighted by the outstanding civilian and military performances. The event includes ground flight simulators, aerobatics, barnstormers, air races, pyrotechnics and sky divers. Parade, entertainment and Kids Hanger. Admission ($20, age 6+) - Discount tickets at area Krogers). (third weekend in June)

FORT RECOVERY

Fort Recovery ***- One Fort Site Street (State Route 49 and State Route 119) 45846. Phone: (419) 375-4649. www.fortrecoverymuseum.com Hours: Daily Noon-5:00pm (Summer). Weekends Only (May and September). Admission: $2.00-$5.00 (student and adult). Educators: a link to www.ohiohistorycentral.org online leads you to many related articles that would be useful for research papers.***

The remaining blockhouses with connecting stockade wall are where General Arthur St. Clair was defeated by Indians in 1791. Later, in 1794, General "Mad" Anthony Wayne defended the fort successfully. A museum with Indian War artifacts and dressed mannequins is also displayed on the property. It's super fun for kids to play in/around a real fort!

Greenville

BEAR'S MILL

Greenville ***- 6450 Arcanum Bear's Mill Road (5 miles East on US 36 then South) 45331. Phone: (937) 548-5112. www.bearsmill.org. Tours (self-guided): Wednesday-Saturday 11:00am – 5:00pm (March-December), Sunday 1-5pm. Weekends only (January-February). Guided tours by appointment. Note: Store-sells flours ground at the mill, gift baskets, handmade pottery.***

Bear's Mill, built in 1849, is an authentic example of a stone grinding flour mill of its time. It is still in use today grinding cornmeal, whole-wheat flour, and rye flour. Tour the mill built in 1849 by Gabriel Bear where grinding stones (powered by water flowing beneath the building) grind flour and meal. Everyone who comes to Bear's Mill during business hours is welcome to take a self guided tour of the 4-story structure and take a walk in the scenic woods surrounding the mill. Numbered signs are located throughout the Mill to provide history and additional insight about how the Mill operates. Best times to take the family: Candlelight Open House (first Friday night in December) and Fall Open House (first weekend in October) with entertainment and great seasonal foods.

GARST MUSEUM, ANNIE OAKLEY CENTER

Greenville - *205 North Broadway 45331. www.garstmuseum.org. Phone: (937) 548-5250. Hours: Tuesday-Saturday 10:00am-4:00pm, Sunday 1:00-4:00pm. (February-December). Closed month of January. Admission: $7-$10.00 (age 6+).*

The main feature of the museum is Darke County's most-famous daughter sharp-shooter and entertainer Annie Oakley (artifacts from her professional and private life). View displays about: world-traveler, broadcaster, author and adventurer Lowell Thomas; pioneering aviator Zachary Lansdowne; The Treaty of Greeneville and a lot of other history of the county including 30 individual room settings. Even something on Lewis and Clark, Anthony Wayne, Native American artifacts and Village of shops, too. Crossroads of Destiny is a chronological walking tour that includes 28 displays. Each display has authentic artifacts that relate a story that begins with prehistoric Native Americans and climaxes in 1795 with the signing of the Treaty of Greeneville that included 12 Indian nations and the United States.

KITCHENAID EXPERIENCE & FACTORY TOURS

Greenville - *423 South Broadway/ 1701 KitchenAid Way (I-70 exit US 127 north to town) 45331. Phone: (888) 886-8318. www.kitchenaid.com/experience-retail-center/ Hours: Experience store Monday-Saturday 9am-6:00pm, Sunday Noon-5:00pm. Admission: Tours are $5.00 per person. Tours: Tuesday-Friday at 12:30pm (subject to manufacturing schedules) or groups over 8 with appointment. Enclosed footwear required. Safety glasses provided, must be at least 12 YEARS OLD.*

The site that houses the KitchenAid Experience was the Turpin House Hotel and later a five and dime store. The Greenville connection started way back in 1908 with a mixer produced for commercial bakers. Visit the heritage exhibits, take a kids cooking class, or tour. The work force produces hundreds of mixers every day. Walk through the whole process, peeking over workers shoulders.

ANNIE OAKLEY DAYS

Greenville - Darke County Fairgrounds, SR 49. www.annieoakleyfestival.org. Annie Oakley's hometown celebrates with a parade, live entertainment, a sharpshooter's contest and a contest to name Miss Annie Oakley. (last weekend in July)

AIRSTREAM FACTORY TOUR

Jackson Center - ***419 West Pike Street (I-75 exit 102, SR 274 east) 45334. Phone: (937) 596-6111. www.airstream.com. Tours are: Monday - Friday at 2:00 pm. Friday Tours are after normal production hour. This is a walking tour approximately ¾ mile in length. The tour begins in the Service Lobby and travels outside to the production facility. Eye protection and hearing protection are required. No sandals or open toe shoes. No appt necessary except for groups over 10.***

Airstream, the world's leader in travel trailers and motor coaches, are completely manufactured and assembled in Jackson Center, Ohio. This is your chance to come see how it's done. From chassis assembly through final quality assurance, you'll be able to witness it all, first hand. The Airstream way is no automotive assembly line process mind you. These travel trailers and motor homes are custom assembled, by hand, in stages throughout the manufacturing process. You won't believe your eyes as you watch them come together in this 90-minute tour.

INDIAN LAKE STATE PARK

Lakeview - ***12774 State Route 235 N (US 33, 20 miles east of I-75) 43331. Phone: (937) 843-2717. http://parks.ohiodnr.gov/indianlake***

Indian Lake is an important resting stop for birds such as Canada geese, ducks, grebes, swans, egrets and herons. Many stay over the summer to nest. The present and much larger lake lies along one of the country's major avian migration routes. The Cherokee Trail, a 3-mile easy walk through brushy habitat, is located west of the camp. The Pew Island Trail, a 1-mile path, encircles Pew Island. Access is available to Pew Island from a causeway. This trail affords a spectacular view of Indian Lake. A paved bikeway is located on the West Bank between Old Field Beach and Lakeview Harbor. The bikeway is 3 miles long. Walkers and joggers are welcome to use the bikeway. Two public beaches, Old Field Beach and Fox Island Beach, invite swimmers to relax in the cool waters of Indian Lake. 6448 acres of camping, hiking trails, boating, fishing, swimming and winter sports.

LOCKINGTON LOCKS

Lockington - ***5 miles North of Piqua-Lockington Road (I-75 to exit 83 West on State Route 25A) 45356. www.ohiohistory.org/visit/museum-and-site-locator/lockington-locks Phone: (800) 686-1535. Hours: Daily Dawn to Dusk. Admission: FREE.***

These stair step locks, among the best preserved in Ohio, were part of the

Miami and Erie Canal System, which opened for navigation in 1845 and connected Cincinnati and the Ohio River to Toledo and Lake Erie. For several decades, the canal provided Ohio with valuable transportation and waterpower. View portions of five original locks (elevation adjusters for canal boats) and the aqueduct that lowered boats 67 feet into the Miami-Erie Canal.

LIGHTS AT LUDLOW FALLS

Ludlow Falls - SR 48. (937) 698-3318. Hundreds of thousands of lights & holiday / storybook characters. Daily, evenings. FREE, donations accepted. (Winter Break)

LAKE LORAMIE STATE PARK

Minster - *4401 Ft. Loramie Swanders Road (3 miles Southeast of Minster off State Route 66) 45865. Phone: (937) 295-2011. http://parks.ohiodnr.gov/lakeloramie*

One of the original canal feeder lakes, Lake Loramie State Park offers visitors a quiet retreat in rural Ohio. Swim from the sandy beach, hike along the old canal towpath, stay a night in a shaded campsite or boat the lazy waters of Lake Loramie. The hiking opportunities at Lake Loramie include more than eight miles of trail. A portion of the trail system follows the Miami-Erie Canal from the park to Delphos.

BICYCLE MUSEUM OF AMERICA

New Bremen - *7 West Monroe Street (I-75 exit 102, west on SR 274) 45869. Phone: (419) 629-9249. www.bicyclemuseum.com. Hours: Monday – Friday 9:00am - 5:00pm (til 7:00pm in the summer). Saturday 10:00am – 2:00pm. Admission: $3.00 adult, $2.00 senior, $1.00 student Educators: click on the For Students link and download pdfs to help with research papers.*

A department store has been converted into a showcase of the world's oldest bike (w/out pedals) to the Schwinn family collection (including the 1,000,000th bicycle made). High-wheelers to side-by-side doubles and quads. Celebrity bikes and bikes from balloon tire to banana seat bikes will amuse you. Actual bikes to try: a 2-person car kids can drive that is pedal-powered and a big front wheel bike for you to sit on and try pedaling the old-fashioned way!

PUMPKIN MAZE PLAYLAND

***New Carlisle** - Meadow View Farm, 755 N. Dayton-Lakeview Rd.(I-70 & SR 235) Pumpkin Patches / Hayrides / Corn Mazes / Fall Playland - Admission (average $7.00). Plan on at least two hours playtime. Zipline. Bonfires. Open Saturday, some weekdays (by appointment) and weeknights.www.meadowview.com. (late Sept - late October).*

JOHNSTON FARM & INDIAN AGENCY

Piqua - *9845 North Hardin Road (I-75 to exit 83 County Road 25A West to State Route 66 North/cty hwy 110) 45356. http://johnstonfarmohio.com/ Phone: (937) 773-2522. Hours: Thursday-Friday 10am-5:00pm, Saturday, Sunday and Holidays Noon-5:00pm (June - August). Admission: $9.00 adult, $4.00 student (6-12). Includes canal boat ride. Note: Canal rides a few times during the afternoon in the summer.*

The focal point of the peaceful 200-acre park is John Johnston--farmer, public official, and United States Indian Agent for western Ohio from 1812 to 1829. Tour the Johnston Farm which includes an 1808 massive log barn which is probably the oldest such barn in Ohio. In the farmhouse, the kids will probably be most interested in the beds made of rope and hay filled sacks. Eight girls slept in one room (ages 2-20) and three boys in another. Many youth games of that time period are displayed. The Winter Kitchen is also very interesting – especially the size of the walk-in fireplace. The Farm buildings have costumed guides describing and interacting with youth as they demonstrate chores on the farm. Before you visit the canal, stop in the museum where excellent exhibits, inside and out, explain the treacherous job of building a canal and why. The General Harrison canal boat is powered by two mules which pull the boat down and back on a section of the Old Miami-Erie Canal (Cincinnati to Toledo). The cargo boat was once used to transport produce and meat at a speed limit of 4 MPH. Once the railroads came, canals became obsolete.

BUCK CREEK STATE PARK

Springfield - *1901 Buck Creek Lane (4 miles East of Springfield on State Route 4) 45502. Phone: (937) 322-5284. http://parks.ohiodnr.gov/buckcreek*

The park's recreational facilities center around the 2,120-acre lake, offering endless water-related opportunities. The spotted turtle, a state endangered animal, is found in the area. The shallow waters provide a stopover for thousands of migrating ducks. More than 7.5 miles of hiking trails offer opportunities for nature study, bird watching and other wildlife observation. A scenic 7.5-mile bridle trail is also open to snowmobiling, weather permitting. The Dam Visitors center provides displays, programs and dam operation tours. 4030 acres of camping, hiking trails, boating and rentals, fishing, swimming and winter sports. 26 family cabins with A/C.

FAIR AT NEW BOSTON

Springfield - George Rogers Clark Park. (937) 882-9216 or www.grcha.org. Area where General Clark defeated Shawnee to open NW Territory. Early 1800's frontier life & Indian village. Re-enactors, craft demonstrations, authentic open fire, wood cooked food and folk entertainment. Admission. (Labor Day Weekend)

GRAND LAKE ST. MARY'S STATE PARK

St. Mary's - *834 Edgewater Drive (2 miles West of St. Mary's on State Route 703) 45885. Phone: (419) 394-3611. www.dnr.state.oh.us.*

Originally constructed as a feeder reservoir for the Miami-Erie Canal, Grand Lake St. Mary's was for many years recognized as the largest man-made reservoir in the world. Nature programs. 14,000 acres of camping, boating and rentals, fishing, swimming, sport courts, putt-putt and winter sports. Ohio's largest inland lake. Fur-Ever Friends Dog Park. Camper Cabins may be rented April through October. Winter snowmobiling!

ST. MARY'S FISH HATCHERY: After boating or swimming on Grand Lake, wander through 52 acres of ponds where pike, catfish, etc. are raised. The farm is one of only three in Ohio and is the only farm with a large mouth bass and yellow perch hatchery. (East Side of Grand Lake, Phone: (419) 394-5170, Hours: Daily 7:00am-3:30pm)

KISER LAKE STATE PARK

St. Paris - *4889 N. St. Rt. 235 (17 miles Northwest of Urbana on State Route 235) 43072. Phone: (937) 362-3822. www.dnr.state.oh.us.*

The rolling wooded hills and diverse wetlands add to the beauty of this scenic lake known for its clean, clear waters. Five hiking trails are located within the park and provide 5.1 scenic miles of walking pleasure. Red Oak and the Nature Preserve Boardwalk trails are located near the family camp area.

The North Bay Trail follows the lake shoreline for 1.5 miles. Seven miles of horse trails are located near State Route 235. 870 acres of camping, hiking trails, boating and rentals, fishing, swimming and winter sports.

SYCAMORE STATE PARK

Trotwood - *4675 N. Diamond Mill Road (1 mile North of Trotwood on State Route 49) 45426. Phone: (937) 854-4452. www.stateparks.com/sycamore.html*

The meadows, woodlots and still waters of Sycamore State Park provide the perfect setting for picnicking, hiking, fishing, camping, snowmobiling and horseback riding. The 3-mile Ghost Hedge Nature Trail offers the hiker an opportunity to explore the Wolf Creek Valley. Giant sycamore trees form a picturesque canopy over the trail. The 1.5-mile Beech Ridge Trail explores the surrounding woodlots and meadows. Horsemen can enjoy 15 miles of bridle trail, including the snowmobile routes when not snow covered.

Troy

BRUKNER NATURE CENTER

Troy - *5995 Horseshoe Bend Rd. (Exit # 73 off of I-75, west on SR 55 3 miles) 45373. Phone: (937) 698-6493. www.facebook.com/bruknernaturecenter. Hours: Monday-Saturday 9:00am-5:00pm, Sunday 12:30 - 5:00pm. Admission: Small admission charged on Sundays.*

This 164 acre nature preserve's attractions include 6 miles of hiking trails, a wildlife rehabilitation center and the interpretive center. The 1804 Iddings log house was built by the first settlers in Miami County. The Center's animal rehabilitation has over 65 permanent residents on display. The top floor contains a glass-enclosed vista room for watching and listening to birds as they feed. A ground-level viewing station for mammals is available. They are best known for their Night Hikes, Star Gazes, Wild Journeys and Seasonal events.

IDLE HOUR RANCH

Troy - *4845 Fenner Road (I-75 exit 73 west) 45373. www.idle-hourranch.com. Phone: (937) 339-9731. Hours: Friday, Saturday & Sunday Noon-6:00pm (June - October). Admission: $12.00 adult, $10.00 child (3-12) & senior (65+).*

Ever want to hitch a ride with a kangaroo? See the world from a giraffe's point of view? Unlike a zoo, IHR allows you to get up close & personal with the animals. Interact with & see over 200 animals including: Camels, Kangaroo, Wallabies, Cougar, Zebu, Llamas, Alpaca, Reindeer, Nilgai, Yak, Wolves, Cavies, Horses, farm animals and many, many more! Special areas included: the North American River Otter Exhibit, the Giraffe Observation Deck & the Farm Market. Otter feeding at 3:00pm. Pony rides. Look for "babies" every now and then.

TROY STRAWBERRY FESTIVAL

Troy - Public Square, I-75 exit 73 or 74. The Strawberry Capital of the Midwest. www.troyohiostrawberryfestival.com. Public Square. The first full weekend in June the fountain on Town Square runs pink water! Loads of fresh-picked berries and strawberry foods (donuts, pizza, fudge) are sold. Bed races, waterball, Kids' Crawl & Pie eating contests. Parade, entertainment and hot-air balloons. Free.

CEDAR BOG

Urbana - *980 Woodburn Road (off Route 68 North / I-70 to Springfield / off State Route 36) 43078. Phone: (937) 484-3744. www.cedarbognp.org. Hours: Wednesday-Saturday 10:00am-4:00pm (site closed for major holidays, severe weather & deer season). Admission: $4.00-$5.00 per student or adult. Educators: Nine different tours are offered to school groups for study during themed guided tours. Field Guides: www.cedarbognp.org/fieldguide.htm*

An almost mile long boardwalk guides the visitor through this preserve. Ohio's only fen - a wetland with water that rises to the surface - that is still surrounded with white cedar, just as it was thousands of years ago after the last great glacier disappeared. A bog is a remnant of the Ice Age and public tours take you to the boardwalk over this bog. Below, you'll see the black, wet, slimy muck and chilly dampness created by a constant water table and cool springs. In contrast, see excellent orchid, prairie and woodland wildflowers. The Education Center is sure to highlight features of the bog not seen every day naturally.

FRESHWATER FARMS OF OHIO

Urbana - *2624 US 68 (north of downtown circle) 43078. Phone: (937) 652-3701 or (800) 634-7434. www.fwfarms.com. Hours: Store - Monday-Saturday 10:00am-6:00pm. Closed major holidays. Tours: FREE. Self-guided tour include trout feeding and a sturgeon petting zoo. Guided tours of the fish farm require advanced registration and a small fee, and can include a gourmet sampling of Freshwater Farms smoked trout appetizers and all-natural smoked trout spreads. Note: Bring a cooler if you plan to purchase fish. Supplies for ponds. Produces several hundred thousand trout sold to premium restaurants.*

Visit Ohio's largest indoor fish hatchery and retail fish farm market. Start your tour by petting a sturgeon fish. Why can you touch them, but not catfish? They raise rainbow trout that are bred in large water tanks. Farmer Smith, a marine biologist with a doctorate in nutrition, and his father (an engineer), developed a system of tracks and tanks using re-circulated pure cleaned water. The fish are really pampered with a special diet and solar-heated hatchery.

You even get to "pet" a fish...

View the spring water "ponds" with gravel bottoms (outside) and put a quarter in the machine to get fish food to feed the fish. Other newer exhibits of live fish are the jumbo freshwater shrimp and their "loopy" eyes! These fish are really spoiled, aren't they?

Wapakoneta

ARMSTRONG AIR AND SPACE MUSEUM

Wapakoneta - ***500 South Apollo Drive (I-75 to Exit 111) 45895. Phone: (419) 738-8811 or (800) 860-0142. http://armstrongmuseum.org Hours: Tuesday-Saturday 9:30am-5:00pm. Sunday Noon – 5:00pm. Closed Winter Holidays. Open Spring & Summer Mondays. Admission: $8.00 adult, $4.00 student (6-12). Note: Picnic area.***

The museum honors Neil Armstrong (a Wapakoneta native) and other area aeronauts (like the Wright Brothers) and their flying machines. After greeted by a NASA Skylaneer flown by Armstrong in the early 1960's, trace the history of flight from balloons to space travel. Look at the Apollo crew spacesuits, a real moon rock, or watch a video of lunar space walks. In the Astro Theater, pretend you're on a trip to the moon. Try a lunar or shuttle landing interactive. Look at Space Food, even dessert! Another favorite is the Infinity Cube – 18 square feet covered with mirrors that make you feel like you've been projected into space. Interactives and videos are abundant. Blast OFF! ...and check out the Summer Moon Festival each July.

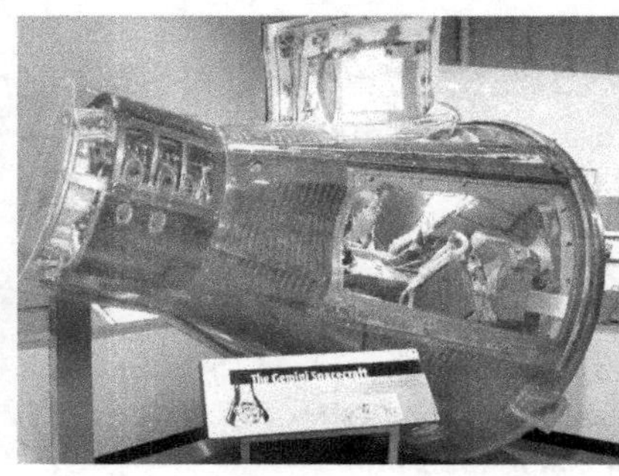

West Liberty

MAD RIVER THEATER WORKS

Zanesfield - ***2790 Sandusky St 43360. www.madrivertheater.com.***

They interview local residents and research historical issues with contemporary relevance (i.e. John Henry, slavery, Casey Jones). This material is used to craft plays with music that are drawn from and produced for the people of the rural Midwest. This is a touring company that is booked for events and special showings each year.

OHIO CAVERNS

West Liberty - ***2210 East State Route 245 (I-70 to US 68 north to SR 507 east) 43357. Phone: (937) 465-4017. www.ohiocaverns.com. Hours: Daily 9:00am-5:00pm (April-October). 10:00am – 4:00pm (November – March). Admission: $19 Adult, $10.00 Children (5-12). Note: On the premises is a park and gift shop with gemstone mining (extra fee).***

This tour is a 45 minute guided regular or historic tour of the largest cave in Ohio. The cave formations are still actively in the process of development. Still photography is welcome to capture you memories. The temperature here is 54 degrees F. constantly so dress appropriately. Look for the Palace of the Gods and stalagmites that look like cacti or a pump.

PIATT CASTLE MAC-A-CHEEK

West Liberty - ***10051 Township Rd 47 (Route 33 West to State Route 245 East) 43357. Phone: (937) 465-2821. www.piattcastle.org. Hours: Daily 11:00am-5:00pm (Summer). Weekends only, 11:00am-4:00pm (mid-April thru late May & early September thru early November). Admission: $13 adult, $11 senior (65+), $7 student (5-15). Note: Hands-on activities for families (summer).***

Castles in Ohio? Catch the eerie, yet magnificent old castles furnished with collections ranging from 150-800 years old. The castle was built in the mid-1800's and give a good sense of the lifestyle of the upper-class.

This self-guided tour is somewhat manageable for school-aged (pre-schoolers not suggested) children and includes lots of land to explore outside. Telling friends they were in a castle is fun too. Because the furniture is original, the homes have an old smell and the rooms look frozen in time. Ceiling paintings and the kitchen/dining area were most interesting.

NATIONAL AFRO-AMERICAN MUSEUM AND CULTURAL CENTER

Wilberforce - ***1350 Brush Row Road (off US 42 - Next to Central State College) 45384. Phone: (800) BLK-HIST. www.ohiohistory.org/visit/museum-and-site-locator/national-afro-american-museum Hours: Wednesday-Saturday 9:00am-4:00pm. Closed holidays except MLK holiday. Admission: $6 adult, $3 student (6-17).***

Wilberforce was a famous stop on the Underground Railroad and became the center (Wilberforce University) for black education and achievements. The University was the first owned and operated by Afro-Americans. Best feature is the "From Victory to Freedom - the Afro-American Experience of 1950 - 1960's". This exhibition chronicles the trends, struggles and social changes that occurred within this crucial period in American history through a variety of photographs and artifacts, but also through life-sized scenes of a typical fifties lifestyles. These include a barber shop, a beauty salon, and a church interior complete with pews, pulpit and choir stand. These exhibits are made real to the visitor through the accompaniment of recorded speaking voices and gospel music.

GREENE COUNTY HISTORICAL SOCIETY MUSEUM

Xenia - ***74 W Church Street (near center of town) 45385. Phone: (937) 372-4606. https://sites.google.com/site/greenehistoricalsociety/ Hours: Tuesday-Saturday Noon-3:30pm. Admission: Donations.***

Tecumseh's famous "courting chair"...

Restored Victorian home and 1799 James Galloway log house where Tecumseh tried to "woo" Rebecca Galloway (actually view the chair Tecumseh sat in near the fireplace!). First, pick herbs from a 1700's garden, smell them and then try to enter the front door of the log house. No door knob or latch? How did they open the door? The Carriage House has a wonderful display of farm equipment, general store (candy), china, books, furniture, toys, railroad exhibit, and school. In the Big House, easily explore the many rooms looking for old-fashioned toys, the kiddie potty, or, the old hair crimpers and curling irons - try one - how does it work? On your way here, stop by Clifton Mill for a hotcake breakfast with freshly milled flour. History and hotcakes is a nice way to make it fun for the kids.

Yellow Springs

JOHN BRYAN STATE PARK

Yellow Springs - ***3790 State Route 370 (2 miles Southeast of Yellow Springs on State Route 370) 45387. Phone: (937) 767-1274. www.johnbryan.org.***

750 acres of camping, hiking trails, fishing and winter sports. The park contains a remarkable limestone gorge cut by the Little Miami River which is designated as a state and national scenic river. Clifton Gorge State Nature Preserve is located adjacent to the park. The Clifton Gorge is a limestone gorge cut by the river (a national natural landmark). Nature lovers can enjoy any of the nine different trails found in the park. Trails follow the scenic river gorge and meander through majestic woodlands. One trail is an old stagecoach trail.

YOUNG'S JERSEY DAIRY FARM

Yellow Springs - *6880 Springfield-Xenia Road (On Route 68, off I-70) 45387. Phone: (937) 325-0629. www.youngsdairy.com. Hours: Daily 6:00am–10:00pm (April-October). Open later in the summer and closes earlier in the winter. Admission: Grounds are FREE. Each activity averages $5.00 per person. Tours: Scheduled groups Monday – Friday (April – October). $5.00 Children – FREE for Teachers and Chaperones. Minimum of 10 paying participants for tours. The one hour tour starts with a short video in the barn full of small animals such as ducks, rabbits and chicks. The video shows the farming process: from feeding cows (amazing how much food they need - 25 gallons of water, over 100 lbs of hay/grain), milking the cows, bottling the milk and making the ice cream (what's their secret?), watching the operations through the processing window, to selling the milk & ice cream in the store and restaurant. The children then visit animals in the big barn. They see what a cow eats, feed the goats and visit with other farm animals. Next is a wagon ride. Finish the tour with some homemade ice cream.*

The Dairy store began in 1960 and is still operated by members of the Young family. Choose from the following activities: Udders and Putters Miniature Golf, Driving Range, Batting Cage, Corny Maze (a 3 acre corn field maze open weekends, August thru October), Wagon Rides & Moo-ver & Shaker Barrel Cart rides on weekends, Petting Area – Baby Jersey (pretty-faced calves) cows, pigs and sheep; or Water Balloon Toss (summertime). Go to the petting area and then the wagon ride with a treat at the end in one of the restaurants. They make and sell 110 flavors a year - try something fun like Cake Batter Rainbow Chip, Green Apple Sorbetto, Cow Chip? or Wooly Wonka. Young's attracts mostly families. Parents and grandparents love to bring children and friends to the farm and visit. Our family has fallen in love with this farm amusement park!

FALL FARM FESTIVAL

Yellow Springs – Young's Jersey Dairy Farm. Pumpkin Patches / Hayrides / Corn Mazes / Fall Playlands. All sites charge admission (average $6.00). Plan on at least two hours playtime. Open weekends & weekdays (by appointment) and weeknights (late September - late October).

MARMON VALLEY FARM

Zanesfield - *7754 SR 292 (off US 33 northwest, exit Mad River Mtn. Area) 43360. Phone: (937) 593-8051. www.marmonvalley.com. Hours: Call for details . Educators: Farm (younger ones) or Ohio Homesteading (upper elementary) field trips offered with instruction.*

Winter and summer activities are available at Marmon Valley Farm. They have live farm animals and a fun barn with rope bridges, rope swings and barn games. Hiking and horseback riding (year-round trail rides, on ponies, or in the indoor arena) are available. When there's snow, you may want to take your sled along for some great riding hills. Overnights combine activities with just enough time left to wander. Activities like archery, fishing, a challenge course, indoor arena sports, and the new indoor barn rock climbing wall fill a sport gal or guy's day. An evening hayride followed by silly barn line dancing and s'mores by the fire pit are a great way to end the day. Overnighters ride the wagon each morning over to the cowboy chuck wagon camp for yummy, open-air cooked, big breakfasts followed by a nature hike with Wrangler Matt. Look to attend their seasonal events if you can't arrange a group visit.

FALL FARM FESTIVAL

Zanesfield – Marmon Valley Farm. Enjoy Farm favorites like horse drawn wagon rides and pony rides. Activities like indoor rock climbing, archery, hay tunnels, a kids fishing derby, leather crafts and pumpkin painting. Experience old west gun fights, stick horse rodeo games, live musical entertainment and contests for kids, too! (Trail rides and some Make-it and Take-it crafts are not included in the admission cost.) Concessions. Barn Dance. Admission. (first Sat in October)

A COUNTRY CHRISTMAS

Zanesfield – Marmon Valley Farm. Costumed characters, carolers, live animals in a presentation of the Nativity story. Hayride wagons take guests to different scenes around the barns and fields. Hot chocolate, goodies, singing, Christmas crafts. By reservation. (First two weekends in December).

Chapter 4
North Central Ohio

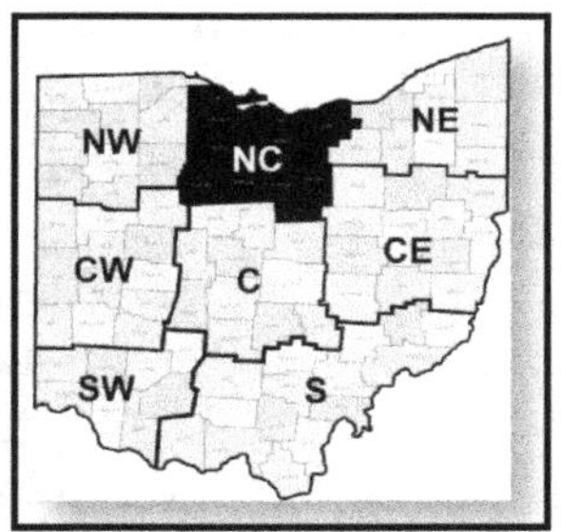

Ashland

- Ashland Balloonfest

Bellevue

- Historic Lyme Village
- Mad River & Nkp Railroad Museum

Bucyrus

- Cooper's Cider Mill Apple Butter & Jelly Factory
- Pfeifer Dairy Farms

Butler

- Prairie Peddler

Castalia

- Castalia State Fish Hatchery

Catawba

- Miller Boat Line Ferries

Elyria

- Apple Festival

Flat Rock

- Seneca Caverns

Fremont

- Hayes Presidential Center

Lakeside

- Lakeside

Lexington

- Mid Ohio Sports Car Course

Loudonville

- Great Mohican Indian Pow-Wow
- Landoll's Mohican CasTle Resort
- Mohican State Park Resort

Lucas

- Malabar Farm State Park

Mansfield

- Biblewalk
- Richland Carousel Park
- Little Buckeye Childrens Museum
- Christmas Wunderland
- Freedom Festival
- Kingwood Center
- Ohio Bird Sanctuary
- Ohio State Reformatory
- Pumpkin Maze Playland
- Spruce Hill Inn & Cottages

Marblehead

- East Harbor State Park
- Kelleys Island Ferry Boat Lines
- Marblehead Lighthouse State Park
- Train – O – Rama

Milan

- Edison Birthplace Museum
- Melon Festival
- Milan Historical Museum

New Washington

- Pumpkin Maze Playland

Oberlin

- Oberlin Heritage Center

Perrysville

- Mohican-Memorial State Forest

Port Clinton

- African Safari Wildlife Park
- Crane Creek State Park & Magee Marsh Wildlife Area
- Great Lakes Popcorn Company
- Jet Express
- Lake Erie Islands Regional Welcome Center
- Lake Erie Islands State Park
- Monsoon Lagoon
- Walleye Madness At Midnight

Put-In-Bay

- Aquatic Visitors Center
- Butterfly House
- Chocolate Café & Museum
- Crystal Cave & Heineman's Grape Juice Winery
- Lake Erie Islands Museum
- Perry's Cave & Family Fun Center
- Perry's Victory And International Peace Memorial
- Put-In-Bay Tour Train
- Stone Laboratory

Rittman

- Apple Festival

Sandusky

- Castaway Bay
- Cedar Point & Soak City
- Goodtime I
- Great Wolf Lodge Indoor Waterpark
- Kalahari Indoor Waterpark Resort
- Lagoon Deer Park
- Maui Sands Indoor Waterpark Resort
- Merry-Go-Round Museum

Tiffin

- Tiffin-Seneca Heritage Festival

Upper Sandusky

- Indian Mill

Vermilion

- Festival Of The Fish
- Woollybear Festival

Wellington

- Findley State Park

Willard

- Celeryville, Buurma Vegetable Farms

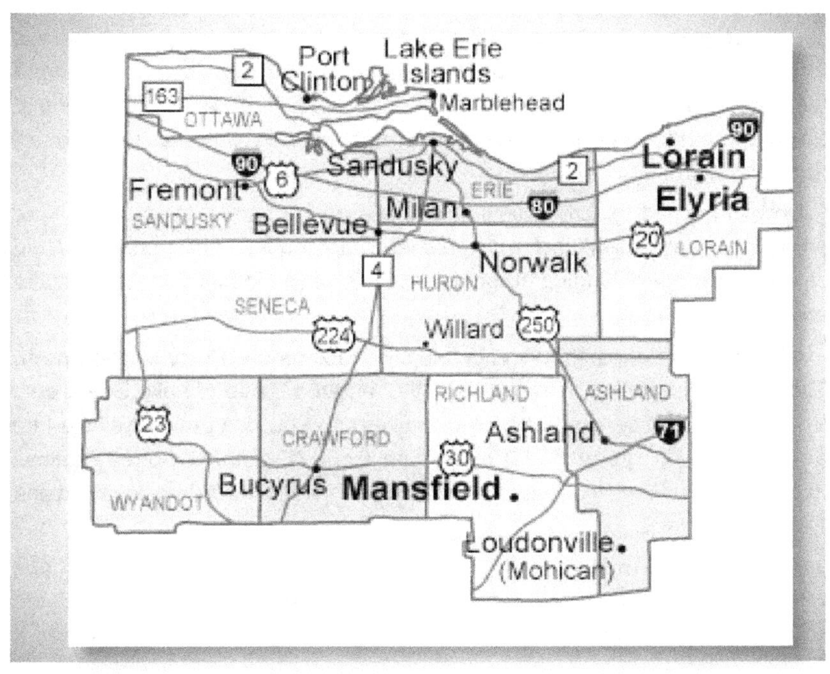

A Quick Tour of our Hand-Picked Favorites Around...

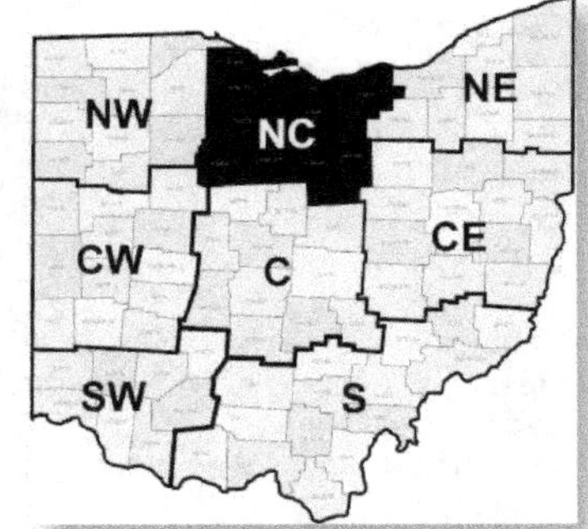

North Central Ohio

Be sure to stop in the **Lake Erie Islands** Regional Welcome Center to view the dioramas of the area and meet the friendly staff. The kids can gaze at the 600 gallon aquarium or do nature rubbings while the parents work out a plan. They can also tell you about eateries in the area that specialize in perch and walleye...any way you like it.

Did you know you could escape to an island, just off the shores of Sandusky? The Islands are a Midwest vacation hot spot. Just a short ferry ride from the mainland, and you'll forget you are in Ohio! Whatever your pleasure, coastal relaxation or on-the-go excitement, the islands have got it covered!

A favorite paradise oasis in any season – Sandusky and its numerous **Indoor Waterparks**, may just be the "Orlando of the Midwest!" Tweens and teens thrive at Kalahari, while the younger set (ages 1-10) are more content at any of the other parks as they're smaller and more manageable with "softer" rides and activities.

Down the road towards **Marblehead** are quaint shops, train or dinosaur attractions, eateries, plus the Marblehead Lighthouse. Their stories of old lighthouse keepers lugging 40 pound buckets of whale oil up those 77 stairs are so interesting.

If history or nature are more your thing, we recommend **Perry's Monument**. The DVD presentation of the War of 1812 and the Battle of Lake Erie are so worth seeing. While island hopping, make sure you don't miss walking into a giant geode (**Crystal Cave**) or walking across **Glacial Grooves** (Kelleys Island). Remember, try to leave Put-in-Bay island by 4:00pm to avoid the "party scene".

Thomas Edison developed the incandescent light bulb, phonograph and early motion picture camera. **Edison's Birthplace**, in Milan (around the corner from the Sandusky area), is where you can count how many tries it took to make the light bulb work; what was first recorded on the phonograph; and what silly thing the first movie was about.

Closer to Central Ohio is **Mohican Country**, near Mansfield...the land of skiing, canoeing, hiking and other outdoor sports. But, several unusual attractions are hidden here too. Ride the Richland Carousel downtown, then grab a bite at the Diner. After lunch, plan to spend a couple hours at **BibleWalk** – the only wax museum in Ohio and full of several choices of themed walkways to explore. It's very emotional, too. You can overnight in the area from your choice of lodge, cabins, tents, or even a castle!

Sites and attractions are listed in order by City, Zip Code, and Name. Symbols indicated represent: Restaurants Lodging

ASHLAND BALLOONFEST

Ashland - Main Street, downtown. www.ashlandballoonfest.org. Hot air balloon races and twilight balloon glow. Ashland is a top balloon manufacturer – factory tours available. (long weekend near 4th of July)

HISTORIC LYME VILLAGE

Bellevue - *5001 State Route 4 (south of SR 113) 44811. Phone: (419) 483-4949. www.lymevillage.org. Hours: Wednesday-Saturday 11:00am-5:00pm (Summer months) Admission: $10 adult, $9 senior (65+), $5 child (6-12). Note: Gift Shop and concessions. Best to visit during special events. No pets allowed on grounds.*

This 19th Century Ohio Village includes the Wright Mansion, Annie Brown's log home that she owned for 82 years (early Ohio settler exhibits inside), a blacksmith shop, schoolhouse, barns, a church, and the Cooper-Fries general store. All original buildings were moved to this location. Of special interest is the National Museum of Postmark Collector's Club (with the world's largest single collection of postmarks) in a restored post office.

PIONEER DAYS

Bellevue – Historic Lyme Village. Early 1800's frontier life & Indian village. Re-enactors, craft demonstrations, authentic open fire, wood cooked food and folk entertainment. (weekend after Labor Day)

CHRISTMAS CANDLELIGHT TOURS

Bellevue – Historic Lyme Village. Take a self-guided tour of the village by candlelight, buildings decorated for Christmas and interpreters located inside with delicious food samples. (second or third Saturday in December)

MAD RIVER & NKP RAILROAD MUSEUM

Bellevue - ***253 Southwest St (Just South of US 20) 44811. Phone: (419) 483-2222. www.madrivermuseum.org. Hours: Daily Noon-4pm (Memorial Day-Labor Day). Adm: $10 adult, $9 senior (60+),$5 child (5-12). Weekends only (May, Sept, Oct)***

Look for steam engines, diesel engines, or the huge snow plow. Once you find them, browse through their collections of full-scale locomotives, cabooses, and mail cars – many that you can climb aboard. The hands-on museum stands on the former Henry Flagler family estate, near the first chartered railroad in the State and the largest railroad museum in Ohio. Tour guide volunteers are retired railway personnel who are knowledgeable and excited to tell you stories about the old railway days.

Bucyrus

COOPER'S CIDER MILL APPLE BUTTER & JELLY FACTORY

Bucyrus - ***1414 North Sandusky Avenue (US Route 30 bypass & State Route 4) 44820. Phone: (419) 562-4215. www.coopers-mill.com. Hours: Open Monday- Saturday 8:30am-6:00pm. Admission: FREE. Tours: Monday-Friday 9:00am-11:30am and 1:00-2:30pm, by reservation usually. Note: Farm Market - taste test jellies and homemade fudge.***

Jelly Factory tour lets you watch fruit spreads being made the old fashioned way. With "Grandma" recipes, watch the cooking of fine jams and apple butter. Take time to go into the screened-in porch to watch the apple butter bubbling in open 50 gallon copper kettles over a wood fire. Or, observe the delicious ripe fruits cooking into jelly. They cook in small batches and use home-canning jars.

PFEIFER DAIRY FARMS

Bucyrus - ***301 S. Sandusky Ave. 44820. www.bucyrus.org. Phone: (866) 562-0720.***

A modern dairy farm milking around 300 cows twice a day. Here their story and see the actual milking of cows the modern way. Plus you may bottle feed a calf if you want. This is an excellent tour to actually experience where milk comes from. Times for this tour are limited to milking times each day.

PRAIRIE PEDDLER

Butler - Bunker Hill Woods, State Route 97. www.prairietown.com. Almost 200 costumed craftspeople offer their items made with frontier style tools, foods cooked over open fires and bluegrass music. Horse drawn wagon rides. Stop by the Medicine Show and buy a bottle of elixir. Admission. (last weekend in September & first weekend in October)

CASTALIA STATE FISH HATCHERY

Castalia - ***7018 Homegardner Road (SR 6 to SR 269 south for 2 miles) 44824. Phone: (419) 684-7499. www.wildohio.gov Hours: Monday-Friday 8am-3pm. Free***

The hatchery raises steelhead and rainbow trout and offers self-guided tours of 90-acres of serene grounds including outdoor raceways, a half-mile section of the Cold Creek and a "blue hole" aquifer. Because the water from the blue hole has no oxygen and high levels of nitrogen, it is treated before being used by the hatchery. The remaining two raceways are supplied with water diverted from Cold Creek. This cold water supply allows the hatchery to raise steelhead and rainbow trout. The facility offers great wildlife viewing opportunities and also offers a limited lottery-style fishing program on the portion of Cold Creek that runs through the hatchery grounds.

MILLER BOAT LINE FERRIES

Catawba - ***Catawba Point (SR 2 to Route 53 north) 43456. Phone: (800) 500-2421 or (419) 285-2421. www.millerferry.com.***

Trips run spring, summer & fall, "family friendly" fares, free mainland parking, Put-in-Bay summer trips every half hour as late as 9:00pm service to Put-in-Bay and Middle Bass Island (early March-October). Low rates $7.50-$10 adult, $1.50-$3.00 child, (one way), most frequent trips. It is the only scheduled service to Middle Bass Island. The ferry trip to Put-in-Bay takes 18 minutes, and 40 minutes to Middle Bass. Cars, motorcycles, RVs, boats, trailers and bicycles are welcome aboard - and Miller Ferry is the only service that takes both passengers and vehicles to these islands. Rental transportation, including bikes and golf carts, available near the dock.

APPLE FESTIVAL

Elyria - Ely Square, downtown. www.elyriaapplefestival.com. Apples & cider. Apple pie eating contests. Apple peeling contests. Apple butter. Candy apples. Wagon/hayrides. Apple Dumplings, Fritters, Donuts, etc. Parades. Pioneer crafts. Petting Zoo. (third weekend in September)

SENECA CAVERNS

Flat Rock - ***15248 Twp. Road 178 (SR 4 off turnpike, south of SR 269) 44811. Phone: (419) 483-6711. www.senecacavernsohio.com. Hours: Daily 9:00am-7:00pm (Summer). Weekends 10:00am - 5:00pm (May, September, October) Admission: $18.00 adult, $17.00 senior (62+), $9.00 child (5-12). Note: Light jacket is suggested as the cave is a constant 54 degrees F.***

"The Caviest Cave in the U.S.A.". The one hour guided tour includes walking and climbing natural stone steps and pathways. The 110 foot deep limestone cave has many small rooms, seven levels and the "Ole Mist'ry River". The cave is actually an earth crack discovered by two boys out hunting in 1872. To make the tour really fun, stop by Sandy Creek Gem Mining and let your little explorers pan for gems.

HAYES PRESIDENTIAL CENTER

Fremont - *1337 Hayes Avenue (Rt. 6), Spiegel Grove (turnpike exit 91, SR 53 south to SR 6 west) 43420. www.rbhayes.org/hayes/. Phone: (419) 332-2081 or (800) 998-7737. Hours: Monday-Saturday 9:00am-5:00pm. Sunday and Holidays Noon - 5:00pm. Closed Winter Mondays, Easter, Thanksgiving, Christmas & New Year's Day. Admission: $20 adult, $18 senior, $10 teen (13-18), $5 child (6-12) Home or Museum. Tours: take place every 30 minutes beginning at 9:30am with the final tour departing at 4pm. They are guided and last 45 minutes. Note: Museum Store. Educators: wonderful biography online.*

Disputed Election? Contested Florida votes? Popular vote vs. Electoral College vote? It all happened in 1876 with the campaign of Rutherford B. Hayes. The iron gates that greet you at the entrance were the same gates that once stood at the White House during the Hayes administration. The 33-room mansion estate was the home of President and Mrs. Rutherford B. Hayes and is full of family mementos, private papers and books. They give you the sense he dedicated himself to his country. The museum displays the President's daughter's ornate dollhouses and the White House carriage that the family used. As 19th President, Hayes contended with the aftermath of Reconstruction in the South, the problems of black citizens, and the plight of the American Indian.

CIVIL WAR ENCAMPMENT & REENACTMENT

Fremont – Hayes Presidential Center. Puts you in the middle of the action as Union and Confederate forces prepare to meet in battle. Walk amid the tent camps of both armies as soldiers prepare meals on open fires, sleep on mattresses of straw, and speak in hushed tones lest the nearby enemy hear them. Re-creation of the Battle of Opequon Creek - a conflict in which Rutherford B. Hayes played a decisive role. Three battle re-creations take place (two Saturday, one Sunday). Small admission. (last weekend in October)

HAYES TRAIN SPECIAL

Fremont – Hayes Presidential Center. A 12 x 24-foot operating model train display featuring six 19th-century-style trains used during the life of the 19th President.

Interactive buttons let visitors control signals, gates, whistles, and more. Victorian Teas. Sleigh/Carriage Rides through Spiegel Grove (end of month). Weather determines if sleighs or carriages will be used. Admission. (month-long in December thru weekend after New Years)

LAKESIDE

Lakeside - ***236 Walnut Avenue 43440. Phone: (419) 798-4461 or (866) 9-LAKESIDE. www.lakesideohio.com.***

Chautaqua – like resort with programs in a historic enclave on Lake Erie. (June – September). The entire area is a Christian family retreat of shops, eateries, entertainment, lectures, worship services and family-rated movies. Daily, weekly and season pass admission prices are charged (average $10.00 per person per day-ages 10+). This gated community is safe for families and offers a huge dock, lake swimming, a sailing area (learn to sail), mini-golf, a town movie theatre, and seasonal festivals. It is like stepping back in time!

MID OHIO SPORTS CAR COURSE

Lexington - ***7721 Steam Corners Road (I-71 exit SR 97 or SR 95, follow signs) 44904. Phone: (419) 884-4000 or (800) MID-OHIO. www.midohio.com.***

Indy Car, Sport Car, AMA Motorcycles, Vintage Car Races. General, Weekend, Paddock (walk through garages & see drivers) passes available. Weekends (May – mid September)

Loudonville

LANDOLL'S MOHICAN CASTLE RESORT

Loudonville - ***561 Twp. Rd 3352 44842. www.landollsmohicancastle.com. Phone: (800) 291-5001.***

Stay overnight in a castle with royal family suites or cottages! Castle suites have fireplaces, jacuzzis, mini-kitchens, heated tile floors, and complimentary euro-style continental breakfast. Euro-gardens and cobblestone paths lead into the 30 miles of hiking/golf cart trails (golf cart rentals available). The royal suites are great for small families, but the Highland Suites are the best for large families or extended family and friends. The patio, two-floor, two-bedroom cottages connect in the middle and each unit sleeps 6+. We loved visiting with friends in the connecting great rooms and were up until late playing board games and watching movies. Both floors have a large deck to sit and watch the leaves change or the flowers bloom.

In colder weather (mid-November thru March), the Landoll's have nearly one million lights outside the castle and all the "kingdom structures". Enjoy the indoor pool/ fitness/gameroom complex - then after a great workout - try the wonderful blueberry jam (made with fresh organic blueberries grown on the property) at the Stepping Stone Restaurant. Kids 10 and younger eat FREE with each paid entree. Overnight stays begin at $200 up to around $400 per night. Reduced off peak.

MOHICAN STATE PARK RESORT

Loudonville - ***3116 State Route 3 44842. Phone: (419) 994-4290 or (419) 938-5411 Resort. www.mohicancamp.com or www.mohicanresort.com.***

The striking Clearfork Gorge, hemlock forest and scenic Mohican River offer a wilderness experience while the resort lodge and cottages provide comfortable accommodations. Most people come to stay at riverfront family cabins (with A/C, fireplaces and cable) or the Lodge rooms (with indoor/outdoor pools, sauna, tennis, basketball and shuffleboard facilities). Family playground activity center. Over 13 miles of trails take the visitor to the more interesting areas of the park and forest. Lyons Falls trail follows Clear Fork Gorge and features two waterfalls. The Hemlock trail leads to the scenic wooden bridge, and Pleasant Hill trail follows the lake shoreline and offers beautiful views of the lake (a favorite trail as it leaves from the lodge and is super scenic). Among the resort's most popular attractions are birds of prey presentations conducted by experts from the Ohio Bird Sanctuary. Nearby activities include visiting four canoe liveries, Mohican Water Slide, five golf courses, two horse stables, and downhill ski resorts. Restaurant serves breakfast, lunch and dinner and kids eat FREE. 1,294 acres of camping, bridle trails, boating and rentals, marina, bike rentals, fishing and winter sports.

GREAT MOHICAN INDIAN POW-WOW

Loudonville - Mohican Reservation Campgrounds & Canoeing. 23270 Wally Road (CR 3175). (800) 766-CAMP. www.mohicanpowwow.com. Nine different tribes gather to a pow-wow featuring foods, music, crafts, hoop dancers and storytellers. Learn proper throwing of a tomahawk or a new Native American custom. Admission. (second weekend in July and third weekend in September)

WOLF CREEK/PINE RUN GRIST MILL

Loudonville - ***1 SR 3 South 44842. www.wolfcreekmill.org. Hours: Open Saturday and Sunday Noon-5pm (May – October as volunteers are available).***

Around 1998, Mark Smith and family were camping at Mohican State Park when they discovered the Wolf Creek Grist Mill there. It had been neglected for years, no windows or doors, leaking roof, unsafe floors & a walk bridge that could barely support itself. Today the Wolf Creek Grist Mill has been restored to operating condition & the Fromme Cabin that was moved to the property several years ago is completed and is the new welcome center. An 1880 saw mill and 7 other historic log cabins have been donated & moved to the site for restoration.

MALABAR FARM STATE PARK

Lucas - ***4050 Bromfield Road (I-71 to Exit 169, follow signs) 44843. Phone: (419) 892-2784. www.malabarfarm.org. Hours: Tuesday-Sunday 11:30am-5:30pm. Weekends only each winter. Admission: $2.00-$4.00 per tour (house or farm). Tours: Guided tours begin at Noon, last tour at 4:00pm. Wagon tours are generally only on weekends during special events. Note: Malabar Inn. 1820's stagecoach stop restaurant.***

A writer and lover of nature, Louis Bromfield, dreamed of this scenic land and home. Today, visitors can see the house and farm existing just as they did in Bromfield's time. The outbuildings and pastures still house chickens, goats and beef cattle. It is still a working farm and the place where Bromfield discovered new farming techniques. The guides at the Big House tell captivating stories. During seasonal events, kids can watch harvesting or planting, ride an authentic wagon, or help with daily chores @ 3:30pm.

The new Visitors Center has easy to understand farm exhibits (even milk a mechanical cow!) and nature study. Over 30 interactive exhibits let visitors explore and experience agriculture, the environment, energy, and Bromfield's legacy as author AND farmer. There are twelve miles of trails for the hiker or horseperson to enjoy. Trails traverse scenic fields and forests. Bridle trails, fishing, hiking trails, camping and winter sports are also available park-wide.

Special note to grandparents...
Humphrey Bogart & Lauren Bacall were married on these beautiful grounds.

MAPLE SYRUP FESTIVAL

Lucas – Malabar Farm State Park. Take a horse-drawn wagon ride and see demonstrations of sugar making through history and pioneer life. Enjoy live music and food. Maple syrup, fudge and other maple products are for sale. FREE (first and second weekend in March)

OHIO HERITAGE DAYS / HARVEST TOURS

Lucus – Malabar Farm State Park. Enjoy demos by 70 traditional crafters, along with vintage farm machinery, draft horse competitions, pressing cider, butter churning, hayride tours, open-fire cooking and eating. FREE (last weekend in September & every weekend in October)

CANDLELIGHT CHRISTMAS TOURS

Lucas – Malabar Farm State Park. Tour the decorated home of Louis Bromfield and enjoy yuletide crafts, refreshments, caroling and holiday stories. Admission. (second week of December)

Mansfield

LITTLE BUCKEYE CHILDREN'S MUSEUM

Mansfield - ***44 West Fourth St 900 Park Avenue West (I-71 exit State Route 30) 44902. Phone: (419) 522-2332. http://littlebuckeye.org Hours: Wednesday-Saturday 10:00am - 4:00pm, Sunday Noon-5:00pm. Open summer Mondays & Tuesdays. Admission: $9.00 (ages 2+).***

Start at the Dino Dig to uncover dinosaur bones, ride a tractor, climb in the Treehouse, shop at the Market, play with money at My Little Bank or don a lab coat in the Baby Doc or Vet play area. The H2O Factory is a favorite water splash/play area with raincoats. Upstairs there's lots of planes, trains, autos and trucks...and a fairytale area.

OHIO BIRD SANCTUARY

Mansfield - ***3774 Orweiler Road (west of Lexington off SR 97, turn north on Bowers Rd, then east) 44903. www.ohiobirdsanctuary.com. Phone: (419) 884-HAWK. Hours: Visitors Center open Tuesday- Saturday 10:00am-4:00pm, Sunday Noon-4:00pm. Trails open daily during daylight hours, restricted winter hours, and group tours by reservation (small fee).***

The Ohio Bird Sanctuary is located on the headwater of the Clearfork River. The marsh and old growth forest offers great birding and hiking. Enjoy seeing birds up close at the Birds Of Prey. The Sanctuary is also a wildlife rehabilitation for native bird species. Nine species of birds of prey including our national emblem, the Bald Eagle, reside in large display areas. If you are a fan of songbirds you will enjoy the walk through Songbird Aviary where birds fly around you and nibble at your hand in search of food. Groups can schedule "Falcon & Friends", a live bird presentation. Picnic tables, gift shop. FREE.

SPRUCE HILL INN & COTTAGES

Mansfield - ***3230 Possum Run Road (I-71 exit 169, Rte. 13 turn up the hill beside Cracker Barrel) 44903. Phone: (419) 756-2200. www.sprucehillinn.com.***

Right next to Snow Trails Ski Resort are sets of cottages (start at $129 peak) and a lodge or house (for groups or extended families) to rent overnight while in the area. Nestled on the hill overlooking the ski trails, you'll have easy access to the slopes. The cottages include a jacuzzi tub in the bathroom, a queen bed and some have a tower room w/ futon bed or an outside deck. Walking around the sloped property and pond is a fun activity. They serve a light continental breakfast at the carriage house each morning. Just minutes from attractions or nearby Mohican Country canoeing, hiking and other outdoor sports.

BIBLEWALK

Mansfield - ***500 Tingley Avenue (I-71 to US 30 West to State Route 545 North) 44905. Phone: (419) 524-0139 or (800) 222-0139. http://biblewalk.us/ Hours: Monday-Saturday 10:00am-5:00pm, Sunday 3:00-7:00pm. Admission: $5.50-$6.50 adult, $5.25-$6.25senior (62+), $4.25-$5.00 youth (6-18), $23.00-$27.00 family. This is the price per museum. There are 6 museums like: Life of Christ, Miracles of The Old Testament, Journeys of Paul, or Heart of Reformation (church history). Discount for families and for combo of all 6 museums. Dinner Theater productions different every season (Saturdays only). Gift Shop.***

The only life-size wax museum in Ohio – it features figures from the Old and New Testaments (non-denominational). Featured stories include the Life of Christ, Daniel in the Lions Den, Jonah and the whale, and Adam and Eve. Your personal tour guide will assist you through dioramas from the Bible, each with its own audio text, music, and some with special effects. At the end of the tour you will be left emotional (a small chapel is available to reflect). What an excellent way to dramatically, unforgettably, walk through the bible and church history.

KINGWOOD CENTER

Mansfield ***- 50 N Trimble Road (I-71 exit State Route 30) 44906. Phone: (419) 522-0211. www.kingwoodcenter.org. Hours: 8:00am - 30 minutes before dusk (April - December). Hall & Greenhouse 10am-5pm. Admission: $5.00 per car.***

Forty-seven acres of gardens, woods and ponds surrounding the King French Provincial mansion. Greenhouses with a specialty of tulips and perennials and short hiking trails are family friendly. Maybe the best time to visit is for the KINGWOOD CHRISTMAS DISPLAY (Thanksgiving thru December)

OHIO STATE REFORMATORY

Mansfield ***- 100 Reformatory Road (I-71 to SR 30 west & SR 545 North) 44906. Phone: (419) 522-2644. www.mrps.org. Hours: Daily 11:00am-4:00pm (April to September). Thursday-Sunday 11am-4pm (October-March). Admission: $15.00 adult, $13.00 student (7-17). Guided tour is $5.00 extra. Tours: (only on summer weekends). Children under 9 and pregnant women should use caution because of stairs and lead-based paint. Best as a "tough love" educational visit for tweens and teens. 45 minutes. Educators: Activities and scavenger hunt on Educational-visits page.***

A castle prison? This 1886 structure was built as a boy's reformatory. The original cellblocks and offices remain intact and were used to film 4 major motion pictures including "The Shawshank Redemption" and "Air Force One" . Ask about the story of the seven-foot Jesus. Tours to choose from:

- BEYOND THE BARS TOUR - wind up the spiral staircase of the Guard Tower for a view of the cemetery in which inmates were buried with only a number on their grave. Stop at the Big Dig underground tunnel system and into the Yard. Lots of stair-climbing.
- HOLLYWOOD TOUR - See the Shawshank Warden's Office and Andy Dufresne's escape tunnels. Take a trip into the sinister "Hole". View the 1886 West Cell Block used as a Russian prison in Air Force One.

PUMPKIN MAZE PLAYLAND

Mansfield - Apple Hill Orchards, 1175 Lex-Ontario Rd. 44903 Pumpkin Patches / Hayrides / Corn Mazes / Fall Playland - Admission (average $6.00). Plan on at least two hours playtime. Scavenger Hunt Kids Day. Open weekends, some weekdays (by appointment) and weeknights. www.applehillorchards.com (late Sept - late Oct).

Marblehead

EAST HARBOR STATE PARK

Marblehead - ***1169 N Buck Road (8 miles East of Port Clinton on State Route 269) 43440. Phone: (419) 734-4424. www.eastharborstatepark.org***

Located on the shores of Lake Erie, East Harbor State Park has unlimited opportunities for outdoor recreation. Boating, fishing, swimming (large sandy beaches), picnicking and camping (large campground) are popular while nature enthusiasts will enjoy the abundance of waterfowl, shorebirds and other species of wildlife found in the park's scenic wetlands. Nature programs. 1,152 acres of hiking trails and winter sports. Disc golf is now available.

KELLEYS ISLAND FERRY BOAT LINES

Marblehead - ***510 W. Main St. (Take 163 E into Marblehead - across from the Police Department, and Fire Station.) 43440. Phone: (419) 798-9763 or (888) 225-4325. www.kelleysislandferry.com. Admission: $6.25-$10 one way.***

They offer the only daily service (passenger & auto) to Kelleys Island with a short enjoyable 20 minute boat ride, departing every half-hour during peak times. Available year-round, weather permitting.

MARBLEHEAD LIGHTHOUSE STATE PARK

Marblehead - ***110 Lighthouse Drive (SR 2 to SR 269 to SR 163 at the tip of the peninsula) 43440. Phone: (419) 798-4530 or (800) 441-1271. www.marbleheadlighthouseohio.org. Hours: Monday-Friday Noon-3:45pm, and on the second Saturday of the month (June-Labor Day). Some Saturdays and Sunday evenings there are pioneer demos at the lightkeeper's house. Admission: $3.00 per person (age 6+). Cash only to climb.***

The oldest working lighthouse on the Great Lakes, Marblehead Point has been known for having the roughest weather along Lake Erie. To warn ships of the danger of being dashed against the rocks by winds from the north, the federal government constructed the Marblehead Lighthouse in 1821. Built of native limestone, it is the oldest light in continuous operation on the Great Lakes.

The reflector lamp originally burned whale oil, lard oil, coal oil, and now it's electric. Their stories of old lighthouse keepers lugging 40 lb. buckets of whale oil up those 77 stairs are so interesting. From the top, you can see Cedar Point rides, Kelley's Island and Put-in-Bay. The cute little museum and gift shop (in the lightkeepers house) have many inexpensive coloring books and puzzles to buy and artifacts to explore. Lifesaving Station now open.

Milan

EDISON BIRTHPLACE MUSEUM

Milan - *9 Edison Drive (off State Route 250, Downtown, near exit 118 off Turnpike) 44846. Phone: (419) 499-2135. www.tomedison.org. Hours: Tuesday-Saturday 10:00am-5:00pm, Sunday 1:00-5:00pm (Summer). Tuesday-Sunday 1:00-5:00pm (April-May and September-October). Friday-Sunday 1:00-5:00pm (February-March and November-December). Closed Easter and January. Admission: $9.00 adult, $8.00 senior (59+), $5.00 child (6-12). Free Military. Note: The Milan Historical Museum Complex is across the street. The birthplace is not wheelchair or stroller accessible. Educators: look at their downloads link for bios, timelines, inventions and video.*

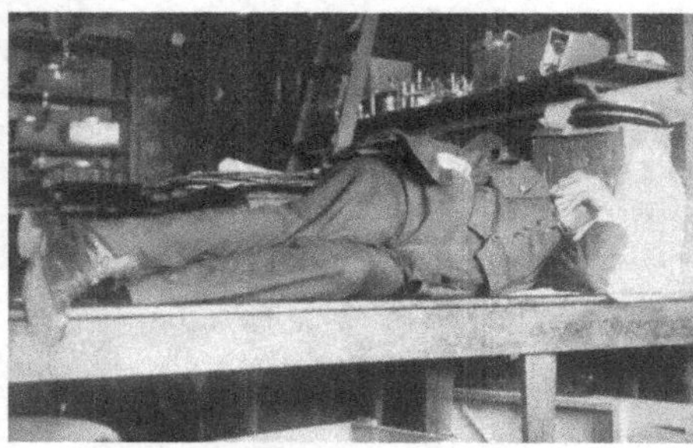

Thomas Edison enjoying one of our favorite inventions...the Power Nap!

Edison was born here in 1847 and raised in this home until age 7. Your tour guides may be one or two of Edison's great-great-great-grandnieces. The original family mementos give you a feeling of being taken back in time. The room full of his inventions (he had 1,093 American patents) gives you a sense of his brilliance! Most famous for his invention of the light bulb and phonograph (first words recorded were “Mary had a little lamb”), you may not know he was kicked out of school for being a non-attentive/ slow learner! So, his mother home-schooled him. Part of the Edison family belongings include slippers, Derby hat, cane, Mother Edison's disciplinary switch (still hanging in the original spot in the kitchen), butter molds and “Pop Goes the Weasel” yarner. Two practical inventions of the time you'll want to see are the pole ladder (a long pole that pulls out to a full size ladder) and the slipper seat (a cushioned little seat, low to the ground, so it is easier to put your slippers or shoes on).

MILAN HISTORICAL MUSEUM

Milan - ***10 Edison Drive (off SR 113, Turnpike exit 118) 44846. Phone: (419) 499-2968. www.milanhistory.org. Hours: Tuesday-Saturday 10am-5pm, Sunday 1-5:00pm (Summer). Friday-Sunday 1-5:00pm (Feb-May, September-December) Admission: $9 adult, $6 senior, $5 child (6-12). Note: Gift Shop with video and slide presentations. Educators: Excellent school tour packets of study. FREEBIES: Search the Museum for hidden clues in a FREE scavenger hunt sticker book.***

Tour includes several buildings in a complex featuring different themes like the Galpin Home of local history, dolls, toys and a collection of mechanical banks. There are several other homes along with a blacksmith and carriage shop and everything you might want to buy from the 1800's is sold in the general store. On a chilly day the warmth of the pot-bellied stove drew menfolk to linger for a game of checkers (try a game on their giant game board). Sign the Captain's Log book and try your strength at the Canal Weight Station. Be sure to add this to your visit to Edison's Home, one block away.

MELON FESTIVAL

Milan - Downtown, SR 113. (419) 499-4909. www.milanmelonfestival.org. Melons in baskets, sliced, muskmelon ice cream & watermelon sherbet. Melon eating contests. Parade, rides, crafts and kiddie pedal tractor pull. Free. (Labor Day Weekend)

OBERLIN HERITAGE CENTER

Oberlin - ***73 South Professor Street, James Monroe House (State Route 38 and State Route 511) 44074. www.oberlinheritage.org. Phone: (440) 774-1700. Hours: Tuesday, Thursday, Saturday 10:30am and 1:30pm. The tour is of most interest to adults and children above the age of 10 years. Tours last 1.25 hours and walking is involved. Summer Saturdays have more family-oriented programming suitable for children (most are FREE). Admission: $6 per adult. Shorter Sneak Peak Tours are $3 per adult. Educators: Oberlin History for Kids link with suggested games, crafts & books. http://www.oberlinheritage.org/researchlearn/historyfaqs.***

Oberlin is a town with strong ties to the Underground Railroad. The First Church in Oberlin served as headquarters for the Oberlin Anti-Slavery Society, and Oberlin's public school system was an early proponent of integration. Learn about abolition and the Underground Railroad, student life around campus through the years, and a little red school house with a collection of lunch pails and McGuffey Readers. Start the tour in James Monroe's home. He was an important abolitionist, advocate of voting rights for African Americans, and friend of Frederick Douglass. Monroe taught at Oberlin College.

On display in the Jewett House is an exhibit on "Aluminum: The Oberlin Connection" that includes a recreation of Charles Martin Hall's 1886 wood shed experiment station. Maybe you'll also want to catch a movie at the Apollo, the local one-screen movie theatre that's been operating in Oberlin since the 1910s, and which introduced the "talkies" to Oberlin in 1928. (Showings cost a whopping $3.00 every day except Tuesday and Thursday, when admission is $2.00. That's hard to beat!)

HOLIDAY OPEN HOUSE

Oberlin – Oberlin Heritage Center. Jewett House, (440) 774-1700. Gingerbread house contest display.

MOHICAN-MEMORIAL STATE FOREST

Perrysville - *3060 County Road 939 44864. www.dnr.state.oh.us. Phone: (419) 938-6222.*

4,498 acres in Ashland County. Hiking trails (24 miles), bridle trails (22 miles), “Park & Pack” camping sites (10), snowmobile trails (7 miles - weather permitting), state nature preserve. Also War Memorial Shrine and Mohican State Park is adjacent.

AFRICAN SAFARI WILDLIFE PARK

Port Clinton - *267 Lightner Road (Off State Route 2 exit SR 53, follow signs) 43452. Phone: (419) 732-3606 or (800) 521-2660. www.africansafariwildlifepark.com. Hours: Daily 10:00am-5:00pm (March-May, September-November). Daily 9:00am-7:00pm (Memorial Day-Labor Day). Admission: $16.00-$24.00 per person (summer). $5.00 discount (spring & fall). Admission ages 3+. Online coupons. Note: Safari Grill and gift shop. Jungle Junction Playland and petting zoo.*

See more than 400 animals (including llamas, alpacas, and zebras) as they wander freely around your vehicle as you drive through a 100-acre park. This is the only drive through safari park in the Midwest. The giraffe lean their long necks over to check you out through your car windows. The friendliest animals are the camels and ponies and you can ride them, too (at no additional charge). The ugliest are probably the warthogs. Another favorite is the “Porkchop Downs” pig races. Boy, do they snort loud when they’re trying to win!

CRANE CREEK STATE PARK & MAGEE MARSH WILDLIFE AREA

Port Clinton - ***13531 W SR 2, Oak Harbor (Rte. 2, west of Port Clinton) 43452. Phone: (419) 898-0960. Hours: Open dawn to dusk, year-round. www.stateparks.com/crane_creek.html.***

Located on the scenic shore of Lake Erie, Crane Creek State Park offers a vast freshwater marsh and spacious sandy beach for enjoyment. This coastal environment is home to more than 300 species of birds. Herons, waterfowl, warblers, gulls and the magnificent bald eagle make this park one of the best birdwatching areas in the country. We loved the boardwalk viewing, the beach and especially, the Eagle's Nests and spring migration. It's amazing how many birds come thru this area! The park was named for the abundance of blue herons - misidentified as cranes years ago. Park also has boating and swimming access to Lake Erie shores.

GREAT LAKES POPCORN COMPANY

Port Clinton - ***60 N. Madison Street (downtown) 43452. Phone: (419) 732-3080 or (866) 732-3080. www.GreatLakesPopcorn.com. Hours: Wed-Thurs 11:00am-5:30pm, Fri-Sat-Sun 11:00am-4:00pm. Extended Seasonal hours. Tours: Available for school-age children.***

Look for the bright red & white awning and listen for the "island music" as you and your children find this fun adventure! All of their equipment is located within view of customers standing at the counter. They turn the coaters at an angle so you can see inside of them and see the popcorn churning in the machines. Sample many varieties of popcorn including "Bubble Gum", "Root Beer", "Jelly Bean" and "Wild Walleye". The "Popcorn Tasting Station" is where kids and families alike can sample any, or all, of the 30 plus flavors.

JET EXPRESS

Port Clinton - ***5 North Jefferson Street (docks at foot of Perry Street Bridge, SR 163) 43452. Phone: (800) 245-1JET. www.jet-express.com. Admission: Children 5 and under ride FREE! Each way is $20.00 for adults, $7.50 youth (12-16), $3.00 child (6-11) and $3.50 more for bikes. (April-October)***

Indoor and outdoor seating on the fastest catamaran to Islands. 22 minute trip with some boat facts weaved in. Nice ride and the docks are located right in the hub of activity. Free parking nearby or parking fee at terminal.

LAKE ERIE ISLANDS REGIONAL WELCOME CENTER

Port Clinton - ***770 S.E. Catawba Road (just off Rte. 2 & Rte. 53 N) 43452. Phone: (800) 255-3743. www.shoresandislands.com.***

The clever silhouette building design and replica dioramas inside really orient you to all the area has to offer. The kids can gaze at the 600 gallon aquarium or do nature rubbings while the parents work out a visitors plan. Their movie theater highlights the Lake Erie region. A Kids play area resides within a replica of Oliver Hazard Perry's flagship, THE LAWRENCE, from the Battle of Lake Erie during the War of 1812. Gander at replicas of the Tin Goose, the first airplane to service the Lake Erie Islands. The Birdwatching display has an interactive telescope. Look for the replica of the Marblehead Lighthouse or listen for a Talking walleye, plus more surprises. They can also tell you about eateries in the area that specialize in perch and walleye...any way you like it.

LAKE ERIE ISLANDS STATE PARK

Port Clinton - ***4049 E. Moores Dock Road 43452. Phone: (866) 644-6727 for camping. http://parks.ohiodnr.gov/kelleysisland Hours: Daylight hours.***

Limestone cliffs, historic wineries, crystal caverns and a shimmering Great Lake greet visitors to the Lake Erie Islands state parks. These five state parks offer unique island retreats with an atmosphere both festive and casual. Fishing, boating and swimming can be enjoyed at each park.

CATAWBA ISLAND STATE PARK: (419) 797-4530, off SR 53.

SOUTH BASS ISLAND: (419) 285-2112 seasonally. Some overnight camping is available. See separate attraction descriptions under Put-n-Bay city listings.

KELLEY'S ISLAND STATE PARK: (reached only by ferry or boat) Six miles of hiking trails lead to scenic vistas, historic sites and two nature preserves. The islands were formed during the glacial period when massive ice sheets entered Ohio. **GLACIAL GROOVES STATE MEMORIAL** is a must see and a great way to study Ohio geology.

Located on the north side of the island, the largest easily accessible grooves were formed when ice once covered solid limestone bedrock. Looking safely over fence, you see a giant groove passage that seems unbelievable. Placards along the trail detail the history of glaciers moving through the area.

See actual groves made by huge glaciers "creeping along"...

Prior to the War of 1812, the Lake Erie Island region had been occupied by Ottawa and Huron (Wyandot) Indian tribes. A testimony to their existence on the islands is carved in **INSCRIPTION ROCK PETROGLYPHS**. The flat-topped limestone slab displays carvings of animals and human figures. Discovered partly buried in the shoreline in 1833, the 32 feet by 21 feet rock is now entirely exposed (protected by a roof and viewing platform).

Archaeologists believe the inscriptions date from sometime between AD 1200 and 1600. (866) 921-5710 (Rock) or (419) 797-4025 (Grooves).

WATERING HOLE SAFARI & WATERPARK

Port Clinton - ***1530 S. Danbury Rd. N (Danbury N Road exit off Rte. 2) 43452. Phone: (419) 732-6671. https://wateringholeatmonsoon.com/. Hours: Generally 11:00am-dusk (Memorial Day weekend-Labor Day) Admission: Rates range $15.00-$30.00 per day. Zoo $9.00-$12.00. Coupons online. Admission must be paid for entrance, even if not swimming. Note: Picnics and coolers are not allowed as well as any outside food. Monsoon Lagoon offers a concession stand with very reasonable prices.***

They have Adventure Island with 150 water toys, a lazy river, two giant water slides plus eatery, mini-golf, bumper boats, go-karts and a game room. Take a ride on the six great waterslides, including the three stories tall Slide Tower or.... Splash around on the Adventure Island Tree House with one-hundred and five water play stations on seventeen different levels. Little ones can splash and play in the Little Squirts Play Pool. And Mom and Dad can relax in the adult pool. THE ZOO & SAFARI PARK features animals from all around the world including giraffes, zebras, camels and more! Souvenir photos with your favorite exotic animals. Exhibits are rotated frequently. Feed animals too.

WALLEYE MADNESS AT MIDNIGHT

Port Clinton - downtown. Family oriented non-alcoholic event with indoor & outdoor activities such as kid's/parent's food, entertainment & crafts, and a countdown to midnight. Watch a 20 foot fiberglass walleye descend during countdown to the New Year. http://wyliewalleyefoundation.com/. Adm. (New Years Eve)

Put-in-Bay

AQUATIC VISITORS CENTER

Put-in-Bay - *Peach Point 43456. Phone: (419) 285-1800. www.ohioseagrant.osu.edu/visit/avc/ Hours: Wednesday-Saturday 10:00am - 5:00pm. (mid-June to early September). Admission: FREE.*

The Ohio Division of Wildlife invites kids to learn about fish and fishing. Displays highlight the story of this historic fish hatchery, live fish exhibits, and recreational fishing activity offered on Lake Erie. A children's playroom includes a touch tank, coloring activities, wooden puzzles, wildlife videos and a hands-on fishing game. Kids can fish off the docks with rod and bait provided.

BUTTERFLY HOUSE

Put-in-Bay - *979 Catawba Avenue (on grounds of Perry's Cave Family Fun Center) 43456. Phone: (419) 285-2446. www.perryscave.com. Hours: Daily 10:00am-6:00pm (summer - May thru September). Spring & Fall 10am-5pm. Admission: $8.00 adult, $5.00 child (6-12).*

Walk among hundreds of exotic butterflies in the fully-enclosed garden. Enjoy the tranquil environment with soothing fountain, Koi fish pond, lush flowers and soothing music. The kids enjoy the secret walkways throughout the garden to get up close with the butterflies. A 15-minute educational presentation is included. Stay as long as your heart desires. Unique educational gift shop including nature gifts, candles & ceramics, butterfly & Put-in-Bay souvenirs.

CHOCOLATE CAFÉ & MUSEUM

Put-in-Bay - *820 Catawba Avenue 43456. www.chocolateohio.com. Phone: (419) 734-7114. Hours: Daily 8:00am-8:30pm (May-September).*

Featuring South Bend Chocolate Company handmade chocolates (our favorite Indiana chocolate factory tour!), learn the history and making of chocolate while viewing a fine collection of antique chocolate collectibles. Learn even more about chocolate - watch a film, or have your picture taken with Lucy at the Chocolate Factory. The unique bistro celebrates fine chocolate & coffee along with decadent cheesecakes and ice cream treats.

CRYSTAL CAVE & HEINEMAN'S GRAPE JUICE WINERY

Put-in-Bay - ***978 Catawba Ave. 43456. www.heinemanswinery.com. Phone: (419) 285-2811. Hours: Daily (early May-Late September). Call for schedule (basically 11:00am-5:00pm except Noon on Sundays) Admission: $8.00 adult, $4.00 child (6-11).***

The Crystal Cave (located below the factory) is well worth the visit! Discovered by workers in 1897 while digging a well for the winery 40 feet above them. The walls of this cave are covered in strontium sulfate, a bluish mineral called celestite. These crystals range from 8 to 18 inches long. The original cave was much smaller than what appears today, as crystals were harvested and sold for the manufacturing of fireworks. You'll walk right into the world's largest geode! Every crystal (mostly bluish green) has 14 sides. We promise a WOW on this one! Another tour option is the juice/wine factory. Although you may be hesitant to have children tour a winery, they really put emphasis on the grapes (varieties, flavor, color, etc.) and the chemistry of making juice. Did you know they use air bags to press the juice out of grapes?

LAKE ERIE ISLANDS MUSEUM

Put-in-Bay - ***443 Catawba Avenue (adjacent to the Put-in-Bay Town Hall parking lot) 43456. Phone: (419) 285-2804. www.leihs.org. Hours: Daily 11:00am-5:00pm (May-October). Admission is $4.00-$5.00 Note: Bicycles can be rented near boat docks. Children's seats & helmets are available. Golf carts are also available. Rates range from $15 per hour, depending on the number of seats.***

Boating, sailors, and shipping industry artifacts. Video shown is an excellent trip to the past. Why did so many Grand Hotels burn? What are the major industries on the island...a hint...one is a fruit! Usually live displays of Box Turtles, Painted Turtles, and island snakes can be seen at the wildlife building. Look for ship models scattered throughout.

PERRY'S CAVE & FAMILY FUN CENTER

Put-in-Bay ***- 979 Catawba Avenue (South Bass Island, 1/2 mile from town) 43456. Phone: (419) 285-2405. www.perryscave.com. Admission: $8.00 adult, $5.00 child (6-12). Other amusements are an additional $5.00-$8.00. Tours: Daily 10:30am - 6:00pm. Tours leave every 20 minutes in the summer. Fewer times rest of year.***

Inside the cave you'll see walls covered with calcium carbonate (the same ingredient in antacids) that has settled from years of dripping water. Rumor says Perry kept prisoners and stored supplies in the cave during the Battle of Lake Erie. At the Gem Mining Company, mine for real gems and minerals. After-hours lantern tours available by reservation. Chart your course around the 18-hole miniature golf course with a War of 1812 theme. In the Antique Car Museum, stroll through the past as you view Ford Model A's & T's as well as the island's oldest automobile. Find your way in Fort Amaze'n or climb the rock wall. The Butterfly House has a separate listing.

PERRY'S VICTORY AND INTERNATIONAL PEACE MEMORIAL

Put-In-Bay ***- 93 Delaware Avenue (Ohio Turnpike to SR 53 and SR 2. There are several ferry lines that service the island, the Jet Express, The Miller Boat Line, and the Rocket) 43456. Phone: (419) 285-2184. www.nps.gov/pevi Hours: Daily 10:00am-6:00pm (mid May to mid-Sept). Daily 10:00am-5:00pm (mid-Sept to early October). Fri-Mon (first half of Oct) Admission: $10.00 per person (age 16 and up). Must climb two flights of stairs first for elevator to top of monument. No fee for Visitors Center. Educators: Biographies of famous characters in the War of 1812 online: www.nps.gov/pevi/historyculture/index.htm***

"We have met the enemy and they are ours"

Built of pink granite, 352 feet high and 45 feet in diameter, this memorial commemorates the Battle of Lake Erie and then the years of peace. Commodore Perry commanded the American fleet in the War of 1812. In September of 1813 he defeated the British and Perry then sent his famous message to General William Henry Harrison "We have met the enemy and they are ours". Interpretive actors outside chat with you on busy days and weekends. The Visitors Center has extensive exhibits, a film with surround sound, and an expanded bookstore. The exhibits tell the story of the Battle of Lake Erie, the

War of 1812, construction of the monument and the international peace that it represents. A live feed camera system provides views from the top of the monument enabling those who are unable or decide not to make the trip to the observation deck to witness the view. The presentation of the War of 1812 and the Battle of Lake Erie are so worth seeing.

JULY 4TH CELEBRATION

Put-in-Bay – Perry's Victory Memorial. 3 days full of parades, rides, entertainment, reenactments and fireworks.

HISTORICAL WEEKEND

Put-In-Bay - Perry's Victory Memorial. www.lake-erie.com or (800) 441-1271. Military living history camps with displays of Indian wars to the present. Boy Scout camporee. Parade, live entertainment. (second long weekend in September).

PUT-IN-BAY TOUR TRAIN

Put-In-Bay - ***154 Delaware Ave, the Depot 43456. www.put-in-bay-trans.com. Phone: (419) 285-2016. Hours: Daily 10:00am-5:00pm (Memorial Day-September). Weekends Only (October). Admission: $12.00 adult, $5.00 child (6-11) Note: South Bass Island State Park, 419-797-4530, 419-285-2112, Reservations: (866) OHIOPARKS. Stone beach, ice skating, flush restrooms with showers (summer only), ice fishing, campsites, cabins, picnic shelter, launch ramp, and fishing pier.***

A tram departs frequently from the village depot for an one hour tour of the island. Stops include Perry's Cave, Heineman's Winery, Crystal Cave, War of 18 Holes Miniature Golf Course, Alaskan Wildlife Museum, and Perry's Victory and International Peace Memorial. Departing every 30 minutes, the train trolley allows passengers to depart and re-board (without additional cost) at any time. The tour is especially interesting and gives a clear understanding of all that occupied the island thru the years.

STONE LABORATORY

Put-in-Bay - ***Field Station, Box 119 43456. Phone: (614) 247-6504 or (419) 285-2341. https://stonelab.osu.edu/. Hours: Workshops (open mid-April thru October). Thursdays in the summer, they co-host Put-in-Bay Eco-History (a.k.a. Passport) tours open to everyone. Admission: Field Station Tours: $10.00 per person. All workshops and tours are prearranged and require transport to the Island from Put-in-Bay or privately.***

Stone Lab's science workshop program offers a variety of activities ranging from water sampling on a research vessel in the lake, to identifying microscopic aquatic organisms you've collected, or dissecting fish in a lab. You can specialize island activities by adding an invertebrate walk, bird walk, edible plant walk, exotic species slide show, or seining. Groups may arrange a one-hour historical/scientific tour of the Gibraltar Island facilities. Cooke Castle, Perry's Lookout, glacial grooves, and brief classroom activities will provide participants with a well-rounded program overview.

APPLE FESTIVAL

Rittman - Bauman Orchards, 161 Rittman Avenue. www.baumanorchards.com. Apples & cider. Apple pie eating contests. Apple peeling contests. Apple butter. Candy apples. Wagon/hayrides. Apple Dumplings, Fritters, Donuts, etc. Parades. Pioneer crafts. Petting Zoo. (last two Saturdays in September, first Saturday in October)

Sandusky

CASTAWAY BAY

Sandusky ***- 2001 Cleveland Road (at the entrance to Cedar Point Causeway) 44870. Phone: (419) 627-2106. www.castawaybay.com. Hours: Generally 9:00am-9:00pm. Closed many weekdays (visit website for calendar).***

In the elaborate enclosed natural setting of palm trees, huts, inland lagoons and plenty of water lies numerous water attractions. Highlights include a tall water roller coaster that propels riders uphill, then downhill; a dozen water slides; a large wave pool w/ 3 foot waves; an action pool with water basketball and floating logs; concessions and the center attraction: a gigantic multi-story interactive play area including a 1,000 gallon tipping bucket that downpours every few minutes. The waterpark is open to overnight guests at the resort featuring rooms starting at $99 per night. Day Passes run $29.00 per person (without overnight stay). Each overnight stay includes park admission for three to six, depending on the size of room. All rooms feature extras such as microwave and mini-frig. The resort has two mid-priced restaurants, an indoor pool, whirlpool, exercise room, arcade and adjacent marina.

CEDAR POINT & SHORES WATER PARK

Sandusky ***- State Route 4 (I-80 to Exit 118 or 110. Follow Signs) 44870. Phone: (419) 627-2350. www.cedarpoint.com. Hours: Vary by season. (May-October). Generally open at 9:00 or 10:00am until dark. Admission: $45.99 onine, Small***

children (under 48") have reduced fees. Children age 2 and under are FREE. Separate admission for Soak City ($39.99). Combo, 2 day & Starlight rates. Parking $20.00. Note: Stroller rental. Picnic area. Food Service. Miniature golf. CHALLENGE PARK (additional admission).

More rides than any other park in the world! The amusement extravaganza on the shores of Lake Erie includes 17 Roller Coasters and a total of 70 rides. Most new rides are super thrillers, not for kids, but maybe the parents. Here are some of the themed areas or rides: SHORES – wave pool, water slides, Adventure Cove, Eerie Falls (get wet in the dark). LIVE SHOWS MILLENNIUM & MAGNUM XL - tallest and best coasters. MAVERICK in Frontiertown. CAMP SNOOPY, PLANET SNOOPY & KIDDY KINGDOM - with piped-in kids music and child sized airplanes, a family coaster, and Speedway. Also Sing-along with Peanuts characters and traditional carousels and classic rides. Cedar Point continues to hold the title of "Best Amusement Park in the World."

GOODTIME I

Sandusky - ***(docked at Jackson Street Pier) 44870. Phone: (419) 625-9692 or (800) 446-3140. www.goodtimeboat.com. Admission: $10.00 - $28.00 (ages 4 and up) Tours: Depart 9:30am, Arrive back 6:30pm (Memorial Day-Labor Day). Tuesday night cruises available.***

The M/V Goodtime I is a sleek all-steel vessel built for ocean-going cruises. She is 117 feet long and Coast Guard approved to carry 355 Passengers. The Goodtime I Departs from Sandusky, Ohio daily on a Daytime Island Hopping Cruise. Stop for awhile at each island.

GREAT WOLF LODGE INDOOR WATERPARK

Sandusky - ***4600 Milan Road (SR250) (Ohio Turnpike, exit 118, north on SR250) 44870. Phone: (419) 609-6000 or (888) 779-BEAR. www.greatwolflodge.com. Hours: Waterpark daily 9:00am-10:00pm. Wristbands are good day of arrival until closing the next day. Checkout is 10:30am. Admission: Lodge room suites include 4-6 waterpark passes. Rooms vary from $100-$300+ per night. Additional waterpark passes $20 each. Day Passes (limited) $45-$60/day. Note: All suites: Family, KidCabin (log cabin in room with bunk beds), microwave, refrigerator. Arcade and outdoor pools, gift shops. Bring Coast Guard approved swim vests for non-swimmers (limited number of vests available at park, too). This park is excellent for kids 11 and under. Check out the wonderful holiday theme packages they offer for Easter, Fall Harvest, Thanksgiving and Christmastime.***

Even though it's a resort...it still was comfy for the both kids and parents. Bring you own food to prepare or eat in at GITCHIE GOOMIE GRILL. All the kid's menu prices are around $5.00. Several nice snack bars too.

The minute you step into the Outdoor/ Northwoods ambiance (and gently heated, no musty or chlorine smell) you have hours of fun. Play in the 4-story interactive fun center featuring 12 levels of water based antics or get "dunked" by the giant bucket. If you don't scream from excitement in the Fort, you're sure to on the giant inner tube slides (best for elementary ages and up). In 5 pools (all age levels), 7 waterslides, and the water fort you'll find watchful and helpful lifeguards - there for safety and are excellent crowd control. Smaller guests will delight in Soak'n Oak Springs, a water play fort, just for toddlers, complete with slides and water spouting bear cubs. Teens and Tweeners can take on the challenge of climbing an Aqua Rock Wall (additional fee). Two areas for the 10 and under crowd are the nightly Story time by the lobby fireplace (come in your pajamas) or the craft room, Cubs Cabin. The staff and quality of craft received high ratings from our crew! With a little planning of resources, you will get your money's worth in memories and fun for sure!

KALAHARI INDOOR WATERPARK RESORT

Sandusky - ***7000 Kalahari Drive (located on State Route 250, just 10 minutes south of Cedar Point) 44870. www.kalahariresort.com. Phone: (419) 433-7200 or (877) KALAHARI. Admission: Overnight packages (lodging, waterpark, dry play area included) run $199.00-$349.00 per night. Waterpark only: $55.00-65.00 for all day pass. Note: Check-in is 4:00pm, Checkout is 11:00am. You may stay to play after checkout until 3:00pm that day. Other dry spaces include an indoor playground, small indoor mini-golf course, gameroom, Safari Outdoor Adventure Park, and they have daily crafts (especially loved the cookie decorating).***

Welcome to the largest indoor waterpark in the U.S.!!! Guests enter an authentic African-themed environment. With a tween and teen in tow (our fav ages to recommend for this park as it is mostly "high adventure on safari"), we ventured north to find out.

WATERPARK: You can choose from a water treehouse, lazy river or water sport pools, but the kids over 10 spend more time in the rides area. Kids Favs: the Zip Coaster (extreme exhilaration, especially at the beginning-keep your head low) and the Victoria Falls family raft slide. Parents Favorites: the indoor/outdoor hot tub (in the winter, snowflakes melt on your nose!). Brighter lighting comes from the Texlon Transparent Roof over much of the new area. The "intelligent" roof system creates a comfortable vacation "feel" allowing natural light in while softening the acoustics. Now, what do you do first? The extreme Tanzanian Twister ("toilet bowl ride") and the less extreme Rippling Rhino family raft ride (but it was almost totally in the dark). And the Wave Pool – so nice and wide and warm (other indoor wave pools tend to be smaller and cold). The "action" waves ride longer than most making this our family's favorite indoor waterpark wave pool! Now, with two indoor Flow Riders – your tweens and teens don't have any excuse to not try the ride. (Preschool Note: under 42" youngster set in tow? The new indoor Kids Safari is a much needed area for them – its two tall giraffes welcome kids to a "safe" play area just for them – set off to the side away from the "buzz" of action).

OUTDOOR WATERPARK: features activity pools, hot tubs, dry play, expanded sun deck, sand volleyball courts, shuffleboard courts and much more!

SAFARI OUTDOOR ADVENTURE PARK: Attractions Include: (additional fee of $7.00-$14.00 per activity): •Ropes Course- Sky Trail Explorer - Three level course featuring 48 elements spanning over 750 feet of thrilling African-themed ropes adventures. •Zip Line Tour •Adventure Climbing Walls •Safari Adventures Animal Park feature up-close and educational animal encounters.

DINING: The Great Karoo Marketplace Restaurant features a lavish buffet with some African/Asian inspired items. Unusual breakfast casseroles and the cinnamon buns were the hit in our family. Other "snack stops" were the Café Mirage (the 20" Big Kahuna is the biggest pizza we've ever had) and B-Lux Grille. The Café is across from the arcade – so, with a twenty minute wait – we HAD to use the time wisely playing games. We also liked having the Grille right smack in the middle of the rides – with plenty of tables to sit down and eat at. Because they make fresh product most every day, the Candy Hut's (located in main lobby) dipped pretzels and cheese/caramel corn were crunchy and perfectly seasoned. (dining budget note: every room has a minimum of a mini micro/frig unit). We noticed in-house Pizza Pub room service deliveries were abundant. Use discount coupons and order extra for reheats later. Plus, almost every guest checking in brought a large cooler – full of snacks, sodas and frozen entrees maybe?)

ROOMS: All rooms and suites include waterpark wristbands, at least one TV, micro/frig and coffee makers. Add bunk beds, Murphy beds or sofa beds for four or more guests. The Village Suite is just perfect for large parties as each family has their own "space" for privacy yet a large communal full kitchen, dining and family room for fellowship. (Budget note: check out their online specials – if you're somewhat flexible with your dates, you can get a room for $139.00 per night/family. And their packages/add-ons are a nice value treat. Get a wonderful mother/daughter pedicure or try a cabana rental).

LAGOON DEER PARK

Sandusky - ***1502 Martins Point Road, State Route 269 (between State Route 2 and US 6) 44870. Phone: (419) 684-5701. www.lagoondeerparkohio.com Hours: Daily 10:00am-6:00pm (May - mid-October). Admission: $9.00 adult, $5.00 child (3-12). Pay Fishing available in stocked lake.***

Hand feed and pet hundreds of deer, llamas, miniature donkeys and other tame species. Altogether, they have 250 exotic animals from Europe, Japan, Asia, South and North America. Approximately 75 baby animals are born here each year.

MAUI SANDS INDOOR WATERPARK RESORT

Sandusky - ***5513 Milan Road (intersection of SR 250 & SR 2 44870. Phone: (888) STAYMSR. www.mauisandsresort.com. Hours: Daily Noon-11:00pm. Admission: Day Passes run $29.99 per day (age 3+). Day Passes are provided based on resort occupancy. Lodging rates vary from $129 to $269 base (waterpark admission included). Note: 70 cabanas for rental. Overnight Rooms (connected to waterpark): Guests can choose from five choices that include unique suite and room types.***

Maui Sands Indoor Waterpark Resort is the second-largest indoor waterpark in Sandusky..second only to Kalahari…and introduces a few water rides that are new to the area. Riders get to experience a bowl ride, which shoots people down a slide into a bowl that will eventually pull them through the bottom. Also inside the park is the SurfRider attraction. The SurfRider is a stationary wave that creates a never-ending two-foot high Waikiki breaker. It is the only deep-water standing wave generator in existence in North America and riders use a real finned surfboard. The kiddie areas feature milder waterslides and an aquatic play structure.

Then there's a teen activity center equipped with hoops, two 40-person heated whirlpool spas (one inside and one outside), and a lazy river. On the dry side is a huge video game arcade and a full-service salon and spa. Several dining options all feature either seafood or American fare with an Hawaiian flare.

MERRY-GO-ROUND MUSEUM

Sandusky - ***West Washington and Jackson Streets (State Route 6, downtown) 44870. Phone: (419) 626-6111. www.merrygoroundmuseum.org. Hours: Monday-Saturday 11:00am-4:00pm. Sunday Noon - 4:00pm (Summer). Weekends Only (February). Wednesday - Sunday (Rest of the Year). Admission: $6.00 adult, $5.00 senior (60+), $4.00 child (4-14). Includes carousel ride. Tours: Guided tours of the current exhibition are scheduled. Note: Gift Shop.***

This colorful, bright, big museum was the former Post Office. Once inside, you'll see all sorts of carousel memorabilia and history. Each year, a new exhibit space is filled with colorful displays of carousel designers or companies. Next, tour the workshop to watch craftsman make carousel horses with authentic "old world" tools. Then, ride the Herschel 1930's merry-go-round.

INDIAN MILL

Upper Sandusky - ***State Route 23 and State Route 67 to Route 47 (along the banks of the Sandusky River) 43351. www.ohiohistory.org/visit/museum-and-site-locator/indian-mill. Phone: (800) 600-7147. Hours: Thursday – Sunday 1:00 – 4:30pm (May – October). Admission: $2.00 Adult, $1.00 Youth (4-12).***

In a scenic location along the Sandusky River, Indian Mill, built in 1861, is the nation's first educational museum of milling in its original structure. The restored three-story structure replaces the original one-story building that the U.S. government built in 1820 to reward the loyalty of local Wyandot Indians during the War of 1812. Many exhibits are placed around the original mill machinery. The restored miller's office displays the history of milling from prehistoric times to the present.

FESTIVAL OF THE FISH

Vermilion - Downtown. Victory Park. www.vermilionohio.com. Walleye and perch sandwiches, "crazy" craft race, entertainment, crafts and a lighted boat parade. FREE. (Fathers Day Weekend)

WOOLLYBEAR FESTIVAL

Vermilion - Downtown. Main Street. www.vermilionohio.com. (440) 967-4477. An annual tribute to the weather "forecasting" woollybear caterpillar with a huge parade, caterpillar races, woollybear contests for kids, crafts and entertainment. FREE. (first Sunday in October)

FINDLEY STATE PARK

Wellington - ***25381 State Route 58 (3 miles South of Wellington on State Route 58) 44090. Phone: (440) 647-4490. http://parks.ohiodnr.gov/findley.***

Once a state forest, Findley State Park is heavily wooded with stately pines and various hardwoods. The scenic hiking trails allow nature lovers to view spectacular wildflowers and observe wildlife. One area of the park is set aside as a sanctuary for the Duke's skipper butterfly, an extremely rare insect. 931 acres of camping, hiking trails, bike rentals, nature programs, boating and rentals (paddles and electric only), fishing, swimming with beach and winter sports. 3 "Conestoga" camper cabins are available from April through October to overnight camp.

CELERYVILLE, BUURMA VEGETABLE FARMS

Willard - ***4200 Broadway (Route 224 West to Route 103 South to Celeryville) 44890. Phone: (419) 935-3633. www.buurmafarms.com. Hours: Weekdays (June-September) just watching. Tours: 20+ people required.***

Judged one of the best industrial tours in the state, this is a 3000-acre organic "muck" vegetable garden. On tour you'll see greenhouses, celery and radish harvesting machines in action, and vegetable processing (cleaning, pruning) and packaging. You'll love the facts and figures it takes to produce veggies. Although started with celery growing, the area now never grows celery (soil conditions prevent it).

Chapter 5
North East Ohio

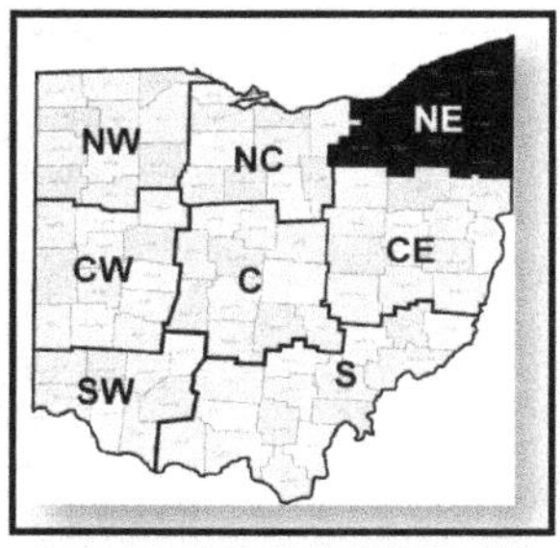

Akron

- Akron Aeros
- Akron Symphony Orchestra
- Akron Zoo
- All American Soap Box Derby
- First Night Akron
- Portage Lakes State Park
- Stan Hywet Hall
- Weathervane Playhouse

Amherst

- Pumpkin Maze Playland

Andover

- Pymatuning State Park

Ashtabula

- Ashtabula Marine Museum
- Covered Bridge Pizza
- Hubbard House And Underground Railroad Museum

Avon

- Duct Tape Festival

Bath

- Hale Farm And Village

Berlin Center

- Noah's Lost Ark Animal Sanctuary

Brecksville

- Cuyahoga Valley National Park

Brunswick

- Mapleside Farms
- Mapleside Farms Restaurant

Burton

- Century Village Museum & Store

Canfield

- Canfield Fair

Chardon

- Geauga County Maple Festival
- Pioneer Waterland And Dry Park

Cleveland

- A Christmas Story House
- Cleveland Botanical Garden
- Cleveland Childrens Museum
- Cleveland Lakefront State Park
- Cleveland Metroparks Zoo & Rainforest
- Cleveland Museum Of Art
- Cleveland Museum Of Natural History
- Cleveland National Air Show
- Cleveland Orchestra
- Cleveland Playhouse
- Cleveland Sports
- Corner Alley
- Federal ReserVe Bank Learning Center And Money Museum
- Good Time III
- Great Lakes Science Center
- Greater Cleveland Aquarium
- Lolly The Trolley Tour
- Memphis Kiddie Park
- Nasa Glenn Research Center
- Nautica Queen
- Rock And Roll Hall Of Fame Museum
- Steamship William G. Mather Museum
- U.S.S. Cod
- Western Reserve History Museum

Cleveland (Berea)

- Irish Cultural Festival

Cleveland (Brookpark)

- Cleveland Christmas Connection
- I-X Indoor Amusement Park

Cortland

- Mosquito Lake State Park

Fairport Harbor

- Fairport Harbor Marine Museum

Geneva

- Geneva State Park
- Great Lakes Medieval Faire

Hinckley

- Buzzard Day

Jefferson

- Ashtabula Covered Bridge Fest
- Jefferson Depot
- Victorian Perambulator Museum

Kirtland

- Holden Arboretum
- Lake Farmpark

Lake Milton

- Lake Milton State Park

Medina

- Ice Festival

Mentor

- Lawnfield - Garfield Home Site

Middlefield

- Middlefield Cheese House
- Pumpkin Maze Playland

Newbury

- Punderson Manor House Resort
- Punderson State Park Resort
- Westwoods Park

Niles

- McKinley Birthplace & Museum

Painesville

- Headlands Beach State Park

Peninsula

- Cuyahoga Valley Scenic Railroad

Portage

- Tinker's Creek State Park

Ravenna

- West Branch State Park

Twinsburg

- Twins Days Festival

Vienna

- Wagon Trails Animal Park

Warren

- Most Magnificent McDonalds
- National Packard Museum

Youngstown

- Butler Institute Of American Art
- Children's Museum Of The Valley
- First Night Youngstown
- Gorant Candies
- Mill Creek Park
- Youngstown Historical Center Of Industry & Labor

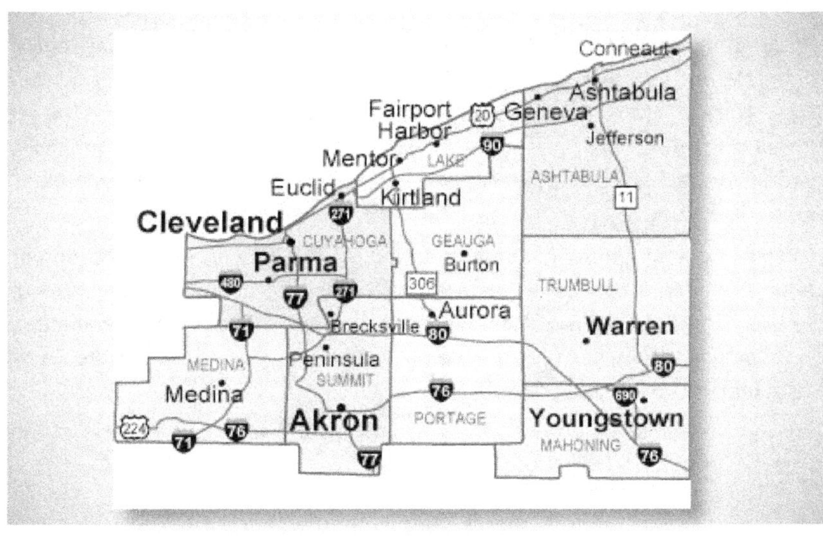

A Quick Tour of our Hand-Picked Favorites Around...

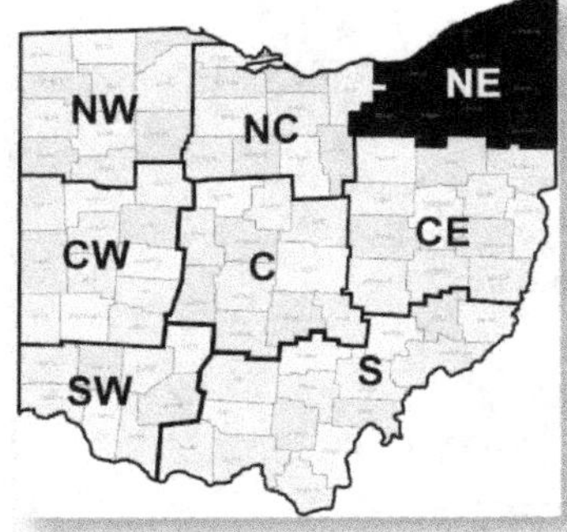

North East Ohio

On your way to visit a major well-known attraction in the Cleveland/Akron area, you might not realize there are some very unique kid-friendly places hidden just around the corner. **Lake Farmpark** (Kirtland, far east side of Cleveland) – not really a farm – it's a park about farming - is a good example. Their focus is to discover where food and natural products come from so on any given day you might be able to milk a cow, card wool, watch honeybees at work or go down below the earth to see where plants get their start!

Many folks know about Marblehead lighthouse but few have visited **Fairport Marine Museum** in Fairport Harbor, near Mentor. The highlight of this museum has to be the real lighthouse (and the inexpensive admission price)! After you proudly climb the 69 steps, catch your breath with a beautiful view of Lake Erie.

Still want more of the outdoors? Two favorite parks of ours are in this region of the state: **Cuyahoga Valley National Park** (south of Cleveland) and **Mill Creek Park** in Youngstown. Some of the best kept, cleanest parks you'll want to visit offer more than just great hikes – they also offer canals, gristmills, gardens or train rides and, best of all, seasonal festivals to engage little ones' sense of wonder.

You'll find some pretty old stuff around this area, too. Meet a mastodon or Dunk, a fearsome 16-foot long armored fish with huge self-sharpening jaws at the **Cleveland Museum of Natural History**. More "old stuff" and characters pretending like they're really from the old days is well-played out at **Hale Farm and Village** in Bath, near Peninsula.

Or, get real close with the fishies in the nation's longest sea tube at the **Greater Cleveland Aquarium**.

Sites and attractions are listed in order by City, Zip Code, and Name. Symbols indicated represent: Restaurants Lodging

STAN HYWET HALL

Akron - ***714 North Portage Path (I-77 or I-71 to State Route 18, follow signs into town) 44303. Phone: (330) 836-5533. www.stanhywet.org. Hours: Tuesday-Sunday 10:00am-6:00pm. Admission closes at 4:30pm (April-New Years). Admission: $15.00 adult, $6.00 child (6-17) - self guided. Add several dollars for a guided tour. Seniors and Military half off admission on Tuesdays. Note: Family Members can also join the Kids Club. Museum Store, Carriage House Café. Nooks and Crannies tour is more of an adventure into secret passages and doors (added cost). Family Friendly Days and Vintage Baseball games select weekends during the summer.***

Want to pretend you're visiting old rich relatives for tea? – this is the place. The long driveway up to the home is beautifully landscaped. You can park right next to the home and carriage house (vs. a block away) and are greeted as an invited guest. The actual family photographs of the Seiberling Family (Frank was the co-founder of the Goodyear Tire and Rubber Company) scattered throughout the home make you feel as if you know them. Being an English Tudor, it is rather dark inside with an almost "castle-like" feeling. Try to count the fireplaces (23) and discover concealed telephones behind the paneled walls. The Corbin Conservatory, a 7,600 square-foot Gothic replication of the original 1915 building, is a complimentary addition to the grounds. Track Butterflies in Flight (seasonally) or explore other garden exhibits.

STAN HYWET'S DECK THE HALL

Akron - The manor House is decorated for the holidays and the grounds and gardens offer a winter wonderland of lights. The Carriage House Museum Store is open with specially selected gift items, and the Café serves hot chocolate, cookies, and other holiday fare. (daily except Mondays late Nov thru Dec)

AKRON ZOO

Akron - ***500 Edgewood Avenue (Perkins Woods Park, I-77 exit 21C, Route 59 east) 44307. Phone: (330) 375-2525. www.akronzoo.com. Hours: Daily 10:00am-5:00pm (May-October). Daily 11:00am-4:00pm (November-April). Closed New Year's Day, Thanksgiving, Christmas Eve and Christmas Day. Admission: $12.00 adult, $10.00 senior, $9.00 child (2-14). Small parking fee. Reduced winter admission. Note: Concessions. You are permitted to bring food into the zoo. There are several picnic areas available. Educators: click on " Animals" link for info and pics about each animal (great start for reports).***

The 50-acre Akron Zoo is an accredited world conservation zoo. Here, you'll come nose-to-nose with more than 700 animals, including endangered Humboldt penguins, snow leopards, jaguars and Komodo dragons. The zoo features Monkey Island, The River Otter Exhibit, and an Ohio Farmyard petting area. Visit the Asian Trail with Tiger Valley, the red pandas, and the barking deer. The exhibit "Wild Prairie" includes prairie dogs and black-footed ferrets. Check out the Jellyfish exhibit and It's a Wild World Show.

SNACK WITH SANTA

Akron – Akron Zoo. Bring the kids and grandkids to the zoo to feed the penguins, decorate cookies, create a holiday craft and have a picture taken with Santa. Admission. (second & third weekend in December)

AKRON RUBBERDUCKS

Akron - *Canal Park, downtown 44308. Phone: (330) 253-5151 or (800) 97-AEROS. www.akronrubberducks.com*

Minor league baseball with ticket prices ranging $5.00-25.00. AA affiliate of the Cleveland Indians. Special events like Little League Nights and fireworks. .

AKRON SYMPHONY ORCHESTRA

Akron - *92 N. Main, 44308. www.akronsymphony.org. Phone: (330) 535-8131.*

Professional orchestra offers pops, classical and educational concerts. Performances at EJ Thomas Hall, Civic Theatre, and Lock 3. Family & Kids series like the Odyssey Series, Picnic Pops in the Park & Youth Symphony.

WEATHERVANE PLAYHOUSE

Akron - *1301 Weathervane Lane 44313. www.weathervaneplayhouse.com. Phone: (330) 836-2626.*

Offers mainstage and children's productions, Young Actors Series, Spring Puppet show (ex. Snow White, Sound of Music).

PORTAGE LAKES STATE PARK

Akron - *5031 Manchester Road (SR 93) 44319. www.stateparks.com/portage_lakes.html. Phone: (330) 644-2220.*

The wetlands of the park attract thousands of geese and waterfowl during spring and fall migration periods. Mallards, wood ducks and Canada geese nest in the wetlands each year. Five miles of hiking trials lead visitors to the woodlands and marshes of the park. Turkeyfoot Lake offers a public swimming beach. 4,963 acres of camping, hiking trails, boating, fishing, swimming and winter sports.

ALL AMERICAN SOAP BOX DERBY

Akron - Derby Downs, 1-77 & State Route 244 East. www.soapboxderby.org. The annual gravity "grand prix" of soap box derby racing is still run the same way since 1934. Youths from over 100 local competitions participate and learn workmanship, completing a project and competing. Parade at 10:00am. Admission. (late July weekend)

PUMPKIN MAZE PLAYLAND

Amherst - Hillcrest Orchard, 50336 Telegraph Road 44001. Pumpkin Patches / Hayrides / Corn Mazes / Fall Playland - Admission (average $6.00). Plan on at least two hours playtime. Open weekends, some weekdays (by appointment) and weeknights. www.hillcrestfunfarm.com. (late September - late October).

PYMATUNING STATE PARK

Andover - *Lake Road (6 miles Southeast of Andover off SR 85) 44003. Phone: (440) 293-6329. www.pymatuning-state-park.org*

In a setting with the mystery of an old swamp forest and the excitement of a water recreation area, Pymatuning State Park invites outdoor lovers of all ages to enjoy one of the finest walleye and muskellunge lakes in the country. Camping, swimming and boating opportunities as well. Two miles of well-marked Hiking trails and an assortment of casual, furnished family cabins.

Ashtabula

COVERED BRIDGE PIZZA

Ashtabula (North Kingsville or Andover) - SR 85 or US 20. (440) 969-1000 or (440) 293-6776. Open daily for lunch and dinner. Casual. Actual covered bridge (late 1800s) was cut in two and rebuilt into pizza parlors! Located in the heart of Ashtabula County (Ohio's populous of covered bridges), historical pictures of the history of the bridge are displayed on the walls of the shop.

ASHTABULA MARITIME MUSEUM

Ashtabula - *1071 Walnut Blvd. (Point Park in Ashtabula Harbor) 44004. (440) 964-6847. www.facebook.com/ashtabulamarinemuseum. Hours: Fri-Sun Noon-5pm (June-August). Weekends only (September). Admission: $3-$5.00 (age 6+).*

Holds treasures of the Great Lakes. It is housed in the former residence of the Lighthouse Keepers and the Coast Guard Chief that was built in 1898.

Contains models, paintings, marine artifacts, photos of early Ashtabula Harbor and ore boats and tugs, miniature hand-made brass tools that actually work, and the world's only working scale model of a Hulett ore unloading machine. Expansive view of the harbor from the hill. Feel like you're captain of the high seas in the actual pilothouse from the steamship.

HUBBARD HOUSE AND UNDERGROUND RAILROAD MUSEUM

Ashtabula - ***1603 Walnut Boulevard (and Lake Avenue near the Ashtabula Harbor) 44004. Phone: (440) 964-8168. www.hubbardhouseugrrmuseum.org. Hours: Friday-Sunday 1:00-5:00pm (Memorial Day weekend-September). Closed on holidays. Admission: $3.00-$5.00 (age 6+).***

> The Hubbard House, known as Mother Hubbard's Cupboard, is the only Ohio Underground Railroad terminus, or endpoint, open to the public.

There are three distinct features of the Hubbard House: the circa 1841 home of William and Catharine Hubbard on the first floor, the Underground Railroad exhibit area on the second floor; and the Civil War and Americana exhibit area in the basement. This is recognized as a northern terminal that was part of the pathway from slavery to freedom in the pre Civil War era. Ashtabula County was instrumental in John Brown's famous attack on the Federal arsenal at Harper's Ferry, Virginia. Of the nineteen men who charged the arsenal with John Brown, Sr., thirteen were from Ashtabula County.

DUCT TAPE FESTIVAL

Avon - Veteran's Memorial Pk, I-90 to Rte. 254 Detroit Rd. The annual Avon Heritage Duct Tape Festival kicks off just in time to celebrate Father's Day. The festival is an all-weekend event. This three-day event celebrates duct tape, its enthusiasts and its wacky and fun uses. The festival also honors the history and heritage of the city that is proclaimed the "Duct Tape Capital" of the world—Avon, Ohio—the home of Duck brand duct tape. From sculptures and fashion to games and a parade, everything at the festival revolves around duct tape. FREE. www.avonducttapefestival.com. (Fathers Day Weekend in June)

Bath

HALE FARM AND VILLAGE

Bath - 2686 Oak Hill Road (I-77 exit 226 or I-271 exit 12 (Rte. 303), follow signs) 44210. Phone: (800) 589-9703 or (330) 666-3711. www.wrhs.org Hours: Wednesday-Sunday 10:00am-5:00pm (Memorial Day - Labor Day). Weekends only (September/October). Special Weekends (November-March). Admission: $10.00 adult, $5.00 child (3-12). Note: Museum Shop (you can purchase crafts made on site) and Cafe. Map and sample questions to ask towns people provided. Summer Family Fun days are old-fashioned fun geared towards kids. Remember, authentic dirt roads throughout the village.

Jonathan Hale moved to the Western Reserve from Connecticut and prospered during the canal era building an elaborate brick home and farm typical of New England. The gate house prepares guests with an orientation movie.

Begin your adventure around the homestead area. Wheatfield Village is a small Ohio town struggling with the impact of the War Between the States. Period tools and machines provide wood- working demonstrations. Other barns serve as shops for a blacksmith, glass-blower, candle or broom-maker and basket maker.

The Hale House (bricks made on site by Hale family and still made today) has pioneer cooking (and sampling!) demonstrations. Across the street, visit with mothers, daughters, sons and fathers (they are first person 1860s) as they share with you thoughts of the day. You will feel like you're part of mid-1800's life as crops are planted and harvested, meetings attended, letters written, textiles spun, barters made, and church and school attended. Kids are asked to help with chores and schoolwork. Maybe you'll even get to "knead" the dough for bricks (with your feet!) or card wool or roll clay marbles. Samples of crafts worked on are given to the kids as souvenirs. We liked the mix of some buildings set in the present, some set in the Civil War era - it's amusing and interesting.

HOLIDAY LANTERN TOURS

Bath – Hale Farm & Village. Take a leisurely guided tour around the Village, circa 1862. Visitors can enter the "homes" around the village green and see what holiday celebrations during the Civil War era were like. Admission. (Friday nights in Dec)

NOAH'S LOST ARK ANIMAL SANCTUARY

Berlin Center - ***8424 Bedell Road (off SR 224) 44401. Phone: (330) 584-7835. www.noahslostark.org. Hours: Tuesday-Sunday 10:00am-5:00pm (May-August). Weekends only until 4:00pm (September-October). Admission: $10.00 adult, $7.00 child (2-17).***

Tour the no-frills Exotic Animal Park. The facility is dedicated to providing a permanent safe haven for unwanted and abused Exotic animals. Hands-on interaction with unusual, uncommon international animals (camels, pot-bellied pigs, antelope). Wagon rides thru farm. The newly constructed large cat compound featuring Tigers, Lions, Ligers, Servals, Leopards, Caracals and Bobcats or the Primate Area are favorites.

CUYAHOGA VALLEY NATIONAL PARK

Brecksville/Peninsula - ***6947 Riverview Road, SE corner of Riverview and Boston Mill roads 44264 (I-271 exit 12, Rte. 303). Phone: 330-657-2752. www.nps.gov/cuva/index.htm or www.dayinthevalley.com. Hours: Visitor Center open Fall, Winter, and Spring: Daily 9:30 a.m. - 5 p.m. Summer: Daily 9 a.m. - 6 p.m. Closed Christmas and New Years Day. Park hours vary by season. Some smaller Visitors Centers scattered throughout the park have more restricted hours in the cooler months (non summer break) and are closed except weekends. Admission: FREE entrance fee. Educators: Online lesson plans - www.generationscvnp.org/education.aspx. NPS Junior Ranger programs. Note: Hale Farm & Cuyahoga Valley Scenic Railroad all within park. See separate listings for details. No overnight camping within park, however some available near the perimeter.***

Learning how a lock works...

Visitors enjoy picnicking, hiking, bike trails, bridle trails, winter sports, golf, fishing, and ranger-guided programs. Some of the park attractions are:

<u>CANAL VISITOR CENTER</u>: 7104 Canal Road, intersection of Canal and Hillside roads Valley View, Ohio 44125. Permanent exhibits illustrate 12,000 years of history in the valley, including the history of the Ohio & Erie Canal. The canal-era building once served canal boat passengers waiting to pass through Lock 38. A 20-minute slide program about the park is shown by request. Hours: 10:00am-4:00pm daily except winter holidays. Just down the street is the Frazee family home, typical of the era (only open summer weekends).

OHIO & ERIE CANAL TOWPATH TRAIL: Once a mode of transportation of goods and people, the canal (dry and overgrown in places) makes for a nice path for over 19 miles of biking, hiking, running or walking. As you enjoy the Towpath Trail each summer, you may chance upon musicians playing banjo, harmonica, and other instruments. HUNT HOUSE, 2054 Bolanz Road, between Riverview and Akron Peninsula Roads, Peninsula, Ohio 44264. Hunt House offers child-friendly nature exhibits, a rest area along the Towpath Trail, and information about nearby attractions.

BRANDYWINE FALLS: A boardwalk trail allows a close view of the roaring water (best after lots of rain).

THE LEDGES OVERLOOK: Hikers can climb to the top of the valley walls to view lots of greenspace.

BOSTON MILL VISITOR CENTER: 1836 general store functions as a museum with exhibits on canal boat construction. Learn the storied history of this rehabilitated 1905 Cleveland-Akron Bag Company general store and the park's wider rehabilitation of the Cuyahoga Valley and its river.

Brunswick

MAPLESIDE FARMS

Brunswick - ***294 Pearl Road, US 42 (on US 42, between Rte. 82 and Rte 303 off I-71 exits) 44212. Phone: (330) 225-5577 store. www.mapleside.com. Tours: Scheduled. Minimum 12 people. $6.00-$12.00 per person. Teachers are FREE. Tuesday-Sunday (Labor Day-October) Note: Gift shop, bakery /ice cream parlor.***

They harvest over 20,000 bushels of apples each year from 5,000 apple trees. Many of the 20 different varieties are kept fresh in controlled atmosphere storage so they can be enjoyed year around (what's the secret?). Fall group tours of the orchards include sample apples (some picked, some from packing room); a tour of apple orchards and production areas with explanation of growing and processing apples; a cup of cider and bakery; a visit to Harvest Hideout playland; and a small pumpkin for each child.

JOHNNY APPLESEED FESTIVAL

Brunswick – Mapleside Farms. This event features craft exhibits, a corn maze, live bands, horse-drawn wagon rides, bag your own, apple butter making, cloggers, apple products and kids activities. Admission. (mid-Sept wkend)

PUMPKIN VILLAGE

Brunswick – Mapleside Farms. Pumpkin patches, hayrides, corn mazes, fall playland. Giant Jumping Pillow. Admission. (late September-late October)

CENTURY VILLAGE MUSEUM & STORE

Burton - *14653 E. Park Street (State Route 87 & SR 700) 44021. Phone: (440) 834-1492. www.centuryvillagemuseum.org. Admission: $8.00 adult, $5.00 child (6-16). Tours: Saturday 11am & 1pm, Sunday at 2:00pm (May-October).*

Tour the magnificent century homes on the Village grounds, hear stories of early settlers, and view a collection of 9,000 toy soldiers. A restored community with 12 buildings (log cabin, church, barns, schoolhouse, marshal's office and train station) containing 19th Century historical antiques and a working farm. Best to attend during Festivals or Pioneer School Camp when the village comes alive with visiting "villagers."

CANFIELD FAIR

Canfield - Canfield Fairgrounds, off Rtes. 46, 11, and 224. www.canfieldfair.com or (330) 533-4107. Grandstand headliners, the World's Largest Demolition Derby, Truck and Tractor Pull, agricultural displays, milk a cow, pet pigs, Elephant Encounter. Admission. (Wednesday - Sunday-Labor Day week)

PIONEER WATERLAND AND DRY PARK

Chardon - *10661 Kile Road (off US 6 or SR 608/US 322) 44024. Phone: (440) 285-0910. www.pioneerwaterland.com. Hours: Daily 10:00am-7:00pm (Memorial Day-Labor Day). Extended weekend hours. Admission: $27.95 and up. Discount tickets online. Dry activities are a few dollars each. Less than 40" tall FREE. Note: Picnic Area, Food Service, and Video Arcade. Parking $5.00.*

Little ones frequent the toddler play area and waterland. Others can explore the water slides, paddleboats, inner tube rides, volleyball nets, Indy raceway, batting cages, miniature golf or driving range. All adjoining a chlorinated crystal clear lake with beaches.

GEAUGA COUNTY MAPLE FESTIVAL

Chardon - Downtown, Chardon Square. I-90 exit to Rte. 44 south. www.maplefestival.com. Sap Run contest, midway, parades, bathtub races and maple syrup production and sales. (long third weekend in April)

Cleveland

CLEVELAND SPORTS

CLEVELAND BROWNS - Browns Stadium, lakefront. (440) 224-3361 tours. www.clevelandbrowns.com. NFL Football, Dawg Pound. Largest scoreboard in NFL Football. Kids Club. Tours by appointment give you facts and figures plus a peek at locker rooms and press boxes. (Sept-December)

CLEVELAND CAVALIERS - Quicken Arena (The Q). (216) 420-2200 or www.nba.com/cavs. Professional Basketball. (September – April).

CLEVELAND INDIANS - Progressive Field. www.indians.com. (866) 48-TRIBE. Kids Club. $10-$27 tickets. (April – Oct). Tours (fee of $10) include Kidsland, a press box, a suite, a dugout, a fun video, lasts one hour (Mon-Sat 10am-2pm, some summer Sundays).

CLEVELAND BOTANICAL GARDEN

Cleveland - ***11030 East Blvd. (University Circle, I-90 to MLK exit) 44106. Phone: (216) 721-1600. www.cbgarden.org. Hours: Tuesday-Saturday 10:00am-5:00pm and Sunday Noon-5:00pm. (Hershey Children's Garden closes all winter) Admission: $15.00 adult, $10.00 child (3-12).***

Display gardens changing each season (best April-October for color). Most like the Knot Garden and the newer areas: the spiny desert of Madagascar and the cloud forest of Costa Rica. With its wheelchair-accessible tree house, dwarf forests, scrounger garden, worm bins and watery bog, Hershey Children's Garden is an exciting destination for families. Lots of adventure paths to explore and splash in water spouts. Flowers in a bathtub - oh my!

CLEVELAND MUSEUM OF ART

Cleveland - ***11150 East Boulevard (University Circle, near the Botanical Gardens) 44106. Phone: (216) 421-7340 or (888) 262-0033. www.clevelandart.org. Hours: Tuesday, Thursday, Saturday & Sunday 10:00am-5:00pm. Wednesday & Friday 10:00am-9:00pm. Check website for updates on hours. Admission: FREE general admission. Note: Café open daytime. Families Learning Together creation days each month. Educators: Online interactive In the Attic visual tour & learning site.***

See the large collection of objects from all cultures and periods including European and American paintings, medieval, Asian, Islamic, pre-Columbian, African masks, Egyptian mummies and Oceanic art. The kids really like the Armor Court (knights in shining armor).

CLEVELAND MUSEUM OF NATURAL HISTORY

Cleveland - ***1 Wade Oval Drive (University Circle, I-90 and Martin Luther King Dr. exit) 44106. Phone: (216) 231-4600 or (800) 317-9155. www.cmnh.org. Hours: Monday-Saturday 10:00am-5:00pm, Sunday Noon-5:00pm. Also, Wednesdays open until 10:00pm (September-May only). Closed holidays. Admission: $17.00 adult, $14.00 youth (3-18) and senior (60+). Note: Gift shop. Modern Planetarium and interactive pre-show activities (extra fee) plus Observatory open Wednesday evenings. Live animal shows daily. Café lunch. Parking fee. Educators: thematic teaching kits and updated teacher guides online.***

Meet "Happy" the 70 foot long dinosaur, "Jane" the teenage dino, or "Lucy" the oldest human fossil. Look for real dino eggs and touch real dino bones! Highlights of Ohio Natural History are: Johnstown Mastodon -- A long-ago Ohio resident and Dunk - this fearsome 16-foot-long armored fish with huge self-sharpening jaws is a native Clevelander found in the shale of the Rocky River Valley (look low, then look high - oh my!). The Ringler dugout is the oldest well-dated watercraft ever found in North America (found in 1976 in Ashland, OH). Also look for the Glacier that Covered Cleveland; the Diorama of Moundbuilders - shown in layers depicting what might be found; or the Wildlife Center & Woods (outside, partially enclosed) where natural habitats are home to raptors, songbirds, turkey, river otters, fox and many other species found in the state. The lower level of the museum has Ohio Botany, Ohio Birds & Insects and Ohio Ecology. In the Discovery Center, kids can use microscopes or view live insects and reptiles. Lots of touch and feel toys and games. Or, experience an earthquake in Ohio - are we ready? Kids visiting here are first amazed at the large scale of the prehistoric skeletons and also love that many prehistoric artifacts came from Ohio. As you might have guessed, you need several hours or many visits to explore every corner of this place!

Meet the famous "Dunk"

CHILDREN'S MUSEUM OF CLEVELAND

Cleveland - ***3813 Euclid Ave. (in Cleveland's MidTown neighborhood) 44106. Phone: (216) 791-7114 www.facebook.com/CMCCleveland/ Hours: Thursday: CLOSED. Mon, Tues, Wed & Fri: 9 am – 4 pm. Saturday: 10 am – 5 pm. Sunday: 12 – 5 pm. Admission: $12.00 (age 1+)***

The museum's permanent exhibits include:

Adventure City: From a market to a two-story climber to construction site, the largest exhibit space invites children to build, work, climb, and explore this bustling city. The multi-level environment, comprised of cozy corners and tall overlooks, encourages pretend play.

Wonder Lab: Enter a world of water and wonder in this industrial science laboratory. Children explore whirlpools, jets, rivers, and more in two fun-filled water tables as other friends build ball tracks on the magnetic wall, make scarves fly through the air, and create cascades of bubbles.

Making Miniatures: Nestled in a series of colorful rooms at the very top of the museum, children discover fascinating dollhouses featuring the Lincoln Collection and including a replica of CMC's new home, the Stager-Beckwith mansion. Children learn how miniaturists make pint-sized objects, design tiny rooms, and build small houses. As they explore this exhibit, children can search for a hidden logo, and, through hands-on play, create their own miniature world.

Arts & Parts: In this sun-filled art studio, children design, construct, and experiment to create unique objects to take home or add to a communal project. Activities include explosions of color and investigations of art techniques as children unleash their inner artists.

CLEVELAND ORCHESTRA

Cleveland - ***11001 Euclid Avenue 44106. Phone: (216) 231-1111 www.clevelandorchestra.com.***

Concerts in beautiful Severance Hall (September-May), outdoors at Blossom Music Center (Summer). The COYO (Cleveland Orchestra Youth Orchestra) performs concerts also. Family Concerts are specially designed for children 6 and older. These narrated concerts are structured around a theme and include collaborative artist such as young musicians, singers, dancers and actors.

CLEVELAND PLAYHOUSE

Cleveland - ***8500 Euclid Avenue 44106. www.clevelandplayhouse.com. Phone: (216) 795-7000.***

America's longest running regional theatre presents contemporary and classical children's series plays during the school year. Classics include A Christmas Story or popular fairy tale themes.

FEDERAL RESERVE BANK LEARNING CENTER AND MONEY MUSEUM

Cleveland - ***1455 East 6th Street (corner of Superior Ave. and East 6th St, downtown) 44108. www.clevelandfed.org. Phone: (216) 579-3188. Hours: Monday-Thursday 9:30am-2:30pm, closed holidays. Admission: FREE. Educators: Education, Curricula, Classroom Activities Money games: www.clevelandfed.org/Learning_Center/For_Teachers/ . FREEBIES: Kids Guide to Money - www.clevelandfed.org/Learning_Center/Online_Activities/great_minds_think/index.cfm***

Does money grow on trees? Was paper money always used? The Museum and Learning Center includes exhibits of ancient currency such as tiny cowrie shells from Indian Ocean Islands and giant stones from the Pacific Island of Yap. Check out the 23 ft. Money Tree featuring replicas of U.S. currency. Want to see what your face looks like on a dollar? Older kids may even learn a little about economics and money management.

WESTERN RESERVE HISTORY MUSEUM

Cleveland - ***10825 East Boulevard, University Circle (I-90 to MLK exit 177) 44106. Phone: (216) 721-5722. www.wrhs.org. Hours: Tuesday-Sunday 10:00am-5:00pm. Admission: $12 adult, $10 senior, $6 child (3-12). Includes Mansion, History, Costume Wing and Crawford Museum. Check website for seasonal special offers. Note: We strongly suggest hands-on programs and guided tours for families. FREEBIES: activities, paper dolls, stories - www.wrhs.org/explore/for-kids/.***

Cleveland's oldest cultural institution boasts a tour of a grand mansion recreating the Western Reserve from pre-Revolution War to the 20th Century. The look (but mostly don't touch) displays include: farming tools, clothing and costumes and over 200 classic automobiles (Cleveland built cars, oldest car, and heaviest car) and airplanes (Crawford Auto-Aviation Museum). Look for an original Morgan Traffic Signal (native Clevelander) or LeBron James Cavalier championship items.

KIDZIBITS: In Backyard of History, children dress in historic clothes, do a little shopping at a recreated West Side market, or build Cleveland's skyline. They also create a family tree, give puppet shows and play with old-fashioned toys. In the Crawford Kidzibits, test out the hottest selling foot-powered car in America the Little Tikes Cozy Coupe. Time and Place Space delves into activities to discover how our clothes, cooking, travel and more have changed over time. Kids can cook over a fire, hearth, range, and microwave oven. They can explore traveling via horse, carriage, car, and plane. Activities encourage intergenerational conversations about the past and how it shapes the future.

MARTIN LUTHER KING PROGRAM

Cleveland – Western Reserve History Museum. (216) 231-1111. In observance of the Martin Luther King Jr. Day holiday, many museums and attractions in University Circle offer free or discounted admission on that day...plus, Orchestra Concert. (Martin Luther King Day-January)

UNIVERSITY CIRCLEFEST

Cleveland - University Circle area. (216) 791-3900. FREE admission to University Circle museums plus holiday carolers and Santa. FREE. (first Sunday in Dec)

CLEVELAND LAKEFRONT STATE PARK

Cleveland - *8701 Lakeshore Blvd., NE (off I-90, downtown) 44108. Phone: (216) 881-8141. www.clevelandmetroparks.com/main/aquatics1/edgewater-Beach-2.aspx*

Cleveland Lakefront State Park provides natural relief to the metropolitan skyline. Sand beaches, tree-lined picnic areas and panoramic views of the lake are found within the park along the Lake Erie shoreline. The annual Erie fish catch nearly equals the combined catches of all the other great lakes. Dominant species are perch, smallmouth and white bass, channel catfish, walleye and freshwater drum. Facilities include: Edgewater Park - This park is divided into upper and lower areas connected by a paved bicycle path and fitness course; East 55th Marina; Gordon Park; Euclid Beach - 650-foot swimming beach with shaded picnic areas and a scenic observation pier; Villa Angela; and Wildwood. 450 acres of boating and rentals, fishing, swimming, and winter sports.

FESTIVAL OF FREEDOM

Cleveland – Lakefront State Park, Edgewater Park. July 4th celebration including downtown parades, rides, entertainment and fireworks. Edgewater park.

A CHRISTMAS STORY HOUSE

Cleveland - *3159 W 11th Street (I-71 exit W. 14th St., around traffic circle and turn right onto Rowley Ave.) 44109. www.achristmasstoryhouse.com. Phone: (216) 298-4919. Hours: Daily 10:00am-5:00pm. Closed all major holidays. Admission: $10.00-$13.00. Admission (age 3+). Tours run every half hour starting at 10:15 (12:15 on Sundays). The last tour is at 4:30pm.*

Purchased by a longtime fan, this is the very home where the movie was filmed. The house was returned to its Hollywood appearance and opened in celebration of the 1983 film.

Across the street is a museum dedicated to the movie, with behind-the-scenes photos, items donated by actors and original props. Among the props and costumes are the toys from the Higbee's window, Randy's snowsuit and zeppelin, the chalkboard from Miss Shields' classroom and the family car.

CLEVELAND METROPARKS ZOO & RAINFOREST

Cleveland - *3900 Wildlife Way (I-71 exit Fulton Road or East 25th Street) 44109. Phone: (216) 661-6500. www.clevelandmetroparks.com/zoo Hours: Daily 10:00am-5:00pm. Closed only Christmas and New Year's Day. Admission: $16.95 adult (12+), $14.95 senior (62+) $12.95 child (2-11). Free Parking. Look online for Great Deals coupons and discounts. Note: Outback railroad train ride, camel rides and adventure rides are $3.00 extra. Concessions and cafes. Zoo trams run daily for FREE. Coolers and picnic baskets are allowed on Zoo grounds.*

Discover animals from every corner of the world. A rainforest with animal and plant settings like the jungles of Africa, Asia, and South America is the most popular exhibit to explore. The rainforest boasts a storm every 12 minutes, a 25-foot waterfall, and a walk-through aviary. Wolf Wilderness is a popular educational study exhibit where you can view thru a giant window the wolves acting "naturally" in the day and night. Wolf Wilderness is part of Northern Trek, where everyone can learn about the Zoo's winter-loving animals including reindeer, Siberian tigers, polar bears and wolves. The Australian Adventure has a kookaburra station, wallaby walkabout and koala junction (55 ft. treehouse and play area with petting yard). African Elephant Crossing has a webcam so you can watch any day/any time. The Center for Zoological Medicine allows zoo guests to view veterinary care through three observation windows. Cameras in the operating rooms allow procedures to be seen up close, and the vets don't shy away from letting people view every stage in an animal's life. New animals are born here often so check their website for who's new!

DECEMBER DAYS & BRUNCH WITH SANTA

Cleveland – Cleveland Metroparks Zoo. December Days offers seasonal activities to enjoy including animal programs, seasonal music, eco-friendly crafts, holiday cookie decorating and more. And, Santa Claus will greet visitors daily through December 24. Stroll Zoo grounds on foot or ride aboard a complimentary heated shuttle, the Sleighbell Express, past monkeys. Hop off for a stop in the seasonal

greenhouse or Pachyderm Building. Take an invigorating walk through Northern Trek to see many of the Zoo's winter-loving animals including reindeer, bears, tigers and wolves. Admission. (December long weekends 11:00am-3:00pm, and school winter break).

GREATER CLEVELAND AQUARIUM

Cleveland - *2000 Sycamore Street (Station: Powerhouse @ Nautica, west bank of Flats) 44113. Phone: (216) 862-8803. www.greaterclevelandaquarium.com. Hours: Daily 10am-5pm. Closed Christmas and Thanksgiving Day. Admission: $19.95 adult, $17.95 senior (60+), $13.95 child (2-12). Military discounts.*

Visitors can wave to the smiling Rays as they glide overhead at the Aquarium's SeaTube, a 145' walk-through tunnel considered to be the nation's longest sea tube. Walk under a shark or high five a scuba diver. Touch a skink and be tickled by a cleaner shrimp. Not only does the facility feature diffferent habitats, such as a Louisiana Bayou, but it also features the creatures found in local rivers and streams.

LOLLY THE TROLLEY TOURS

Cleveland - *1101 Winslow Avenue (at the Cleveland Aquarium) 44113. Phone: (216) 771-4484 or (800) 848-0173. www.lollytrolley.com. Hours: Early morning or afternoon departures. More available on weekends (even early evening). Weekends only in winter. Admission: $10-$15 (1 hr.) or $15-$25 (2.5 hr.). Tours: 1 or 2 hours, Reservations Required. 1 hour tour is suggested for preschoolers. Note: Lots of specialty tours or Holiday Tours.*

"Lolly the Trolley", an old fashioned bright red trolley, clangs its bell as you take in over 100 sights around the downtown area. The tour includes Cleveland's North Coast Harbor featuring the world's only Rock & Roll Hall of Fame and Museum and the Great Lakes Science Center; Downtown Cleveland; The Warehouse District, The Flats, a river port by day and a bustling entertainment center by night; Ohio City, with many Victorian homes and the county's oldest church; and the West Side Market, one of the world's largest indoor/outdoor food and produce markets; Playhouse Square and University Circle, a focal point for cultural educational and medical institutions. Your tour concludes with a brief stop at the Cleveland Gardens and a drive along the Lake Erie shoreline back to the station. A great way to show off the city to visitors or get an overview of sites to decide which you want to visit.

CORNER ALLEY & FOURTH STREET GRILL

Cleveland - ***402 Euclid Avenue, Cleveland 44114. Phone: (216) 298-4070. www.thecorneralley.com. Lunch, dinner and late night.***

A fun dining experience for the whole family, this grill restaurant is located at a downtown bowling alley. Enjoy contemporary American cuisine with a kid's menu to boot (~$6 each w/drink for the kids12 and under). Now, rent some bowling shoes ($3) and play a family game of bowling ($4.25) before you head back out. (extra per lane rental fee on wkend nights after 4pm).

GOOD TIME III

Cleveland - ***825 East 9th Street Pier (Behind Rock & Roll Hall of Fame) 44114. Phone: (216) 861-5110. www.goodtimeiii.com. Admission: $20.00 adult, $17.00 senior, $10.00 child (age 5-12). Add $15 extra for lunch. Tours: Tuesday-Saturday, Noon and 3:00pm, Sunday times vary (mid-June to Labor Day). Weekends (Friday-Sunday) only in May and September. Note: Food Service Available. Lower deck is air-conditioned and heated. Parking on the pier. They sail rain or shine.***

The quadruple-deck, 1000 passenger boat takes a two hour excursion of city sights along the Cuyahoga River and Lake Erie. The word Cuyahoga is Indian for "crooked". You'll see tugboats and the largest yellow crane boats in the country. See all the industry in the Flats including concrete, pipe, transportation, limestone, and coke businesses. Collision Bend used to be so narrow that many boats got tangled up. Since then, they have dredged the curve and it's now very wide.

GREAT LAKES SCIENCE CENTER

Cleveland - ***601 Erieside Avenue (E 9th Street and I-90, North Coast Harbor, Downtown) 44114. Phone: (216) 694-2000. https://greatscience.com/ Hours: Tuesday-Saturday 10:00am-5:00pm, Sunday Noon-5pm. Only closed Thanksgiving and Christmas. Open summer Mondays. Admission: $13.95-$16.95. Omnimax additional $9-$11.00. Discount combo tickets. Note: Gift Shop OmniMax Theater – 6 story domed screen image and sound. Bytes sandwich restaurant on location. Polymer Funhouse is a ball pit and playplace just for those 7 and under. Educators: Printer Projects are found under the icon "Think!" online.***

Located on the shores of Lake Erie is one of America's largest interactive science museums. You can't miss the iconic wind turbine and solar panel canopy at the entrance. Over 400 interactive exhibits – especially fun on the second floor. Pilot a blimp, test your batting skills, or bounce off the walls in the Polymer Funhouse.

The science playground museum focuses on the Great Lakes region and its environment (Sick Earth, Cloud Maker, Nitrogen Fixation). Young lab scientists (guests) can create a tornado or create light. Here, visitors can touch an indoor tornado, watch the power of lightning and learn about the environment all within several feet of each other. BioMedTech Gallery, Virtual Sports, Electric Shows & one of the largest video walls east of the Rockies.

The **NASA Glenn Visitor Center** interactive exhibit space called the Aero Adventures houses displays on a space shuttle, satellites, zero gravity chamber, wind tunnels, and space environmental tanks. The Apollo Command Module (used on Skylab 3) is the most popular area. Look for the moon rock, major league baseball, and space suit used by astronauts (audio explanation) The Launch Control Center allows you to conduct a countdown sequence towards a simulated launch of a rocket. After following the steps, actual footage is played from one of the experiments conducted in space. Other areas allow kids to operate a wind tunnel or a DropTower - Boom!

NAUTICA QUEEN

Cleveland - ***1153 Main Avenue (West Bank Flats) 44114. Phone: (216) 696-8888 or (800) 837-0604. www.nauticaqueen.com. Hours: Monday – Thursday Noon, 7:00pm; Friday Noon, 7:30pm; Saturday 11:00am, 7:30pm; Sunday 1:00pm (April-December). Reservation Required. Admission: $16.95-$23.95 child (Adult prices add $10-$15).***

Experience the excitement of the Nautica Queen, Cleveland's luxury cruise dining ship, offering a unique adventure in lakefront and river cruise dining for people of all ages. 3 Hour Dinner Cruise or 2 hour Lunch/Brunch Cruise. Many cruises include entertainment with special themes like pirates or shipwrecks.

ROCK AND ROLL HALL OF FAME MUSEUM

Cleveland - ***One Key Plaza, 1100 Rock and Roll Blvd. (9th Street exit north, downtown waterfront) 44114. www.rockhall.com. Phone: (216) 781-ROCK or (800) 493-ROLL. Hours: Daily 10:00am - 5:30pm (open until 9:00pm on Wednesdays & summer Saturdays). Closed Thanksgiving and Christmas. Admission: $28 adult, $18 youth (6-12). Note: Cafe & Store.***

Visit Cleveland's own Rock and Roll Hall of Fame, the world's largest single collection of rock and roll memorabilia. Each level has interactive listening exhibits. As parents reminisce, kids will probably giggle at most of the many exhibits including: Cinema (documentary films), Induction Videos, Radio Station and the Hall of Fame. The Beatles and Michael Jackson exhibits are classic favs for the family.

The Garage is a new hands-on exhibit featuring 12 instrument stations with instruction and a jam session room. Even create your own band logos. Please check in with Visitor's Services before you explore here - they'll let you know which areas have PG and above ratings - you'll know which areas to overlook.

STEAMSHIP WILLIAM G. MATHER MUSEUM

Cleveland - ***Docked at 601 Old Erieside Avenue (Dock 32 at Northcoast Harbor Park, just behind Science Center) 44114. www.glsc.org/mather_museum.php Phone: (216) 574-6262. Hours: Tuesday-Saturday 11:00am-5:00pm, Sunday Noon-5:00pm (summer). Weekends Only (Friday-Sunday - May, September, October). Admission: $8.95 adult, $5.95 youth (3-12). Combo discounts w/ Science Center. Note: Best for preschoolers and older because of dangerous spots while walking. Films play continuously.***

The floating Mather is an iron freighter once used to carry ore, coal and grain along the Great Lakes. Little eyes will open wide in the 4 story engine room and they will have fun pretending to be the crew in the cozy sleeping quarters or the elegant dining room.

Group tours are treated to programmed learning fun in the Interactive Cargo Hold area. Make a sailor hat or a boat made from silly putty (why does a boat float?). Learn to tie sailors' knots with real rope or pretend you're at sea as you move the ship's wheel. In the pilothouse area, kids use navigation charts, working radar, and a marine radio to plan a trip.

U.S.S. COD

Cleveland - ***1201 N Marginal Road (next to Burke Lakefront) 44114. Phone: (216) 566-8770. www.usscod.org. Hours: Daily 10:00am-5:00pm (May-September). Admission: $12.00 adult, $10.00 senior (62+), $7.00 youth (5-16). FREE for military in uniform. Note: Recommend airport parking lot. NOTE: Because the COD has not been altered from her wartime configuration, visitors must enter and***

exit through the original hatchways and climb up and down ladders. Caution by persons with small children, the elderly and the handicapped.

We started our visit at the Aristotle periscope on shore that gives you a view of Lake Erie and puts you in the mood to explore the WW II submarine that sank enemy shipping boats. The ninety-man crew lived in cramped quarters. The eight separate compartments, tight quarters, ladders to climb and plenty of knobs to play with give an authentic feeling of submarine life. The best part of this tour is the fact that the sub was actually used in wartime and still remains pretty much the same...very authentic presentation.

SWEETIE CANDY COMPANY

Cleveland - *6770 Brookpark Road (I-480 exit Ridge Road south. West on Brookpark Rd just a few blocks). 44129. (216) 739-2244 or www.sweetiescandy.com.*

Candy for breakfast? Probably not, but maybe Moon PIes? From wax lips to the world's largest PEZ dispenser collection, this amazing candy superstore has every delight for every sweet tooth.

CLEVELAND AIRPORT MARRIOTT

Cleveland - 4277 W 150th Street. 44135 (offI-71, just a few miles north of airport exits). (216) 252-5333 or www.marriott.com/cleap. Each room features artwork from local Cleveland artists, indoor pool, shuttle service to airport, restaurant on premises. Best part: the rooms are very plush yet comfy. ____________

MEMPHIS KIDDIE PARK

Cleveland - *10340 Memphis Avenue (I-71 to West 117th/Memphis Avenue Exit) 44144. Phone: (216) 941-5995. www.memphiskiddiepark.com. Hours and Admission: 10:00am-8:00pm, seasonal. Pay per ride (~$2.50 each). %5.50 for mini golf. Discounts for books of tickets. FREE parking and no entrance fee. RIDERS MUST BE UNDER 50 INCHES TALL FOR MOST RIDES.*

With many of the original rides still in place, Memphis Kiddie Park is truly a landmark of the Cleveland area which has thrilled generations of children. Memphis Kiddie Park consists of eleven miniature amusement rides, a concession stand, an arcade, and an eighteen hole miniature golf course. The park is mainly for youngsters anywhere from about a year old on up to around eight. Little tots rides like a ferris wheel, roller coaster and carousel.

CLEVELAND NATIONAL AIR SHOW

Cleveland - Burke Lakefront Airport, downtown. www.clevelandairshow.com. (216) 781-7747. Military jet demonstrations and civilian aerobatics performers. Thunderbirds and Blue Angels Flybys. Admission. (Labor Day weekend). INTERNATIONAL WOMEN'S AIR & SPACE MUSEUM on premises (the museum is open during normal airport hours year-round). Discover the achievements of women in aviation and space through exhibits that include an aerobatic plane, a flight simulator and a hands-on mission control console. In "Living & Working in Space" get into a vertical sleeping bag, and work with space gloves. Learn about women pilots who underwent secret astronaut testing.

I-X CENTER INDOOR AMUSEMENT PARK

Cleveland (Brookpark) - One I-X Center Drive, next to airport 44135. (216) 265-2586 or www.ixamusementpark.com. Hours vary daily. Admission: $23-$26.00. Food service. After riding the World's Tallest Indoor Ferris Wheel (10 stories high) you can SCREAM through 150 rides! Also features a video arcade, miniature golf, laser karaoke, Kidzville, and live entertainment. (month-long starting later March thru mid-April)

IRISH CULTURAL FESTIVAL

Cleveland (Berea) - Cuyahoga County Fairgrounds, 164 Eastland Blvd. Irish culture at its best with dancing, music, arts & crafts, storytelling and workshops. Admission. www.clevelandirish.org. (third weekend in July)

CLEVELAND CHRISTMAS CONNECTION

Cleveland (Brookpark) - IX Center, near Hopkins Airport. (216) 676-6000. Gifts, arts and crafts, regional entertainment, Santa, train rides, giant indoor ferris wheel rides, nice free gift craft area for kids, variety of ethnic food. www.ixchristmasconnections.com. Admission. (long weekend before Thanksgiving)

MOSQUITO LAKE STATE PARK

Cortland - *1439 SR 305 (10 miles North of Warren off State Route 305) 44410. Phone: (330) 637-2856. http://parks.ohiodnr.gov/mosquitolake*

Several hiking trails allow visitors to explore the woodlands and scenic shoreline of the park. Ten miles of bridle trails give horsemen access to the park's interior. Snowmobilers have access to 14 miles of shoreline and 15 miles of wooded trails. Mountain biking is permitted on 5 miles of multiple-use trails. 11,811 acres of camping, boating and rentals, fishing, swimming at sandy beach and winter sports. Near the lake, look for the 12 bald eagles that reside in the area.

FAIRPORT HARBOR MARINE MUSEUM

Fairport Harbor - *129 Second Street (I-90 to SR 44 north to SR 2) 44077. Phone: (440) 354-4825. http://fairportharborlighthouse.org Hours: Wednesday, Saturday, Sunday and Holidays. 1:00 – 6:00pm (Memorial Weekend – third wkend in September). Admission: $5.00 adult, $4.00 senior and $3.00 child (6-12).*

Pretend you're on a sea voyage as you explore an old pilothouse with navigation instruments, maps and charts and a large ship's wheel. Find out what number of whistles you use to indicate the ship's direction. This room is large enough to really romp around. The highlight of this museum has to be the real lighthouse (although it's a steep climb up and out to the deck). After you proudly climb the 69 steps, catch your breath with a beautiful view of Lake Erie. Our favorite lighthouse & museum combo!

Geneva

GENEVA STATE PARK

Geneva - *4499 Padanarum Road (Shore of Lake Erie, I-90 to Geneva Exit 218) 44041. Phone: (440) 466-8400 or (800) 801-9982 lodge. http://parks.ohiodnr.gov/geneva. Note: ERIEVIEW PARK - www.erieviewpark.com. Located on the "strip" with arcade, kiddie rides and water slides. Food service and picnic areas. Ride or day pass admissions (~$2.50 per ride). No fee to wander park area.*

Located on Ohio's northeastern shoreline, Geneva State Park reflects the charisma of Lake Erie. Vacationers enjoy fishing and boating, swimmers love the beautiful sand beach, while nature enthusiasts retreat to the park's freshwater marshes and estuaries. Three miles of multi-use trails traverse the park. They are used by hikers and cross-country skiers. 698 acres of camping, boating and jet ski rentals, and large cottages for rentals.

The **LODGE & CONFERENCE CENTER** at Geneva State Park (www.thelodgeatgeneva.com) is an upscale resort with a spectacular view of Lake Erie. The resort includes 109 guest rooms, a restaurant, indoor pool, outdoor pool, fitness center, game room and gift shop. Bicycle rentals are available for guests who would like to experience the NorthCoast from atop a bike. In addition, direct access to Lake Erie is available at the beach and marina located in the State Park.

GREAT LAKES MEDIEVAL FAIRE

Geneva - 3033 State Route 534. www.medievalfaire.com. The Great Lakes Medieval Faire is a shaded, 13th century family fun theme park filled with fine continuous entertainment, crafts & artisans, jugglers, jesters, musicians, rides & interactive games, and foods fit for a King. Step back in time to an age of romance and chivalry, where brave knights battle on the jousting field for the favor of the Queen, fair damsels, and the roaring crowd. Join King Arthur, Queen Guinevere, and the Knights of the Round Table as they visit the village of Avaloch for a day of Celebration and Festivities! Admission. (weekends July to mid-August)

OUR LITTLE WORLD ALPACA FARM

Grafton - ***16800 Cowley Road, Grafton, OH 44044. Phone: 440- 724-7070. http://www.ourlittleworldalpacas.com/***

Quality Huacaya Alpacas and Fiber Products.They open the farm several times a year to the public and do private tours for families and small groups who want to come see these wonderful animals. You are welcome to take a walk around our farm, enjoy the calm quiet gentleness of the alpacas and while you are here, shop from a selection of products made from alpaca fiber and our own brand of alpaca yarn.

BUZZARD DAY

Hinckley - Cleveland Metroparks Reservation. (440) 351-6300. www.hinckleyohchamber.com Annual migration of the buzzard with breakfast watch. Cleveland Metroparks naturalists on-hand to talk about the history of the birds and why they return to this same spot year after year. Activities include: Naturalist-led Hikes (including an "Early Bird" hike; Shuttle Hikes (to Top'O Ledges and Worden's Ledges); An Official Buzzard Scoreboard; EarthWords Nature Shop; Live Musical Entertainment; Buzzard Bingo; Children's Craft; Storytelling; Live Animal Programs; Historical Bus Tours of Hinckley; and an Exhibit Area. FREE. (mid-March Sunday)

JEFFERSON DEPOT

Jefferson - ***147 E. Jefferson Street (SR 46 and downtown) 44047. Phone: (440) 293-5532. www.jeffersondepotvillage.org. Admission: $7.00 donation accepted. Tours: Guided Tours every Saturday & Sunday, 1:00-4:00pm during June, July, August and September. Open Mondays & Thursdays from 10am-4pm. School tours are early fall and late spring with hands-on activities and themes.***

Travel back in time to the 1800's. Costumed kinfolk will let you peek back into the past! See the ornate 1872 LS&Ms Railroad Station on the National Register, the quaint 1848 "Church in the Wildwood," 1849 Church barn, 1918 Caboose, 1838 Spafford One-Room School House, Hohn's General Store, Early Pharmacy and 1888 House. The Blacksmith shop and Post Office are newer buildings on the property.

ASHTABULA COUNTY COVERED BRIDGE FESTIVAL

Jefferson - Ashtabula County Fairgrounds, 25 West Jefferson Street. (440) 576-3769 or www.coveredbridgefestival.org. Ashtabula is known as the working covered bridge capital of the Western Reserve. Enjoy a tour of 16 covered bridges during the beautiful fall season, plus entertainment, crafts, and draft horse contests. Admission. (second weekend in October)

HOLDEN ARBORETUM

Kirtland - *9500 Sperry Road 44094. Phone: (440) 946-4400. www.holdenarb.org. Hours: Daily 9:00am-5:00pm. Closed Christmas and Thanksgiving. Admission: $10.00 adult, $4.00 child (6-18). Canopy Walk extra $2-$4.00 Dogs are welcome!*

Tour the many trails, which offer a variety of lengths and difficulty, from easy to rugged. 3000 acres of gardens and walking trails (focus on woody plants). Holden Butterfly Garden is directly behind the Visitor Center. This fabulous garden is over two acres and home to two ponds, a waterfall and a profusion of plantings geared to attract caterpillars, butterflies and hummingbirds. Guided or self-guided hikes. $2.00 Tram Tour.

Canopy Walk at Holden Arboretum features a 500 ft. long elevated walkway suspended 65 ft. above the forest floor. It gives visitors a truly unique perspective of the forest and the animals that live among the trees. And as an added bonus, there's an observation tower on site that takes you up even further up—so much further that you end up above the trees.

LAKE FARMPARK

Kirtland - *8800 Chardon Road (I-90 to SR 306 south to SR 6 east) 44094. Phone: (800) 366-FARM. www.lakemetroparks.com/parks/farmpark. Hours: Tuesday-Sunday 9:00am-5:00pm. Closed major winter holidays. Admission: $8.00 adult, $7.00 senior (60+), $6.00 child (2-11) Note: Gift Shop. Restaurant. Comfortable walking or tennis shoes are best to wear on the farm. Wagon rides throughout the park are included. Wagon rentals are available. Barnyard - ostriches, poultry, sheep petting. Pony rides are $2.00. Seasonal events are fantastic!*

Not really a farm - it's a park about farming (and the cleanest farm you'll ever visit!). Most of their focus is to discover where food and natural products come from. In the Dairy Parlor, you can milk a real cow and make ice cream from the cow's milk. Wander over to the Arena and watch the sheep show or a horse show. What products can be made with the help of sheep? Use special brushes to clean their wool and then spin some by hand. Some of the cutest exhibits are the babies...look for them all around the Arena. Exhibits are ready to be played with all day in the Great Tomato Works.

A giant tomato plant (6 feet wide with 12-ft. leaves) greets you and once inside the greenhouse, you can go down below the earth in the dirt to see where plants get their start. Sneak up on a real honeybee comb, but mind the words on the sign, "DO NOT DISTURB - HONEYBEES AT WORK". This visit generates lots of questions about the food you eat. Great learning!

MAPLE SUGARING WEEKEND

__Kirtland__ – Lake Farmpark. Syrup making demos. Pancake dinners/breakfasts. Sugarbush tours by foot or by wagon or by train. (second weekend in March)

VILLAGE PEDDLER & PUMPKIN HARVEST WEEKENDS

__Kirtland__ – Lake Farmpark. Pumpkin patches, hayrides, corn mazes, fall playlands, festive foods and crops. Admission. (select long weekends in October)

COUNTRY LIGHTS

__Kirtland__ – Lake Farmpark. Horse-drawn sleighbell rides through the light show; live entertainment; baby calves, chicks and pigs; miniature railroad displays; delightful holiday horse shows; and, best of all, the life-like Toy Workshop where elves help kids make an old-fashioned wooden toy to take home. Holiday food served at the Visitor's Center, too. By reservation only! Extra Admission (select days in December)

LAKE MILTON STATE PARK

Lake Milton - *16801 Mahoning Avenue (1 mile South of I-76 off State Route 534) 44429. Phone: (330) 654-4989. http://parks.ohiodnr.gov/lakemilton*

Lake Milton's reservoir offers the best in water-related recreation. Boating, swimming and fishing are popular. A 600-foot beach has restrooms, change booths, showers, playground, basketball court and sand volleyball court. The scenic shoreline provides a habitat for waterfowls and shorebirds. 2,856 acres of boating (unlimited horsepower), fishing, swimming and winter sports.

ICE FESTIVAL

Medina - Downtown. Uptown Square. (800) 463-3462. www.mainstreetmedina.com/medina-ice-festival/. Cash prizes and medals for an ice carving competition. Sculpting demos and a "parade" of ice sculptures in front of uptown merchants' businesses. FREE. (mid-February Presidents weekend)

LAWNFIELD - GARFIELD NATIONAL HISTORIC SITE, JAMES A.

Mentor - *8095 Mentor Avenue (I-90 exit Rte. 306, turn right 2 miles East on US 20) 44060. Phone: (440) 255-8722. www.nps.gov/jaga. Hours: Daily 10:00am-5:00pm.n-*

5:00pm (May-October). Long weekends only (November-April). Admission: $10.00 per person (age 16+). Educators: online biography for research papers. Note: Gift Shop. Summer Fun Programs (weekdays at 2:00pm) are recommended for hands-on. If touring with school-aged kids, ask for the Young People's club worksheet of puzzles & games. Not recommended for preschoolers. Garfield Birthplace Site & Monument east of Cleveland (440-248-1188).

The Victorian farmhouse mansion was the home of President James A. Garfield. Notice the tiles in the dining room fireplace were painted by family as a craft project. The walk-in safe is neat (contains the wreath sent to his funeral by the Queen of England). Like to drape your legs over the side of a chair? See Garfield's office Reading Chair. Who killed him and why? A great museum explains his politics and death. Shortly after his election, an opponent at a railroad station in Washington D.C. assassinated him. See a video showing his life as a preacher, teacher and lawyer plus Garfield's campaign on the front porch of his home in 1880. Journalists standing on the lawn covering the campaign nicknamed the property "Lawnfield". Other structures on the 7.82 acre site include the carriage house (visitor center), the campaign office, the 75-foot tall pump house/windmill and barn. Be sure to spend as much time in the Visitors Center as on tour.

Did You Know?

The wallpaper in James A. Garfield's home and a side table in the Memorial Library have a spider web motif. Victorians believed that house spiders brought good luck and good fortune to the inhabitants.

PRESIDENTS DAY AT THE GARFIELD HISTORIC SITE

Mentor – Lawnfield. Join their annual President's Day program and take part in a new game, Presidential Squares. Join Presidents Lincoln and Garfield, along with several other presidents and their first ladies, in an interactive game of trivia tic-tac-toe for all ages. Crafts and activities in the afternoon. Small fee for each craft and discounted tickets for tours of the Garfield Home will be sold in honor of the event. (President's Day in February)

CHRISTMAS OPEN HOUSE

Mentor – Lawnfield. Buildings decorated for holidays, Santa visit, entertainment and light refreshments served. Great way to expose younger ones to historical homes that might be boring otherwise. Admission. (winter break at 2:00pm)

Middlefield

ROTHENBUHLER CHEESE CHALET

Middlefield - ***15815 Nauvoo Rd State Route 608 (north of Rte. 87) 44062. Phone: (440) 632-6000. www.rothenbuhlercheesemakers.com Hours: Monday – Saturday 8:00am – 5:30pm.***

Approximately 25 million pounds of Swiss cheese are produced here each year. Did you know that it takes nearly 6 quarts of fresh milk to make one pound of Swiss Cheese? Your tour begins with a film describing the cheese-making process. Then wander through the Cheese House Museum with Swiss cheese carvings, antique cheese-making equipment, and Amish memorabilia. Lastly, sample some cheese before you buy homemade cheese, sausage and bread for a homemade snack on the way home.

PUMPKIN MAZE PLAYLAND

Middlefield - 5488 Kinsman Rd, Ridgeview Farm (SR 87, west of SR 45) 44062. Pumpkin Patches / Hayrides / Corn Mazes / Fall Playland - www.ridgeviewfarm.com. Pig races. Petting barn. Admission (average $6.00). Plan on at least two hours playtime. Open weekends, some weekdays (by appointment) and weeknights. (late September - late October).

PUNDERSON MANOR HOUSE RESORT

Newbury - Punderson State Park, (440) 564-9144 or www.pundersonmanor.com. Become a royal guest in an English Tudor-style mansion. The charming rooms, modernized indoor and outdoor pools and cozy cabins combine enchantment with relaxation (Rooms run ~$125+ and Cabins run ~$135.00+). They have board games and videos to check out at the front desk. There are sport courts (including horseshoes and volleyball) and a playground or two. The restaurant is upscale English/American for dinner, but lunch offers a more casual, moderately-priced fare (ever tried Welsh Rarebit?). Weekly summer activities for kids include: playing tag, Storytime, sand art, chalk art, nature walks, and a variety show. The resort has indoor/outdoor pools, tennis, basketball, toboggan and winter chalet. And when it's time for rest, you can hideaway in your room, the tower library or lounge by a fire. Lots of seasonal getaway packages are available.

PUNDERSON STATE PARK RESORT

Newbury - ***(2 miles East of Newbury off State Route 87) 44065. Phone: (440) 564-2279. http://parks.ohiodnr.gov/punderson***

Nature programs. Tennis. 996 acres of camping, hiking trails, boating and rentals, fishing, swimming and winter sports. Family cabins with A/C and fireplaces. Just the right size for small family getaways in the woods. Activities abound year-round in this beautiful setting. Enjoy the tranquility of relaxing at the indoor and outdoor pools. Wade a while at the sandy beach, play tennis, volleyball, basketball. Combine that with 15 miles of natural hiking trails (some are nature walks with signs) that wind past deer, squirrel, beaver, giant maples, and scented pine trees. You might even catch a wink of a busy beaver working on his dam. When winter comes, you can snowmobile, cross-country ski, ice fish or race downhill on a giant grooved sled hill.

SLED DOG CLASSIC

Newbury – Punderson State Park. Dog sled racing in Ohio? Yes! See sled dog racers mush their teams through challenging race courses. Fee for racers. Spectators are admitted FREE. (one weekend in January, depending on weather)

WESTWOODS PARK

Newbury - *9465 Kinsman Road (Route 87) (I-90 to Route 306. Travel south on Route 306 for approximately 12.7 miles to Route 87. Turn east on Route 87) 44073. Phone: (440) 286-9516. www.geaugaparkdistrict.org/parks/westwoods.shtml. Note: Geauga County Parks are nearby.*

They had an excellent Ice Age exhibit that has left, but the Ice Age theme continues throughout the year through outdoor adventures.Take home a souvenir glacier rock. Other exhibits highlight the geology, hydrology, and diverse ecology of the county's lands. More than 5 miles of trails traverse through woodlands, across streams and past outcroppings of conglomerate sandstone. Other trails lead past "black swamp" pools, past Sunset Overlook, or to Ansel's Cave. This is a one-stop place for studying glaciers in northeast Ohio.

MCKINLEY BIRTHPLACE MEMORIAL AND MUSEUM

Niles - *40 North Main Street (SR 46 to downtown) 44446. Phone: (330) 652-1704. https://mckinleybirthplacemuseum.org/ Hours: Monday-Wednesday 9:00am-5:00pm. Thursday 9am-3pm. Admission: FREE. Educators: Lesson Plans online.*

The classic Greek structure with Georgian marble which houses a museum of McKinley memorabilia. Also see artifacts from the Civil War and Spanish-American War. McKinley was the 25th President and the first to use campaign buttons. He was assassinated in office.

HEADLANDS BEACH STATE PARK

Painesville - *State Route 44 (2 miles Northwest of Painesville) 44060. Phone: (440) 881-8141. http://parks.ohiodnr.gov/headlandsbeach*

The trademark of Headlands Beach State Park is its mile-long natural sand beach, the largest in the state. In addition to its popularity during the summer season with picnickers and swimmers, the area is home to many plant species typically found only along the Atlantic Coast. 125 acres of hiking trails (adjacent nature preserve), fishing, swimming and winter sports. **HEADLANDS DUNES STATE NATURE PRESERVE** - is located on the east end of the park, and one of the last remaining examples of Lake Erie beach and dunes. Preserve open daylight hours.

CUYAHOGA VALLEY SCENIC RAILROAD

Peninsula - *Cuyahoga Valley National Recreation Area (Independence Depot is off I-77 exit 155, follow signs) 44264. Phone: (330) 657-2000 or (800) 468-4070. www.cvsr.com. Hours: Departs Wednesday-Sunday, Morning and early Afternoon (June-October). Weekends, Morning and early Afternoon (Rest of the Year) Admission: $10.00-$15.00 per person (age 3+). Reservations highly recommended. $15 - $35 for themed family excursions. Note: Gift Shop Car/Concession Car, Park Ranger/Volunteer available for nature information. Main train trips depart from Independence, Peninsula & Akron. Bring a picnic lunch to eat in transit or at a stopover. Wheelchair car available.*

Ride in climate controlled coaches built between 1939 and 1940 on the very scenic 2 - 6½ hour ride to many exciting round trip destinations. Meadowlands, pinery, marsh, rivers, ravines, and woods pass by as you travel to Hale Farm and Village, Quaker Square, Akron Zoo, Canal Visitor Center, Stan Hywet Hall or just a basic scenic tour (best if small kids take shorter trips or ones with layovers). Narration of views and history of changes in the area included. The Canal Limited is the only excursion which begins at the depot in Peninsula on a trip north to Canal Visitor Center. The center is a restored house on the Ohio & Erie Canal. Learn about the canal days in the museum and watch the canal lock demonstrations held every weekend during the summer and periodically in early fall.

The conductor punches tickets...

This is a fun way to spend the day family style (grandparents too!) and see one other attraction along the way. Be sure your little engineers get a blue or pink cap to wear along the trip as a memory of their first train ride! Preschoolers look forward to the summer special rides on the "Little Engine that Could". All kids love the holiday themed train rides.

HOLIDAY EXPRESS, CHRISTMAS TREE ADVENTURE OR POLAR EXPRESS

Peninsula – Cuyahoga Valley Scenic Railroad. Train Trip in decorated coaches with Santa. Songs and Treats. Some are pick your own tree or ride in pajamas. Dress warmly. Advance tickets necessary. Weekends and some weekdays.

TINKER'S CREEK STATE PARK

Portage - *10303 Aurora Hudson Rd. (2 miles West of State Route 43) 44266. Phone: (330) 296-3239. http://parks.ohiodnr.gov/tinkerscreek*

Herons, ducks, geese and beaver can be found in the spring-fed waters, while cattail, buttonbush and swamp white oak line the shores of this beautiful park. Tinker's Creek State Nature Preserve is located adjacent to the state park and features extensive marshes. A 1.5-mile trail, known as the Seven Ponds Trail, features a boardwalk through the wetlands. An observation deck has been constructed to allow visitors excellent views of waterfowl. The preserve is open during daylight hours and is accessible only on foot. Parking is available on Old Mill Road in Aurora. 60 acres of fishing trails, swimming and winter sports.

WEST BRANCH STATE PARK

Ravenna - *5708 Esworthy Road (5 miles East of Ravenna off State Route 5) 44266. Phone: (330) 296-3239. http://parks.ohiodnr.gov/westbranch*

West Branch State Park's large lake with its many forks and coves is extremely popular with fishermen, boaters and swimmers. The park's meadows and woodlots provide an excellent backdrop for camping, hiking and horseback riding. Nature programs. More than twelve miles of hiking trails provide access to a portion of the state's Buckeye Trail passing through the park and is linked to the campground by a two-mile spur trail. The park offers extensive snowmobile trails when conditions permit. Mountain biking is permitted on trails in the snowmobile area.

TWINS DAYS FESTIVAL

Twinsburg - I-80/90 to SR-91, follow signs. www.twinsdays.org. The largest gathering of twins in the world (usually over 2500) includes twins contests, entertainment, fireworks and the nationally televised "Double Take" parade. Small fee for non-twins. Twinsburg was originally named by the Wilcox twins in the early 1800s. Admission. (first full weekend in August)

WAGON TRAILS ANIMAL PARK

Vienna - *907 Youngstown-Kingsville Road (SR 193) 44473. Phone: (330) 539-4494. www.wagontrails.com. Hours: Daily, except Tuesday 10:00am-4:00pm (June-August). Weekends only (May, September, October)Admission: $16.95 adult, $13.95 child (2-12). Tours: Include wagon ride, bucket of feed and petting zoo. Wagon and zoo are wheelchair and stroller accessible.*

From horse-drawn wagons, you'll see and feed animals from the farm to the Outback. Your safari will now take you over a bridge where you will feed colorful koi fish in the pond. Then your safari will go to new heights as your safari truck takes you up the new "mountain" where you'll get a view of the animals. Knowledgeable safari guides narrate your tour through 60 acres of woods, ponds and animals. Zoo food included with your admission. Get up close and personal as you feed the animals. Don't forget your camera!

NATIONAL PACKARD MUSEUM

Warren - *1899 Mahoning Avenue NW 44482. www.packardmuseum.org. Phone: (330) 394-1899. Hours: Tuesday-Saturday Noon-5:00pm, Sunday 1:00-5:00pm. Admission: $8.00 adult, $5.00 senior (65+), $5.00 child (7-12).*

Watch a video about Packard's family of vehicles and personal family stories. See memorabilia about the manufacturer's history from 1899 – 1958. Look for vehicles named "Wingfoot", "Caribbean" or "flying". Also Packard Electric history display.

The famous Mary Poppins-like Silver Bridge

MILL CREEK PARK

Youngstown - *123 McKinley Avenue (South of Mahoning Avenue off Glenwood Avenue) 44406. Phone: (330) 740-7115 (Lanterman's Mill). (330) 740-7107 (Ford Nature Center) or (330) 740-7109 (Winter). www.millcreekmetroparks.com. Hours:*

Tuesday-Saturday 10:00am-5:00pm, Sunday Noon-5:00pm (Center/Mill). Note: Gift Shop. Lanterman's Mill (May - October), small admission.

This park has your basic scenic trails, lakes, falls, gorges, gardens and covered bridges but it also has more.

FORD NATURE CENTER is a stone house with live reptiles and hands-on exhibits about nature. Recorded messages are available for the different stations along the trail beginning outside the Center.

LANTERMAN'S MILL is a restored 1845 water-powered gristmill with a 14-foot oak wheel. While in the mill, observe the pioneer ingenuity involved in the early production of meal and flour. Smell the aroma of freshly ground grains. Hear the gentle trickle of water as it flows toward the wheel. Feel the rumblings of the stones as they whirl, grinding the various grains. Later, try baking some Johnny Cakes made with stone-ground corn meal.

As you travel through the park, be on the look out for the Silver Bridge (reminiscent of Old England and Mary Poppins). Fellowship Riverside Gardens is a colorful mixture of greens and flowers. The best community park system (and very well kept) you'll find anywhere!

OH WOW! CHILDREN'S CENTER

Youngstown - ***11 West Federal Street 44503. Phone: (330) 744-5914. http://ohwowkids.org Hours: Daily 10:00am-4:00pm. Admission: $7-8.00 (age 3+). Educators: lesson plans - http://ohwowkids.org/educators-groups/lesson-plans/***

The Children's Museum of the Valley provides regional educational opportunities for hands-on interaction. Activities and exhibits explore the culture, art, drama, construction, science, and natural history connected to the Mahoning Valley. Be a mad scientist and perform real science experiments yourself. The Phenomenal Puzzle Place is where you test your puzzle prowess as your try to solve the wide variety of puzzles. Come and learn more about your world, region, and state with giant maps. Test your navigation and mapping skills about your community. Visit Culture Central and live the culture of one of the more than one hundred countries from which people came to the Valley. Or, be a television or stage star and play with art and writing displays.

BUTLER INSTITUTE OF AMERICAN ART

Youngstown - ***524 Wick Ave. 44502. Phone: (330) 743-1711. www.butlerart.com. Hours: Tuesday – Saturday 11:00am - 4:00pm, Sunday Noon - 4:00pm.Admission: FREE. Note: Cafe open for lunch.***

Showcases American art from colonial times to the present. Children's Gallery (hands on) and American Sports Art Gallery. FREE Sunday Family Programs and FEE paid "gift art" classes available.

YOUNGSTOWN HISTORICAL CENTER OF INDUSTRY & LABOR

Youngstown - ***151 West Wood Street (Wood Street is off of Market Street two blocks north of downtown) 44503. www.ohiohistory.org/visit/museum-and-site-locator/youngstown-historical-center-of-industry-amp-labor Phone: (330) 743-5934. Hours: Wed-Fri 10am-4pm, Saturday Noon-4pm. Closed winter holidays. Admission: $7 adult, $3 student (all ages). Educators: the link ohiohistoryteachers.org provides info before you tour and activities, word search and a puzzle.***

If your family has a heritage of steelworkers in the family, then this is the place to explain their hard work. The history of the iron and steel industry in the Mahoning Valley area can be viewed easily looking at the life-sized dioramas titled, "By the Sweat of Their Brow" or from the numerous videos shown throughout the building. Rooms are set up like typical steel mill locker rooms, company houses, and a blooming room. They certainly give you the "feel" of the treacherous work at the mill.

YOUNGSTOWN SYMPHONY

Youngstown - ***260 Federal Plaza West 44503. www.youngstownsymphony.com. Phone: (330) 744-4264.***

Performs Pops Concerts with guest artists in Powers Auditorium (tours). Community site Storytyme concerts provide opportunities for the Symphony to engage young people in programs on their common ground. Youngstown Symphony Youth Orchestra and Youngstown Symphony Symphonette.

GORANT CANDIES

Youngstown - ***8301 Market Street (State Route 7, Boardman) 44512. Phone: (800) 572-4139 Ext.1236. www.gorant.com Tours: Tuesday-Thursday until 1:30pm (usually March only). Maximum 50 people. 1st grade and above. Note: Candy store. Displays of chocolate history. Hair net (provided) must be worn.***

Put on your paper hat and watch up to 375,000 pieces of chocolate candy being made each day. See the 2000-pound chocolate melting vats and color-coded rooms. The brown walls are the molding room where chocolate is poured and shook on vibrating tables (takes out the air bubbles). The yellow room is the coating room. A personalized hand dipper (only one) dips 3600 candies a day. Receive a free candy bar at the end of the tour.

Chapter 6
North West Ohio

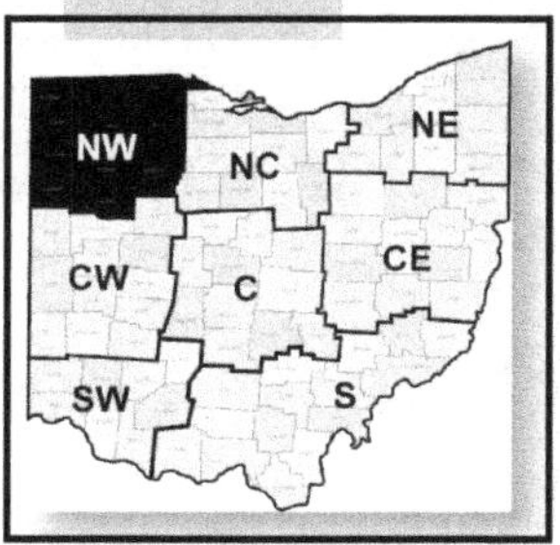

Archbold

- Sauder Village

Attica

- Oak Ridge Festival

Bluffton

- Bluffton Blaze Of Lights

Bowling Green

- American Civil War Museum Of Ohio
- Bg Wind Farm
- Snooks Dream Cars Museum

Bryan

- Spangler Candy Factory (Dum Dum Pops Candy)

Defiance

- Auglaize Village Farm Museum
- Independence Dam State Park

Delphos

- Museum Of Postal History

Fayette

- Harrison Lake State Park

Findlay

- Dietsch Brothers Fine Chocolates & Ice Cream
- Mazza Collection Museum
- Northwest Ohio Railroad Preservation

Grand Rapids

- Canal Experience
- Mary Jane ThurstOn State Park

Lima

- Allen County Museum
- Apple Festival

Sylvania

- Fossil Park

Toledo

- Imagination Station
- Lagrange Street Polish Festival
- National Museum of Great Lakes
- Sandpiper Canal Boat
- Toledo Botanical Gardens
- Toledo Firefighters Museum
- Toledo Mud Hens Baseball
- Toledo Museum Of Art
- Toledo Symphony Orchestra
- Toledo Zoo
- Tony Packo's Café
- Wolcott House Museum Complex

Toledo (Maumee)

- Children's Wonderland

Toledo (Oregon)

- Maumee Bay State Park

Toledo (Perrysburg)

- Fort Meigs

Toledo (Swanton)

- Cannaley Treehouse Village

Van Buren

- Van Buren Lake State Park

Van Wert

- Kernel Coopers Corn Maze

Whitehouse

- Butterfly House

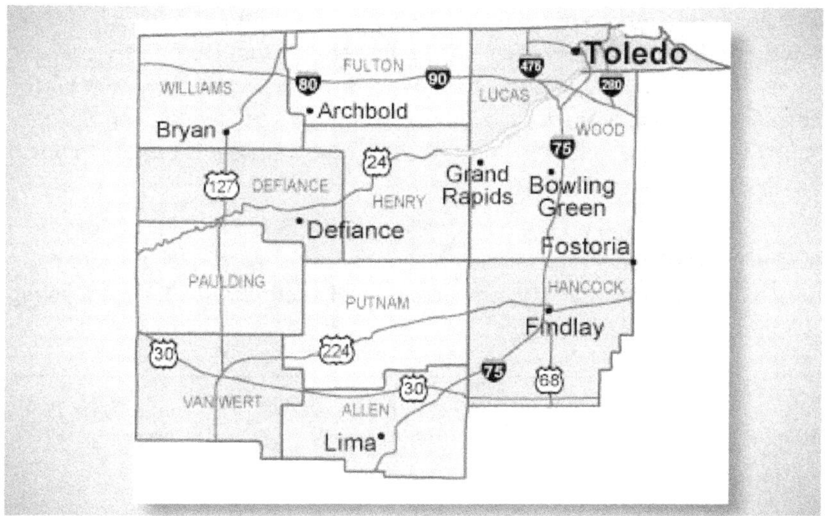

A Quick Tour of our Hand-Picked Favorites Around...

North West Ohio

Giant freighters pour into the Toledo harbor and you can even tour one plus visit the new **National Museum of the Great Lakes** along the riverfront. The most kid-friendly fort in the Midwest is located down the road at **Fort Meigs** - with plenty of dress up clothes to try on and green space to run on. Built up an appetite for some crazy food? Stop by the original **Tony Packo's** and take a bite of a Packo's Hungarian Hot Dog while viewing framed hot dog buns signed by celebrities. We told you - crazy stuff...

Do your kids love candy? What about spending the day sampling chocolates, ice cream and hard candies? You're in the right place! This region of the state has **Dietsch Brothers** (Findlay) old-fashioned ice cream and chocolates and **Spangler Candy Factory** (Bryan), the makers of Dum Dum Pops suckers. Tours are not too hard to coordinate (weekdays) or tag along on. Try wacky flavors like Cream Soda, Cotton Candy, "Everything but the Kitchen Sink," or "Snick-a-Ripple" flavors. You can't miss on these visits – just be sure to brush your teeth soon after!

After lunch it's time to take a trip back in time at **Sauder Village**. Costumed guides will lead you through hands-on activities and more. Hope you're there on a day the marble maker is around but most every day the ice cream shop is open.

Sites and attractions are listed in order by City, Zip Code, and Name. Symbols indicated represent: Restaurants Lodging

Archbold

SAUDER VILLAGE

Archbold - 22611 State Route 2 (off SR 66, 2 miles Northeast on State Route 2 or off turnpike exit 25) 43502. www.saudervillage.org. Phone: (419) 446-2541 or (800) 590-9755. Hours: Tuesday-Saturday 10:00am-5:00pm. Sunday & Holidays Noon–4:00pm (Late-April – October). Closed 60-90 min. early in the spring and fall. Admission: $20 adult, $14 child (6-16). Special Sunday Rate: Adults $12.00. Free admission for children 16 and under every Sunday (with adult paid admission) $1.00 Carriage, Train or Wagon rides Educators: Wonderful, easy-to-follow study guides and suggested activities for all grades are on the Field Trips-Curriculum Resources Page online. Note: The Barn Restaurant serves wonderful home-style food with a children's menu ($5.00). Meals served buffet or family style. Gift Shop. Bakery. Sauder Store & Outlet - featuring all of the ready-to-assemble furniture made right here in Archbold. Heritage Inn w/ indoor pool with waterfall and hot tub adjacent to the "Great Oak Tree", new game and exercise rooms. Campground - campers can use the pool, hot tub and game room at the Inn.

Like to get inside the mind of a successful entrepreneur? Learn the history of Sauder Woodworking & Erie Sauder. He started from using wood scraps (his teenage woodworking shop is open for touring). Meet famous & very talented glass, pottery and wood crafters (you'll flip over the beautiful giant marbles!). Maybe get locked in jail, trade furs or take a lick from an old-fashioned ice cream cone. In the Homestead (1910), look for baby animals, an old baby walker, a Mother's Bench Rocker or a baby bottle warmer. Walk along the craft village where you can meet a weaver, broom maker, tinsmith

or blacksmith all dressed in early 20th Century clothing. "Erie Express" is a train that takes guests on a 1 1/2 mile ride around the perimeter of the Historic Village. The Natives & Newcomers: Ohio in Transition area is a living-history experience telling the story of Northwest Ohio from 1803 to 1839. Covered with swamps and thick forests, this region of the state was one of the last to be settled by Europeans. The settlement also depicts the family lives of the many Native American nations who called this area home. While focusing on Northwest Ohio, the Pioneer Settlement stories mirror our national story of immigration, community building and technological changes. Workers here love what they do!

OLD FASHIONED 4TH OF JULY AT SAUDER VILLAGE

Archbold – Sauder Village. What better place to celebrate Independence Day than at Ohio's largest living-history village! Join them for a day filled with special activities from hand-cranked ice cream and old-fashioned games, to a reading of the Declaration of Independence and patriotic songs being played on the reed organ. Admission. (July 4th)

APPLE WEEK

Archbold – Sauder Village. Guests can watch the boiling of the cider, the adding of the thinly sliced apples and the cooking of the apples in the copper kettles over an open fire. Admission. (last full week in September)

HOLIDAY LANTERN TOURS

Archbold – Sauder Village. (By Reservation Only). Time: Tours last roughly 90 minutes and will be repeated every half hour from 4:00 – 8:30pm. The flicker of a candle-lit lantern lights the way as a costumed interpreter, through a personalized, guided lantern tour, takes small groups on a journey to meet historical characters in the 1910 Homestead, the District 16 Schoolhouse, Villages' St. Mark's Church and the Train Depot. Guests are invited to experience the holiday customs and celebrations of the 1900s in Northwest Ohio as along the way, your guide shares stories about Christmas' past and the history of Northwest Ohio. Admission. (Saturday after Thanksgiving, first Saturday in December, and second weekend in December)

OAK RIDGE FESTIVAL

Attica - SR 4 & US 224, on Township Road 104. www.oakridgefestival.com. Early 1800's frontier life & Indian village. Re-enactors, craft demonstrations, authentic open fire, wood cooked food and folk entertainment. Admission. (mid-July & mid-October weekend)

BLUFFTON BLAZE OF LIGHTS

Bluffton - Downtown. Hundreds of thousands of lights & holiday / storybook characters. Wagon rides. www.allencvb.lima.oh.us/events.asp. Daily, evenings. Admission. (Thanksgiving - January 1)

PUMPKIN MAZE PLAYLAND

Bluffton (Pandora) - (about 7 minutes from Bluffton) Suter's Produce. www.suterproduce.com. They have a new corn maze theme every year and go all out with costumes and decorations to fit the theme! (Click on "Corn Maze" to see all the past mazes.) Everyone in this area loves the corn maze, the hayride through the woods to the pumpkin patch and watching the old cider press work (on Wed. and Sat. mornings). Admission. (Fall)

Bowling Green

BG WIND FARM

Bowling Green - ***Corner of Route 6 & Tontogany Rds. (I-75 exit 179) 43402. Phone: (419) 354-6246.***

Visit the only wind farm in the state of Ohio (Daily from 9:00am-6:00pm). Four wind turbines swirl through the air to generate electricity to BG and its electric co-op. An informational computerized kiosk is available for visitors to see how these towering turbines were erected.

SNOOKS DREAM CARS MUSEUM

Bowling Green - ***13920 County Home Road, Twp 172 (I-75 exit 179, east on US 6) 43402. Phone: (419) 353-8338. www.snooksdreamcars.com. Hours: Weekdays 8am-4pm. Admission: $5.00-$8.00 per person.***

Begin in a 1940's era Texaco filling station, featuring "automobilia" - everything from hood ornaments to backseat games to seat covers. Operational mechanics area leads to coin-operated amusement games (even a Model T kiddie ride). Remember pedal cars? The showroom has dream cars showcased in themed rooms from the 30's-60's. "We like to consider this a living museum," says Jeff, co-owner, "since all the cars on display are in working condition.

SPANGLER CANDY FACTORY (DUM DUM POPS CANDY)

Bryan - *400 N. Portland Street (10 miles south of 80/90 Toll Road, exit 13, SR 15 south to town, right on Mulberry Street) 43506. Phone: (419) 636-4221 or (888) 636-4221. www.spanglercandy.com. Hours: Wednesday - Friday 10am-3pm (winter). Monday-Friday 10am-3pm (summer). Factory tour prices are: $6.00 Adults, Children 6-17 years $4.00, Children 5 & Under Free with paid Adult. There is no admission charge for the store/museum. Tours: Public tours of the factory are available on the Dum Dum Trolley. There are no reservations. Tours are on a first come, first served basis. Tours not be offered on any day that is a holiday for the factory.*

The Spangler Store & Museum is located at the corner of Portland and Mulberry Streets, next to the world-famous Dum Dum Pop factory! Due to safety and FDA regulations, the trolley tour will not go through the main kitchen areas, but does go through the candy pack-out and warehouse areas (similar to what the Jelly Belly tours do). Candy cooking and forming in the kitchen areas are shown via a DVD player while on the trolley tour. The small, ball-shaped treats are famous for their array of great-tasting flavors, from Cream Soda to Cotton Candy and Butterscotch, which rotate in part based on consumer voting. Consumers can go to www.dumdumpops.com and vote for their favorite Dum Dum flavor, weigh in on newly introduced flavors, and submit suggestions for new flavors.

The museum features historical information in a timeline fashion, along with samples of products and other artifacts from years past. Through the museum experience visitors will learn how their company grew from one man and some baking powder to the world-class hard candy company it is today.

Defiance

BLACK SWAMP STEAM & GAS SHOW

Defiance - Auglaize Village. Working gas tractors and over 30 operating steam engines on the sawmill, threshing wheat and plowing machines. Admission. (second weekend in June)

JOHNNY APPLESEED FESTIVAL

Defiance - Auglaize Village. The historic village is busy with crafts, apple butter, cider and molasses making, and harvest demonstrations. Tractor pulls and train rides. 1840 Encampment. Admission. (first weekend in October)

INDEPENDENCE DAM STATE PARK

Defiance - ***State Route 424 (4 miles East of Defiance) 43512. Phone: (419) 784-3263. http://parks.ohiodnr.gov/independencedam.***

Independence Dam State Park is situated along the banks of the beautiful Maumee River. The river is ideal for boating, fishing or a scenic canoe trip. A three-mile hiking trail, once the towpath of the Miami and Erie Canal, offers the hiker a glimpse into the colorful past of Ohio's canal era. The three-mile access road through the park offers a scenic ride for bicyclists. The park offers the perfect setting for a picnic or overnight camping experience.

HARRISON LAKE STATE PARK

Fayette - ***26246 Harrison Lake Road (4 miles South of Fayette off State Route 66) 43521. Phone: (419) 237-2593. http://parks.ohiodnr.gov/harrisonlake.***

A green island of scenic woodlands in a rich agricultural region. A 3.5-mile hiking trail circles the lake and provides the opportunity to explore the scenic lakeshore and woodlands. Harrison Lake is popular for swimming, fishing, camping and canoeing. 249 acres of camping, hiking trails, boating (no power), fishing, swimming, and winter sports.

Findlay

DIETSCH BROTHERS FINE CHOCOLATES & ICE CREAM

Findlay - ***400 W. Main Cross Street (I-75 exit 157, State Route 12) 45839. Phone: (419) 422-4474. http://dietschs.com/. Hours: Store open daily except Mondays. Tours: Wednesday & Thursday mornings (1st grade & up). (Fall & Spring). ½ hour long, 20 people maximum. Reservations required.***

Three brothers (2nd generation) run an original 1937's candy and ice cream shop. In the summer, see ice cream made with real cream. They make 1500 gallons per week. Fall, heading into the holidays, is the best time to see 500 pounds of chocolate treats made daily. Try some wacky flavors like "Everything but the Kitchen Sink" or "Snick-a-Ripple."

MAZZA COLLECTION MUSEUM

Findlay - ***1000 North Main Street (University of Findlay Campus, I-75 EXIT 159 SR 224) 45840. www.mazzacollection.org. Phone: (419) 424-4777 or (800) 472-9502. Hours: Wednesday-Friday Noon-5:00pm, Sunday 1:00-4:00pm. Closed all holidays. Admission: FREE. Tours: Tuesday-Thursday between 9:00am-2:00pm and Friday 9:00am-Noon. $2.00 per student, $1.00 extra for craft.***

This is the world's first and largest teaching museum devoted to literacy and the art of children's picture books. All the artwork here is based on children's storybooks and the teaching units include such exhibits as printmaking, the Mother Goose Corner, a borders section, the book-making process, an historical art gallery, and an art media exhibit. After a tour, some groups opt to have an art activity where the students get to use the ideas they saw in the galleria to produce their own artwork.

NORTHWEST OHIO RAILROAD

Findlay - ***11600 County Rd. 99 (northeast corner of I-75 exit #161 east and County Rd. 99, north end of Findlay) 45840. www.nworrp.org. Phone: (419) 423-2995. Hours: Generally weekends 1:00-4:00pm (April-December) plus evenings during peak seasonal excursions. Diesel on Saturdays and Steam on Sundays. Admission: $2.00-$3.00 per person.***

Experience the thrill of a coal-burning steam train ride on the nearly 1/2 mile of 15" gauge track layout.

Special events, such as Tracks To The Past in September, the Pumpkin Train in October & Christmas' North Pole Express in December are best times to visit. Tours of their B&O caboose are the first Sunday of each month, April-September. Kids eyes gleem at the Lionel Toy Train layout.

CANAL EXPERIENCE

Grand Rapids - ***Mill Road in Providence Metro Park (I-475 exit 45, US 24 and State Route 578) 43522. www.metroparkstoledo.com/explore-your-parks/providence. Phone: (419) 535-3050 mill or (419) 407-9741canal. Hours: Wednesday-Friday 10:00am-2:00pm, Weekends & Holidays Noon-4:00pm (May-October). Extended weekday hours in the summer. Admission: FREE demonstrations of mill. Canal boat tickets: $7.00 adult, $6.00 senior (60 and over), $4.00 child (3 to 12). Tours: 45 minute mule drawn canal boat rides leave every hour until 4:00pm. Narrated. Note: Fishing below the roller dam, hiking/biking on 8-mile towpath (once occupied by canal mules). Educators: Discovery Walks.***

CANAL BOAT: It's always 1876 at Providence, where people and goods still travel by mule-drawn canal boat at 4 MPH. Grain is still ground in a gristmill and water still powers saws that slice logs. Visitors to the Metropark step back in time to become passengers on the Miami & Erie Canal aboard the "The Volunteer," with a crew of costumed interpreters in character for the first half of a 45-minute, narrated journey.

ISAAC LUDWIG MILL: One of the few mills left in Ohio, this 19th century mill sits on the Maumee River and demonstrates how a flour mill, sawmill and electric generator can be powered by water from the old canal below.

MARY JANE THURSTON STATE PARK

Grand Rapids - ***State Route 65 (2 miles West of Grand Rapids) 43534. Phone: (419) 832-7662. http://parks.ohiodnr.gov/maryjanethurston***

The Maumee is not only scenic, but also provides some of the best stream fishing in Ohio. Boaters have access to the river while history buffs may explore the remnants of the old canal. A one-mile portion of the Buckeye Trail passes through the park following the side cut canal. The trail continues on to the Village of Grand Rapids. A one-mile loop trail winds through the floodplain forest while an easy half-mile trail circles the day use area. Six miles of trails in the North Turkeyfoot Area may be used for backpacking, horseback riding or mountain biking.

ALLEN COUNTY MUSEUM

Lima - ***620 West Market Street (I-75 exit 125 on SR117/309) 45801. Phone: (419) 222-9426. www.allencountymuseum.org. Hours: Tuesday-Sunday 1:00-4:00pm. Closed holidays & Mondays. Children's Museum only open in summer and by appointment in the school year. Admission: Suggested donation of $5.00 per adult. MacDonell House $3.00. Note: While in town, stop for lunch or dinner at the Old Barn Out Back (3175 W. Elm St - www.oldbarnoutback.com) serving country-style food in the "Chicken Coop" or "Pig Pen" - known for their fried chicken and cinnamon rolls.***

Indian and pioneer artifacts. Antique automobiles and bicycles. Barber Shop, Doctor's office, country store, log house on grounds. Next door is MacDonell House (wall of purses). Lincoln Park Railroad exhibit locomotive and Shay Locomotive (huge train) is something the kids will love. The most unusual display is a collection of objects that people have swallowed (ex. Bolts, diaper pins). Try your hand at various trivia games and puzzles located throughout the Children's Center. Each year, they present a new theme in the Children's Discovery Center where kids can assemble and operate exhibit interactives based on relevant themes (ex. Railroads). Experiment with other means of communication. Try your hand at sign language. Learn how to read and write Braille. Play checkers blindfolded. Send signals with flags. Write with hieroglyphs like an ancient Egyptian. Try to decipher a secret code. Make a craft or art project to take home with you.

APPLE FESTIVAL

Lima - Allen City Farm Park, 1582 Slabtown Road. www.jampd.com. Apples & cider. Apple pie eating contests. Apple peeling contests. Apple butter. Candy apples. Wagon/hayrides. Apple Dumplings, Fritters, Donuts, etc. Parades. Pioneer crafts. Petting Zoo. (first weekend in October)

FOSSIL PARK

Sylvania - *5705 Centennial Road (I-75 exit 210 west on SR 184) 43560. Phone: (419) 882-8313. www.olanderpark.com Hours: Saturday 10:00am-6:00pm, Sunday 11:00am-6:00pm (April -late October). Admission: FREE*

Fossil Park, located in an abandoned quarry is an unusual destination for travelers who are interested in rocks, quarries or mines. The park contains some of the best fossils from the Devonian period in the world; even little tyke diggers can easily find corals, brachiopods, echinoderms and trilobites . Visitors are allowed to break the fossils from the soft shale and keep any fossils that they find...but, no tools are allowed.

Toledo

IMAGINATION STATION

Toledo - *One Discovery Way (in the old COSI bldg at the corner of Summit & Adams Streets on riverfront) 43604. Phone: (419) 244-2674. www.imaginationstationtoledo.org. Hours: Tuesday-Saturday 10:00am-5:00pm, Sunday Noon-5:00pm. Admission: $13 general, $11 child (3-12). Note: Science2Go store, Atomic Cafe.*

Classics like the High Wire Cycle, the BOYO, along with Grow U agriculture and farming. Energy Factory allows kids to program a robotic arm or command a colorful oil refinery. In Water Works you'll find the Hurricane Chamber where visitors can stand beneath a gust of rushing air and water play. Smash your food and take on the Wheel of Fire in Eat It Up. They do a bang up job involving kids in life-applicable experiements downstairs

NATIONAL MUSEUM OF THE GREAT LAKES

Toledo - *1701 Front Street (2 miles North of State Route 60 / OH 2 intersection) 43605. www.nmgl.org. Hours: Tuesday-Saturday 10am-5pm, Sunday Noon-5pm. Admission: $11.00 adult, $10.00 senior (65+) and $8.00 child (6-18). Add $6.00 for touring the Schoonmaker.*

The National Museum of the Great Lakes reveals the haunting and fascinating history of our treasured Great Lakes that happen to make up 84 percent of the fresh surface water in North America. The Maritime Center includes: original artifacts (some from horrific shipwrecks like the Edmund Fitzgerald), over 40 hands-on exhibits (for example: direct your own submersible through the wreckage of the lost freighter or keep your own ship afloat by operating a real bilge pump). The real life-size S.S. Col. James M. Schoonmaker Museum Ship sits outside the museum for touring. The Schoonmaker freighter depicts how ships of the Great Lakes worked in teh early to mid-1900s. Visitors are awed by the massive engine room and the galley. And for waterside wonderers - a beautifully landscaped 3.5 acre maritime-themed park.

REAL SEAFOOD CO.

Toledo - 22 Main Street 43605. www.realseafoodcorestaurant.com. Phone: (419) 691-6054. Take a break and relax with a view of the downtown Toledo skyline at one of several restaurants located at the Docks. They bring in fresh seafood from the Atlantic, Pacific and Great Lakes. Many rave about their crab cakes. I liked their selection of locally caught Perch or Walleye. Lunch runs $11-$15. Dinner runs about double. Entrees include two sides. I recommend you try their blue cheese vinaigrette coleslaw with any fish entree. All kids meals include a beverage and the meals (shrimp, burger, tenders, spaghetti, etc) run $5.95. Ona nice day, try to get a patio seat.

WOLCOTT HOUSE MUSEUM COMPLEX

Toledo - *1031 River Road (I-475/23 to exit 4, Rte. 24 east) 43537. Phone: (419) 893-9602. www.wolcotthouse.org Hours: Saturday Noon-3:00pm (May-December). Admission: $6.00 adult, $5.00 senior (60+), $2.50 student. Educators: Teacher Tour Activities online. Tours: 12:30pm and 2:30pm.*

Life in the mid-1800's in the Maumee Valley. Costumed guides lead you through a building complex of a log home, depot, church and gift shop. The seven historic buildings are filled with art and artifacts representative of 19th century life and culture in the Maumee River Valley, beginning with the era of Tecumseh and William Henry Harrison, and continuing through the heydays of the "canal sharks" and the "iron horsemen."

TOLEDO MUD HENS BASEBALL

Toledo - *Fifth Third Field, Warehouse District (I-75 exit 202A or 201 B) 43604. Phone: (419) 725-HENS. www.mudhens.com.*

AAA Semi-professional baseball (farm team for the Detroit Tigers) played in a newly built classic ballpark. See “Muddy” the mascot or sit in "The Roost" bleachers. Also, playground and picnic areas. Tickets $8.00-$13.00. (April-September). Note: the food concessions here are quite good...especially in the suite breezeway.

TONY PACKO'S CAFÉ

Toledo - 1902 Front Street (I-280 exit 9) 43605. www.tonypackos.com. Phone: (419) 691-6054. Built up an appetite for some crazy food? After seeing the "macho" life of "shipsmen" near the Toledo port, try some fiery or authentic ethnic Hungarian food at Tony Packo's Café. The original restaurant is part dining, part museum. Sample a Packo's Hungarian Hot Dog, made famous by Corporal Klinger on the TV show "M.A.S.H." Be sure to look for the 100's of hot dog buns signed by TV stars that have visited the café. Other unique dishes are a Chili Sundae (chili and toppings served in a sundae glass with chips); Fried Pickles; Cabbage Rolls; and Chicken Paprikas.

SANDPIPER CANAL BOAT

Toledo - *2144 Fordway, Riverfront (Jefferson Street Docks, I-75 exit 201B or 202A) 43606. Phone: (419) 537-1212. www.sandpiperboat.com. Admission: Range of $11.00-$19.00. Basically double the price for lunch cruises.*

Replica of a Miami and Erie Canal boat. Educational or historical Cruise up river past riverside estates, downtown or down river. See busy ports, shipyards and dry docks. Public and group tours average 2-4 hours. Mostly weekends (morning/lunchtime). Some evening cruises. Seasonal Fireworks and Fall Cruises. Bring a picnic. Reservations suggested. (May-October)

TOLEDO ZOO

Toledo - *2700 Broadway (I-75 to US 25 - 3 miles South of downtown) 43609. Phone: (419) 385-5721. www.toledozoo.org. Hours: Daily 10:00am-5:00pm (May - Labor Day). Daily, 10:00am-4:00 pm (Rest of the Year). Admission: $22.00 adult, $19.00 senior (60+) and child (2-11). Parking fee $7.00. Military, County residents and special promotion discounts updated seasonally on the website. Note: Carnivore Cafe. Children's Zoo- petting zoo and hands-on exhibits. Wagon/stroller rentals.*

Immerse yourself in the heart of Africa on the Safari Railway through a 5-acre African habitat teeming with giraffes, zebra and all the wilds of Africa. Grab lunch at the Carnivore Cafe before enjoying your whirlwind trip through the Arctic Encounter, Hippoquarium, Nature's Neighborhood, Museum of Science and Aquarium...your journey is endless! The new aquarium was funded by locals, so it's their pride and joy. I particularly loved that the zoo keeps many old structures and recycles them. For instance, the old lion and tiger cages are now the Carnivore Cafe - indoor seating in actual barred cages! They have areas typical of a zoo but they are known for their Hippoquarium (the world's first underwater viewing of the hippopotamus) along with a small enough acreage that is manageable with little ones in tow.

LIGHTS BEFORE CHRISTMAS

Toledo – Toldeo Zoo. Hundreds of thousands of lights & holiday / storybook characters. Daily, evenings (unless noted). Admission. (begins third weekend of November thru most of December)

TOLEDO FIREFIGHTERS MUSEUM

Toledo - ***918 Sylvania Avenue (I-75 exit 206) 43612. www.toledofiremuseum.com. Phone: (419) 478-FIRE. Hours: Saturday Noon-4:00pm. Admission: FREE.***

Feel what 150 years of history of fire-fighting must have meant to the fireman. Learn fire safety tips. In Jed's Bedroom, children are taught how to roll out of bed, keep low in case of smoke, and feel the door for heat with the back of their hand. See actual vintage pumpers, uniforms, and equipment used that trace the growth of the Toledo Fire Department. Located in the former No. 18 Fire Station.

TOLEDO BOTANICAL GARDENS

Toledo - ***5403 Elmer Drive (I-475/US23 exit 13, off North Reynolds Road) 43615. Phone: (419) 936-2986. www.toledogarden.org. Hours: Daily 8:30am-5:30pm. Admission: FREE.***

Fifty-seven acres of meadows and gardens. The outdoor sculpture and storybook garden appeal to kids. A scavenger hunt can be picked up at the Administrative Office for families to enjoy while discovering the Garden. Gallery and gift store. Family Nights are held each season (fee).

TOLEDO MUSEUM OF ART

Toledo - ***2445 Monroe at Scottwood (off I-75) 43620. Phone: (419) 255-8000. www. toledomuseum.org. Hours: Tuesday-Saturday 10:00am-4:00pm, Sunday 11am-***

5:00pm. Open Friday evening til 10:00pm. Admission: FREE (except special exhibits or events). Note: Strollers allowed in most spaces.

Discover treasures from the riches of the medieval, the splendors of a French chateau, and the tombs of Egypt. Also glass, sculpture, paintings. Drop in to the Family Center for themed activities that enliven the world of art for kids of all ages (even those in grown-up guise). The Glass Pavilion is- in itself - a work of art. All exterior and nearly all interior walls consist of large panels of curved glass, resulting in a transparent structure that blurs the boundaries between interior and exterior spaces. You are greeted by a clear glass "fish-looking" Chihuly sculpture and then drawn in further by the live glass-blowing artists at work.

TOLEDO SYMPHONY ORCHESTRA

Toledo - *1838 Parkwood Avenue 43604. Phone: (419) 246-8000. www.toledosymphony.com.*

Regional symphony performs orchestral masterpieces with guest artists, chamber, contemporary, pops, youth and summer concerts. Their Young People's concerts combine other forms of art with classical music (September-May)

LAGRANGE STREET POLISH FESTIVAL

Toledo - Lagrange Street between Central & Mettler Sts. www.polishfestival.org. All kinds of Polish foods, polish bands, dancers, a polka contest, rides and craft area. Free. (first full weekend in July, after the 4th)

CANNALEY TREEHOUSE VILLAGE

Toledo (Swanton) - *3520 Waterville Swanton Rd (Oak Openings Metropark) 43537. https://metroparkstoledo.com/discover/cannaley-treehouse-village/ Phone: (419) 407-9723. Hours: Vary by season. Overnight packages.*

Take a look at this exciting Treehouse Village thanks to the hard work of the Metroparks builders! This is the largest project of its kind in the US and features 4 treehouses plus 3 tent/hammock platforms for camping in the trees. There's also a common treehouse with seating for up to 49 people, a crow's nest, and a canopy walk linking the common treehouse to the crow's nest.

MAUMEE BAY STATE PARK

Toledo (Oregon) - *1400 Park Road #1 (I-280 exit 9 - 8 miles East of Toledo, then 3 miles North off State Route 2) 43618. Phone: (419) 836-7758 park, (419) 836-1466 Lodge or 836-9117 Nature Center. www.maumeebaystateparklodge.com*

Resort cottages and rooms, golf, racquetball, sauna, whirlpool, fitness, tennis, volleyball and basketball are available. The lodge, cottages and golf course are nestled among the scenic meadows, wet woods and lush marshes teeming with wildlife. The park boasts two sand beaches -- on the Lake Erie shore while the other lines the park's inland lake. Developed hiking trails in the park include the Mouse Trail, a 3-mile diverse trail winding through meadows and young woodlands, and several miles of paved combination trails for bicycling and cross-country skiing. Hikers will discover acres of meadow, marshland and woodland. A 2-mile boardwalk traversing swamp and marsh wetlands has interpretive signs, an observation blind and tower, and wheelchair loop.

Improvements include water features in the indoor pool area with seven splash features on a non-skid pad plus a waterfall that spills into the indoor pool; soft play area for children with 5 pirate-themed climbing features on a cushioned floor; snack bar and ice cream shop. 1,845 acres of camping, hiking trails, boating, fishing, swimming and winter sports. Children's recreation is offered most weekends and daily during summer season. This recreation can include games, arts and crafts, hayrides or hikes.

FORT MEIGS

Toledo (Perrysburg) - *29100 West River Road (1 mile Southwest of State Route 25, I-475 to exit 2) 43551. www.fortmeigs.org. Phone: (419) 874-4121 or (800) 283-8916. Hours: Wednesday-Saturday 9:30am-5:00pm. Sunday & Holidays Noon-5:00pm (April-October). Visitor Center ONLY remains open year-round. Admission: $10.00 adult, $8.00 senior (60+), $5.00 child (6-18). Note: Military History Center with Gift Shop at the stone shutterhouse describes role of Ohioans at War. Monthly summer weekend reenactments. Educators: Printable activity sheets (word search and scavenger hunts) are online under Education link. FREEBIES: games and puzzles are found on this page - www.fortmeigs.org/kids*

A War of 1812 era authentic castle-like log and earth fort with seven blockhouses that played an important role in guarding the Western frontier against the British. William Henry Harrison built Fort Meigs on the Maumee River in 1813 to protect northwest Ohio and Indiana from British invasion. The remodeled museum with authentically restored fort is a child's dream! The museum has many unique artifacts, easily displayed with a large gift shop attached. But, the fort's blockhouses, earthen mounds and cannon holes are major "role-playing" spaces! Each blockhouse exhibits a "theme" and the re-enactors add flare

to the scene. March like a soldier or try the "Wheel of Disease". The walls of the blockhouses are 2 feet thick with 4-inch deep windows with cannon hole ports on the second floor. See actual cannons fired as the air fills with smoke. Notice how much manpower was needed to "run" a fort. Our favorite fort in the Midwest!

1813 INDEPENDENCE CELEBRATION

Toledo (Perrysburg) - The 4th of July at Fort Meigs is celebrated with cannon firings, toasts, music, and a day of leisure. War of 1812 soldiers and civilians recreate this day through cannon firings, demonstrations, and hands-on activities for children. The highlight of the day is the eighteen-gun National Salute accompanied by toasts, and fife and drum music starting at 2:00pm on July 4th. A War of 1812 living history encampment, weapons demonstrations, and more take place throughout the weekend. Admission. (July 4th weekend)

FORT MEIGS HOLIDAY OPEN HOUSE

Toledo (Perrysburg) - War of 1812 soldiers and civilians will be on hand to provide demonstrations and answer questions about the War of 1812 and camp life. Enjoy holiday music, hot cider and cookies and hands-on activities. Try your hand at period dancing. No partner or experience is necessary. Shop the museum store for holiday gifts. Tin-smithing demonstrations. Admission. (2nd Sat in Dec)

VAN BUREN LAKE STATE PARK

Van Buren - *State Route 613 (1 mile East of Van Buren, I-75 exit 164) 45889. Phone: (419) 832-7662. http://parks.ohiodnr.gov/vanburen.*

Hiking trails circle the lake. Hikers, horseback riders, and mountain bikers are welcome on 6 miles of multiple-use trails traversing steep ravines and gentler terrain in scenic woodlands. 296 acres of camping, hiking trails, boating, fishing, and winter sports.

BUTTERFLY HOUSE

Whitehouse- *11455 Obee Road, Wheeler Farms. 43571. (419) 877-2733 or www.wheelerfarms.com. Monday-Saturday 10am-5pm, Sunday Noon-5pm (May-August). September closed Monday-Wednesday. October weekends only (corn maze). Admission: $6.50-$9.00 ages 4+.*

Colorful species come from all corners of the world - from Central America, Malaysia, Africa, the Philippines & North America. The 'house' is a 3,000 sq ft. glass house conservatory that recreates a near tropical environment. The gardens surrounding the House are inviting as well, and you may even see the many life cycles of the butterflies occurring outside.

Chapter 7
Southern Ohio

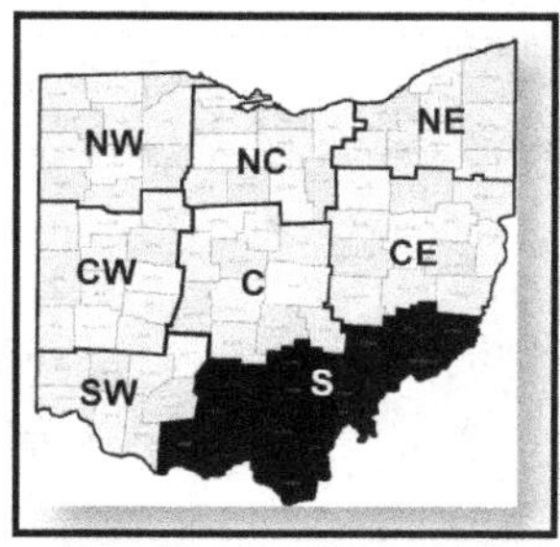

Athens

- Stroud's Run State Park

Bainbridge

- Cave Canyon (7 Caves)
- Magic Waters Theatre
- Paint Creek State Park
- Pike Lake State Park

Chillicothe

- Adena
- Apple Festival
- Feast Of The Flowering Moon
- Great Seal State Park
- Hopewell Culture National Historical Park
- Ross County Heritage Center
- Scioto Trail State Park
- Sumburger Restaurant
- Tecumseh
- Telephone Museum, James M. Thomas

Glouster

- Burr Oak State Park
- Smoke Rise Ranch Resort

Laurelville

- Tar Hollow State Park

Logan (Hocking Hills)

- Hocking Hills STate Park
- Lake Logan State Park
- Washboard Music Festival

Marietta

- Campus Martius
- Marietta Trolley Tours
- Ohio River Museum
- Pumpkin Maze Playland
- Red, White And Blues
- The Castle
- Valley Gem Sternwheeler

McArthur

- Lake Hope State Park

Nelsonville

- Hocking Valley Scenic Railway
- Paul Bunyan Show
- Rocky Boots Factory Outlet & Grill

Oak Hill

- Jackson Lake State Park

Peebles

- Serpent Mound

Portsmouth

- Portsmouth Murals

Reedsville

- Forked Run State Park

Rio Grande

- Bob Evans Farm

Rockbridge (Hocking Hills)

- Great Expectations Cafe
- Hocking Hills Canopy Tours

Waverly

- Lake White State Park

Wellston

- Buckeye Furnace
- Lake Alma State Park

West Portsmouth

- Shawnee State Park

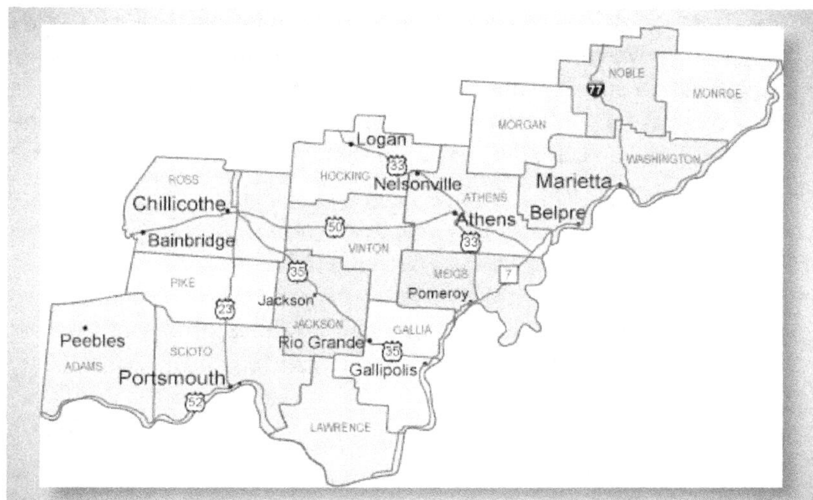

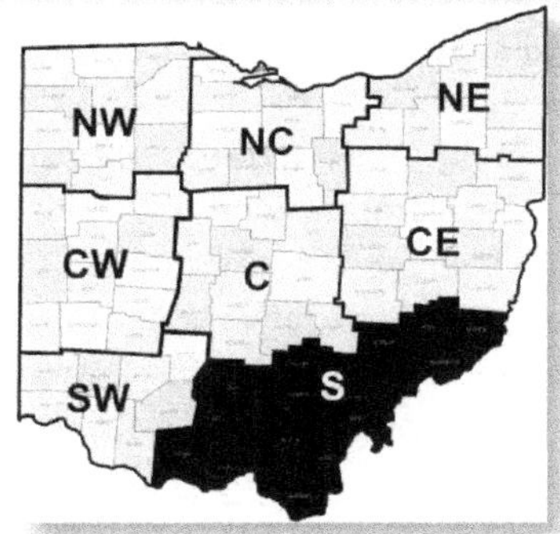

A Quick Tour of our Hand-Picked Favorites Around...

Southern Ohio

Grab your cameras and backpacks and head for southeast Ohio in time to hear the conductor of the **Hocking Hills** Scenic Railway in Nelsonville beckon "all aboard" the old-time passenger train. The cave and trail system (near Logan or Glouster) here attracts visitors from hundreds of miles away but the beauty of the different southern Ohio seasons is really why they came. If you don't have "sure foots" in your crowd, a nice leisurely ride on the train may suit your family best.

Ancient Indians are the name of the game in Chillicothe. Curious? Try to answer these questions: Why did Ancient Hopewell Indians build Mounds? Where did they get seashells and copper from? At **Hopewell Indian Mounds** you may just be able to piece the clues together. To keep with the Indian theme, purchase tickets for your older elementary kids to the **Tecumseh** drama or just catch his tomahawk at **Adena**.

Wear layered clothing and comfortable walking shoes because your family is going on an adventure! **Cave Canyon** (formerly **7 Caves**) is an absolutely wonderful way to spend almost the entire day in nature as you explore a series of small caves you actually peer into. But first, you have to traverse the 100 foot deep canyon surrounded by an enchanting rock-walled gorge. Don't worry, clear paths lead the way...

Have you ever looked at an ugly wall and thought – how can I cover this up? Paint, of course, is the answer. But what if that wall is 2,200 feet long and 20 feet high? About 10 years ago, in the river town of Portsmouth, a committee was formed to begin a project that would take a 20 foot floodwall that protected its city from the Ohio River and transform it into 2,200 feet of magnificent art. Each **Portsmouth Mural** tells the story of the history of Ohio and its people - beginning in the year 1730 and ending in 2002. Which one is your favorite?

At the very tip of the southern region of Ohio is a town that still has an air of the first settlement in the Northwest Territory. The whole downtown Marietta area is one of our favorites to visit during the summer months (festival season) but your family might especially like seeing artifacts from really old Ohio at **Campus Martius**. Things like the oldest house, farm or musical instruments. Some of their murals are so big, you feel you're actually walking into them. Plenty of videos and interactive voices make this old place pretty interesting. Afterwards, lighten the scene by popping into a pasta factory or soda shop and museum.

Sites and attractions are listed in order by City, Zip Code, and Name. Symbols indicated represent: Restaurants Lodging

Athens

STROUD'S RUN STATE PARK

Athens - 11661 State Park Road (8 miles Northeast of Athens off US 50A, Cty Road 20) 45701. Phone: (740) 592-2302. http://parks.ohiodnr.gov/stroudsrun

The first settlers arrived in the Athens County region in 1796. Settlers were encouraged to settle on these college lands to make them attractive, productive and to form a fund for the institution. Fifteen miles of hiking trails meander through the wooded hills of Strouds Run leading to scenic vistas. Excellent bird-watching and nature study can be done along the trail. An 8½ mile bridle trail has been constructed. A 900-foot sand beach on the east side of the lake is open during the summer months. 2,767 acres of camping, hiking trails, boating and rentals, fishing, swimming and winter sports.

Bainbridge

HIGHLANDS SANCTUARY (OLD 7 CAVES)

Bainbridge - *7660 Cave Road (US 50, 4 miles Northwest, follow signs) 45612. Phone: (937) 365-1935. www.arcofappalachia.org/visit/highlands-nature-sanctuary/. Hours: Daily 9:30am-4:30pm (May-September). Weekends only (April & October). Admission: entrance is by donation. Includes Appalachian Forest Museum, orientation slide presentation, and three trails available for hiking on one's own. Note: Many stairs - not stroller accessible. Shelter house. No pets. No food service available. Bring water and packed lunches.*

Wear layered clothing and comfortable walking shoes because your family is going on an adventure! An absolutely wonderful way to spend almost the entire day in nature as you explore a series of small caves you actually peer into. The region abounds with cliffs and canyons, seeps and springs, sinkholes and small caves. An imposing 100 foot deep vertical canyon carved by the Rocky Fork Creek winds through the heart of the preserve, presenting an enchanting rock-walled gorge. Naturalist-led tours include a forest walk and candle-lit cave tours (led Tom Sawyer style - with old-fashioned candle lanterns). Guided tours allow for the kids to learn about the unusual structures as they walk along. Cute, clever names are given to each naturally carved figure. Some areas require following "corkscrew" paths to deep dungeons or grottos. Three different trails lead to caves with cemented walkways, handrails, and lighting showing specific formations. See cliffs, canyons, and waterfalls. About a hundred kinds of birds inhabit The Seven Caves, the Pileated Woodpecker is the rarest. It's a beautiful and humbling experience. A hidden treasure here!

MAGIC WATERS THEATRE

Bainbridge - *7757 Cave Road 45612. www.magicwaters.weebly.com. Phone: (937) 304-0818. Performances: Friday-Saturday 8:00pm, Sunday 7:00pm (mid-June through Labor Day). Pre show picnics available with reservations and additional fee. Admission: $7.00 adult, $4.00 senior, $3.50 child.*

Live outdoor drama in a rustic amphitheater featuring magic shows and kid's theatre (i.e. The Wizard of Oz). Christmas at the Cabin (Oct through December 25) and pre-show dinners are wonderful additions to the regular lineup.

PAINT CREEK STATE PARK

Bainbridge - ***14265 US 50 (17 miles East of Hillsboro on US 50) 45612. Phone: (937) 365-1401. http://parks.ohiodnr.gov/paintcreek***

Located amid the scenery of the Paint Creek Valley, Paint Creek State Park features a large lake with fine fishing, boating and swimming opportunities. A modern campground and meandering hiking trails invite outdoor enthusiasts to explore the rolling hills and streams. Nature programs. On the west side of the lake is Paint Creek Pioneer Farm. The pioneer farm includes a log house, collection of log buildings, livestock, gardens and fields which represent a typical farm of the early 1800's. A walk through Pioneer Farm provides further insight into the settlers' lives. Boating rentals and winter sports. Bicycle rental is available and miniature golf can be enjoyed for a small fee.

PIKE LAKE STATE PARK

Bainbridge - ***1847 Pike Lake Road (6 miles Southeast of Bainbridge) 45612. Phone: (740) 493-2212.***

The surrounding state forest is known for its variety of ferns, mosses, lichens and fungi. The wildflowers are diverse, creating spectacular displays--spring through autumn. The park features 12 standard cottages and 12 family cottages. Six miles of hiking trails provide strenuous and/or casual walks to scenic locations. The adjacent state forest has several miles of bridle trails. Horses are not provided by the park or forest. Nature programs. 613 acres of camping, hiking trails, boating and rentals, fishing, swimming and winter sports.

DOGWOOD PASS

Beaver - ***722 Adams Rd. (20 miles south of Chillicothe) 45613. Phone: (740) 835-1130.*** www.facebook.com/dogwoodpassoldwesttown ***Week day Tours of the town $5.00 per person donations. Weekend events admission varies. Weekend tours are usually 11am, 1pm and 3pm.***

Dogwood Pass Is Home To Wild West Festivals, Major Film Productions, Music Video's, and Special Holiday Events. Throughout the warm seasons Dogwood Pass holds monthly Wild West Festivals, including Period Stage Shows, Old West Shootouts, Period Traders, Pan for Gemstones, Horse Back Riding for kids, Old Time Photography, Food venders, Raffles, and more. Visit the town's Living History Exhibits during festivals, such as the town's blacksmith, the potter's wheel, spinning wheel and loom weaver. Period theatre troupe and Music as well.The old west town also features a Saloon, Jail, Mercantile, Bunk House, Bath House, Bank, Freight Office, Livery Stable, Undertaker, Half Pint Shooting Gallery, Doc's office, Cigar Shop, Gold Mining Camp, 1800's cabins, Bakery, Church, Dress Shop, Barber Shop, Cavalry Office, and a Souvenir Shop.

Chillicothe

ADENA

Chillicothe - ***847 Adena Road (West of State Route 104 off Adena Road) 45601. Phone: (740) 772-1500 or (800) 319-7249. www.adenamansion.com. Hours: Wednesday-Saturday 9:00am-5:00pm, Sundays and Holidays Noon-5:00pm (April-October). Admission: $10.00 adult, $5.00 student (5-12). Tours: Tours of the mansion begin on the hour, from 10:00am-4:00pm, with no tour at noon. Educators: Adena to Go glossary, word search, and bios are on the link: www.ohiohistoryteachers.org.***

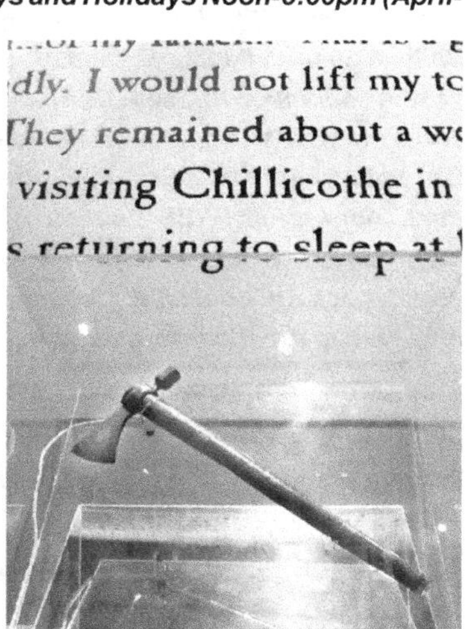

Tecumseh's tomahawk

View the overlook of the hillside that was used to paint the picture for the Ohio State Seal. Adena was the 2000-acre estate of Thomas Worthington (1773-1827), sixth governor of Ohio and one of the state's first United States Senators. The mansion house, completed in 1806-1807, has been restored to look much as it did when the Worthington family lived there, including many original Worthington family furnishings. Look for Thomas Jefferson's invention, a giant dumb waiter - why was it called that? Adena is an important site for many reasons. It is the only plantation-type complex of its kind in the state and the stone mansion was built by the Father of our Statehood. Also visit a tenant house, smoke house, wash house, barn and spring house. Begin at the Visitors Center for an overview. Then, play games in two interactive areas, one dress-up, the other running a supply boat successfully in the early 1800s computer game area. A good area to study early Ohio statehood.

GREAT SEAL STATE PARK

Chillicothe - *Marietta Pike (3 miles Northeast of Chillicothe) 45601. Phone: (740) 773-2726. http://parks.ohiodnr.gov/greatseal*

Great Seal State Park is dedicated to the wilderness spirit of Ohio. The history of the Shawnee nation and Ohio's early statehood is in these hills. Rugged trails take visitors to scenic vistas of distant ridge tops and the Scioto Valley below. The Sugarloaf Mountain Trail (yellow), 2.1 miles, climbs through dense maple-dominated forests to the crest of Sugarloaf. This loop is short and rises almost 500 feet in less than a quarter mile. These very hills are depicted on the Great Seal of the State of Ohio, from which the park gets its name.

HOPEWELL CULTURE NAT'L HISTORICAL PARK

Chillicothe - *16062 State Route 104 (two miles north of the intersection of US 35 and SR 104) 45601. Phone: (740) 774-1126. www.nps.gov/hocu. Hours: Daily 8:30am-5:00pm. Extended closing at 6:00pm in the summer. Closed Thanksgiving, Christmas and New Year's Day, and on Monday/Tuesday during December-February. Grounds open daily dawn till dusk. Admission: FREE. Educators: click on Teachers, then Curriculum Materials for a guide to print. There is popular activity booklet for kids that come to the park. Along with this they also offer Native American games and pottery making for kids.*

The 120-acre park with 13-acre earthwall enclosure is home to 23 prehistoric burial and ceremonial mounds of the Hopewell Indians. The center presents the story of the prehistoric Hopewell culture with exhibits, brochures and the 17-minute video "Legacy of the Mound Builders." The park is a cool place for kids to learn about what happened in Ohio during the last 2000 years. Just wander through the park's museum, watch the short movie about the Hopewell culture, or stroll around the mounds.

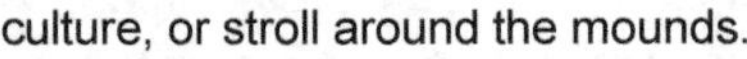

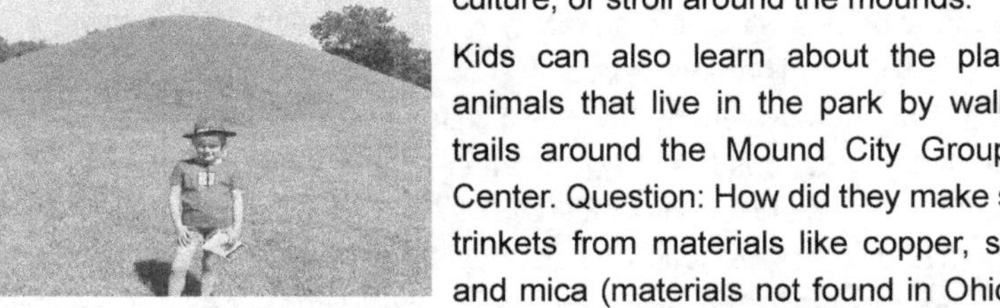

Kids can also learn about the plants and animals that live in the park by walking the trails around the Mound City Group Visitor Center. Question: How did they make so many trinkets from materials like copper, seashells and mica (materials not found in Ohio)? After viewing many effigy (animal-shaped) pipes, maybe purchase a reproduction (inexpensively) as a souvenir.

ROSS COUNTY HERITAGE CENTER

Chillicothe - *45 W. Fifth Street (near Paint Street, downtown) 45601. Phone: (740) 772-1936. www.rosscountyhistorical.org. Hours: Tuesday-Saturday 1:00-5:00pm (April-December). Friday & Saturday only (January-March). Admission: $4.00 adult, $2.00 senior & student.*

See the table upon which Ohio's Constitution was signed and Thomas Worthington's sea chest! See exhibits on early Chillicothe (diorama of town in 1803) and Ohio, Civil War (Camp Sherman -- "Ohio's World War I Soldier Factory,"), World War I and the Mound Builders. Also the Knoles Log House Museum (everyday life in early 1800's Chillicothe) and Franklin House Women's Museum. Kids will be intrigued by stories of olden times like: No garbage pickup? Just throw it in the streets. Or, how did the saying: Peas, Porridge Hot...Peas, Porridge Cold...Nine Days Old" come about (something to do with leftovers!). And, why didn't they use forks? Learn the real "scoop" about Conestoga wagons. Look through an authentic old-fashioned ViewMaster (Megalethoscope). Because this complex showcases the first capital of Ohio, it has early Ohio historical value hidden in every corner!

SCIOTO TRAIL STATE PARK

Chillicothe - *144 Lake Road (10 miles South of Chillicothe off US 23) 45601. Phone: (740) 663-2125. http://parks.ohiodnr.gov/sciototrail*

A small, quiet park nestled in beautiful 9,000-acre Scioto Trail State Forest, this state park is an undisturbed wooded refuge. Twelve miles of hiking trails and 17 miles of bridle trails lead to scenic overlooks and breathtaking vistas. 248 acres of camping, hiking, boating, canoeing, fishing and winter sports.

SUMBURGER RESTAURANT

Chillicothe - 1487 North Bridge Street 45601. Phone: (740) 772-1055. www.sumburger.com. Add to your "telephone" experience in town (Telephone Museum listing), eat a casual lunch or dinner (ordered from table telephones) at Sumburger. If you want an even more authentic 50s experience, drive your auto into a covered spot, order from the menu into the intercom and soon your order is delivered and set on a tray next to your driver window. The house specialty is of course the Sumburger, "a jumbo all beef patty served up on a hot bun with melted cheese, lettuce, and our own special sauce."

TECUMSEH

Chillicothe - ***5968 Marietta Rd, Sugarloaf Mountain Amphitheater (US 23 to Bridge St. exit, left on SR 159, right on Delano Road) 45601. Phone: (740) 775-0700 or (866) 775-0700. www.tecumsehdrama.com. Hours: Monday-Saturday, Show time 8:00pm. Show ends around 10:45pm. Reservations please. (early June to Labor Day weekend) Admission: $15-$25.00 Prehistoric Indian Mini-Museum. Backstage Tour - 4:00 or 5:00pm ($5.00). The stuntmen of TECUMSEH! give a dazzling display of stage-combat and flintlock firing, then pitch headfirst from a twenty-one foot cliff, get up, and explain how they did it. Tours last approximately one hour and also include make-up demonstrations (including mock "yummy" blood bags & Native "tanning" products) and detailed historical information on the drama and area. Note: Gift Shop & Restaurant with buffet (good food & entertainment - $8.95 - $15.95 per person) served a few hours before show. Warning: We recommend the Drama for 4th graders and older who have studied Ohio History and understand the savage, violent conflicts.***

This production has received national attention. Witness the epic life story of the legendary Shawnee leader as he struggles to defend his sacred homelands in the Ohio country during the late 1700's (before Ohio was a state). Fast action horses, loud firearms and speeding arrows make the audience part of the action especially when costumed actors enter the scene from right, left and behind. Lots of lessons learned about courage, honor, wisdom and greed...for kids and adults. We left quietly sobbing. As the actor playing Tecumseh said to us afterwards, "we got it."

TELEPHONE MUSEUM, JAMES M. THOMAS

Chillicothe - ***68 East Main Street 45601. Phone: (740) 772-8200. Hours: Monday-Friday 8:30am-4:30pm. Closed holidays. Suggested $1.00 donation.***

Run by the Chillicothe Telephone Company, it shows the telephone from its invention stages to modern times. The museum features telephone equipment and paraphernalia dating back to 1895. Included are telephone instruments, early local directories, wooden underground conduit and a working section of electro-mechanical "step-by-step" switching equipment. Free tours by appointment.

FEAST OF THE FLOWERING MOON

Chillicothe - Yoctangee City Park, just north of Main Street near the Railroad tracks. www.feastofthefloweringmoon.org. This three-day themed event features Native-American dancing, crafts and village as well as a mountain-man encampment depicting pioneer life in the early 1800's. Extensive quality arts and crafts displays, food, entertainment, and a variety of activities to see and do. Free. (Memorial Day Weekend – Friday thru Sunday)

APPLE FESTIVAL

Chillicothe - Hirsch Fruit Farm, 12846 State Route 772. Apples & cider. Apple pie eating contests. Apple peeling contests. Apple butter. Candy apples. Wagon/ hayrides. Apple Dumplings, Fritters, Donuts, etc. Parades. Pioneer crafts. Petting Zoo. Orchard tours, pick-your-own apples. www.hirschfruitfarm.com. (third weekend in September)

BURR OAK STATE PARK

Glouster - *10220 Burr Oak Lodge Road (6 miles Northeast of Glouster off State Route 13) 45732. http://parks.ohiodnr.gov/burroak. Phone: (740) 767-3570 or (740) 767-2112 Lodge.*

Located in southeast Ohio, quiet and remote Burr Oak State Park has a rustic country charm in its scenery of wooded hills and valley farms. Twenty-eight miles of hiking trails, including a portion of the state's Buckeye Trail, take hikers to scenic vistas and unique rock outcroppings. There are 30 family cottages with air conditioning and cable TV situated near the lodge in the wooded hills overlooking the lake. A public swimming beach offers enjoyment for swimmers and sunbathers. Nature programs, Bridle trails, Guest rooms in the Lodge with an indoor pool, tennis and basketball courts are highlights of this park. Also camping, hiking trails, low power boating and rentals, fishing, swimming, and winter sports.

SMOKE RISE RANCH RESORT

Glouster - *6751 Hunterdon Road (US 33 to SR 78 to CR 92) 45732. Phone: (740) 767-2624 or (800) 292-1732. www.smokeriseranch.com.*

Saddle up and get ready to discover your inner cowboy. Full service campground or cabins. Working Cattle Ranch (Ridin' & Ropin'), Riding Arenas, Trail riding. Activities Include: Round Up Rides , Pool and Hot Tub Parties, Hay Rides, BBQ's , Team Ropings and Team Pennings, Music Events and Dances.

TAR HOLLOW STATE PARK

Laurelville - *16396 Tar Hollow Road (10 miles South of Adelphi off State Route 540) 43135. Phone: (740) 887-4818. http://parks.ohiodnr.gov/tarhollow*

Dense woodlands of scattered shortleaf and pitch pines growing on the ridges were once a source of pine tar for early settlers, hence the name Tar Hollow. Dogwoods, redbuds and a variety of wildflowers color the hillsides in the springtime. The 2-mile Pine Run mountain bike trail begins at the general store. 634 acres of camping, hiking trails, boating, fishing, swimming.

Hocking Hills (Logan)

HOCKING HILLS STATE PARK

Logan - *19852 St. Rt. 664 South (Route 33 south to Route 664, follow signs) 43138. Phone: (740) 385-6841 or (800) HOCKING. http://parks.ohiodnr.gov/hockinghills Hours: 6:00am-Sunset (Summer), 8:00am (Winter).*

In the mid 1700's, several Indian tribes traveled through or lived here including the Wyandot, Delaware and Shawnee. Nature trails are found throughout the park, many of them lead to obscure, out-of-the-way natural creations. The park includes: Ash Cave (an 80 acre cave and stream), Cantwell Cliffs, Cedar Falls, Conkle's Hollow, Rock House, and the most popular, Old Man's Cave (a wooded, winding ravine of waterfalls and caves). The recess caves at Ash Cave, Old Man's Cave and Cantwell Cliffs are all carved in the softer middle rock. Weathering and erosion widened cracks found in the middle layer of sandstone at the Rock House to create that unusual formation.

Old Mans Cave Visitor Center: How about a hike to Old Man's Cave or Cedar Falls or Cantwell Cliffs. Do you realize none of these individual hikes is more than one mile long? While you're at the Center, be sure to check out their Butterfly Habitat or hand feed hummingbirds at Lake Hope St Pk, south of the Caves area. If you're more of the city type and just want one great short hike on a mostly paved trail (wheelchair/stroller accessible), just follow the signs to Ash Cave (near intersection of SR 56 & SR 374) - especially in the spring or fall when rainfall creates a wonderful Cave and Waterfall view!

The Park offers Naturalist Programs year round: weekends in early spring, and weekdays & weekends in summer and fall. Here's a sampling of the FREE programs we liked best: Historic Lantern Tours, Star Gazing at Conkle's Hollow, Stream STompin', Furs, Feathers, and Feet and Fangs (oh my!). And if you like folklore, Naturalist Pat Q loves to tell stories peppered with extraordinary characters. From caves that once served as a hideout for bank robbers or home for a Civil War-era hermit, to abandoned clay kilns from the 1800s, the Hocking Hills are full of stories. Your children's sense of adventure will soar!

Overnight accommodations, bed and breakfasts, camping, cabins with A/C, heat and fireplaces, recreation, picnic grounds, and hiking. Concessions available at Old Man's Cave or dining in the Lodge, seasonally (with outdoor pool). We recommend close supervision on the hiking trails for your child's safety.

HOCKING HILLS STATE FOREST: 9,267 acres in Hocking County. Hiking trails (9 miles), Bridle trails (40 miles), horse campground, see a former fire lookout tower, rock climbing a rappelling area, and state nature preserves.

MAPLE SUGARING IN THE HILLS

Logan – Hocking Hills State Park. Meet at Old Man's Cave Naturalist Cabin behind the Visitors Center. Discover the many methods used to make this tasty treat from maple sap. Free samples available. Pancake breakfast is offered at the dining lodge for a fee. (first weekend in March)

HOCKING FALL COLOR TOUR

Logan – Rockbridge, Hocking State Forest. Enjoy a guided tour at Cedar Falls and a hayride through the fall colors, along with a bean dinner. FREE. (October)

LAKE LOGAN STATE PARK

Logan - *30443 Lake Logan Road (4 miles West of Logan off State Route 664) 43138. Phone: (740) 385-3444. http://parks.ohiodnr.gov/lakelogan.*

One of the best fishing lakes in Ohio, the lake sports northern pike, bass, bluegill, crappie, catfish and saugeye. Across Lake Logan Road from the beach, the one-mile Pine Vista Hiking Trail circles a hilltop, providing opportunities for nature study and wildlife observation. 527-foot public swimming beach is located on the north shore of the lake on Lake Logan Road (CR 3). 717 acres of hiking, boating and rentals, fishing, swimming and winter sports for day-use only.

OLD MANS CAVE CHALETS

Logan - 18905 SR664S. 43138. (800) 762-9396 or www.chaletshh.com/about-old-mans-cave-chalets. Ok so you know how to have fun in all this nature, but where do you base from? We tried a pet-friendly cabin (sleeps six - 2 parents, 2 kids, one grandma and one dog) at Old Man's Cave Chalets. They offer last-minute getaway deals and reduced cost midweek escapes for affordable prices with the added bonus of being clustered near natural attractions (great views). Each unit has fully furnished bedrooms, bath, kitchen and living spaces, plus, our unit had a gas fireplace and an outdoor, canopied large hot tub! If it was cold, we lit the fireplace or climbed in the hot tub. If it rained we stayed indoors and played cards or watched a movie. Best of all, it was a xozy place to come back to after a day being out in nature traversing land and water. And, Snowshoes, the Travel Dog, got to come along! Cabins start at $139/night. ____________

WASHBOARD MUSIC FESTIVAL

Logan - Town Center (Main, Market, Spring Streets). http://washboardmusicfestival.com/ Home to the World's Largest Washboard. Fun filled weekend event for the whole family. Free tours of the Columbus Washboard Company, the only washboard factory left in the United States. Continuous music, factory tours, quilt show and food. FREE. (Father's Day weekend in June)

Hocking Hills (McArthur)

LAKE HOPE STATE PARK

McArthur - *27331 SR 278 (12 miles Northeast of McArthur on State Route 278) 45651. Phone: (740) 596-5253 or (740) 596-0400 restaurant. http://parks.ohiodnr.gov/lakehope*

Lake Hope State Park lies entirely within the 24,000-acre Zaleski State Forest in the valley of Big Sandy Run. It is a rugged, heavily forested region traversed by steep gorges, narrow ridges, abandoned mines, ancient mounds and beautiful scenery. The dining lodge features The Stone Terrace Restaurant, meeting room, General Store, as well as lodge and cottage reservation office. A fine swimming beach is located near the dam. Nature programs. 3,223 acres of camping, family cabins, hiking, boating and rentals, fishing, swimming.

ZALESKI STATE FOREST: The Zaleski State Forest Sawmill is Ohio's only publicly owned and operated sawmill. It began operation in 1967. The "low-tech" approach taken at Zaleski gives the mill an almost historical significance. It is an efficient functioning mill that turns out specialty orders for many public works projects. Additionally, demonstrations and training activities (for example, grading workshops) are held every year at Zaleski. 26,827 acres in

Vinton and Athens counties. Bridle trails (50 miles), 3 walk-in camp areas (self-registration permit - no fee) and sawmill. Lake Hope State Park is adjacent.

HOLIDAY LIGHTS

McArthur – Lake Hope State Park. www.1800hocking.com/whattodo/holiday_trail_of_lights_at_lake_hope_state_park.htm. Hundreds of thousands of lights & holiday / storybook characters. Walk thru. (daily, all month of December)

Hocking Hills (Rockbridge)

GREAT EXPECTATIONS BOOKSTORE AND CAFE

Rockbridge - off US 33 in the Hills Market Complex of shops. www.hockinghills.com/greatexpectations/ The Cafe offers great soup of the day and famous sandwich paninis. The kids loved the Pizza Sandwich. Shop and browse while you wait for your meal. Reasonable prices for lunches (~$6 includes pickle and chips). Their desserts looked tempting. Well-behaved leashed dogs are welcome at the outdoor patio tables.

HOCKING HILLS CANOPY TOURS

Rockbridge - *10714 Jackson Street 43139. www.hockinghillscanopytours.com. Phone: (740) 385-9477. Tours: Scheduled in advance - daily April thru October. Hours change seasonally due to available light.*

Trust us, this is the one extra "high" adventure you should save up for. Professional guides lead you along 10 ziplines and 4 Sky Bridges. Fast, fun, and exhilarating, this 3-hour tour offers guided, instructed tours to zip through the treetops on a network of safety cables and skybridges suspended high above the forest floor. As a mom, I can assure you that not once did I feel my kids or myself were in danger or fear. They really know how to orient you to the "bunny glides" first before you hit the Screaming Eagle! Each season offers new vistas as you swing and swoop like a bird from zero to 70 feet above the ground tree-to-tree over a cave, rock cliffs, a river, and maybe see a beaver dam or even deer. Canopy tour guests finally land in a lush "Garden of Eden" and rappel down a short cable to the final ground platform. Soft adventure, good for anyone who likes mild amusement rides and doesn't have a fear of heights. This experience leaves you floating on air! Course fee: $90-$94.00.

Less expensive Super Zip tours give just a taste of zipping. Over a quarter mile long, and speeds as fast as 50 mph, the SuperZip is the answer to requests for "higher, longer, and faster" zip. $30.00 for 1st zip, $20.00 each additional SuperZip.

Dragonfly Zip is for kids. This tour includes 8 kid-friendly ziplines and 4 adventure bridges. Dragonfly boasts a "continuous-belay" safety system that allows children to stay connected to the cable from start to finish...no transferring necessary. $29.00 per person (ages 5 to 12 and 35 to 140 lbs).

Marietta

CAMPUS MARTIUS

Marietta - *601 2nd Street (2nd and Washington Street ,Downtown) 45750. Phone: (740) 373-3750. www.campusmartiusmuseum.org Hours: Mondays, Wednesday-Saturday 9:30am-5:00pm and Sundays and Holidays Noon-5:00pm (March-October) Admission: $7.00 adult, $4.00 student (K thru college w/ ID). Combo passes offered w Marietta Ohio River Museums. Educators: Treasure hunts & Vocabulary enhanced self-guided tours about settlement, migration, production and pioneer living are online at the ohiohistoryteachers.org*

Campus recreates early development of Marietta as the first settlement in the Northwest Territory. The Putnam House is the oldest residence in Ohio and the smell of old wood and the hearthen floors make this tour authentic to the senses. The home and land office display replicas of the hardships of early pioneer life including old surgical and musical instruments. An exhibit titled "Paradise Found and Lost" highlights migration from farms to cities and from Appalachia to industry. Find videos and interactive computer games on migration. You can actually create a feeling of being taken back in time by walking through the train passenger car and listening to stories of passengers taking a trip to the "big city" for business or jobs (Stories told on telephone handsets). Another interactive area is lined with mining jackets and helmets to try on. See huge photographs of Columbus and Marietta in the early 1900's that take up an entire wall - you'll feel as if you're walking into them!

MARIETTA TROLLEY TOURS

Marietta - *241 Front St (the Armory, I-77 exit 6 towards downtown) 45750. Phone: (740) 350-9852. www.facebook.com/TrolleyToursMarietta. Hours: Saturday 10:00am (May) Tuesday-Saturday 10am and 7pm (June-October). Schedule can vary. Admission: $10.00-$15.00 (ages 5+).*

Narrated one-hour tours describing and viewing historic architecture, shops along Front Street, Marietta College and more. Start with this tour as soon as you get into town as a relaxing orientation. Then, you'll know which Museums are worth the price of your time and money without having to feel like you have to visit them all. While in town, park once and then walk the rest of the day - everything is packed into their quaint downtown.

OHIO RIVER MUSEUM

Marietta - ***601 Second Street (St. Clair & Front Street, Downtown) 45750. Phone: (740) 373-3717 or (800) 860-0145. www.ohiohistory.org/places/ohriver. Hours: Mondays and Wednesday-Saturday 9:30am-5:00pm. Sunday Noon-5:00pm (April - Labor Day). Noon-5:00pm (September-October). Admission: $7.00 adult, $4.00 student (all ages). Educators: find a scavenger hunt worksheet, "turkey" or mussels workshop, or River Explorers workshop online at ohiohistoryteachers.org link. Also, note group tours are early fall and early spring, even though the museum is not open to the public.***

The Ohio River Museum consists of three exhibit buildings, the first of which houses displays depicting the origins and natural history of the Ohio River. The golden age of the steamboat is featured in the second building, along with a video presentation on river steamboats. The last building features displays about boat building, mussels inn the Ohio River system, and tool and equipment from the steamboat era.

The WP Snyder, Jr. moored along the museum is the last surviving stern-wheeled towboat in America. Also, see a model of a flat boat and other scale models of many riverboats. A video titled, "Fire on the Water" describes dangerous early times when boilers might explode, killing many. Diorama (full scale) of wildlife along the Ohio River.

OHIO RIVER STERNWHEEL FESTIVAL

Marietta - Ohio River Levee. https://ohioriversternwheelfestival.org/. Thirty plus sternwheelers dock for the weekend, some for commercial and some for residential use. Continuous musical entertainment, fireworks and grand finale sternwheeler races. FREE. (weekend after Labor Day)

THE CASTLE

Marietta - ***418 Fourth St. 45750. Phone: (740) 373-4180. www.mariettacastle.org. Hours: Daily (Summer); Thursday - Monday (April, May, September-December). Weekdays 10:00am-4:00pm. Weekends 1:00-4:00pm. Admission: $7.00-$10.00 (age 6+).***

Historic area furnishings. Impressive parlor and chandelier. Videos and fun old time entertainment upstairs.

CHRISTMAS OPEN HOUSE - castle is decorated for the holidays and Santa's visit, entertainment and light refreshments. (generally first weekend in December)

VALLEY GEM STERNWHEELER

Marietta - *601 Front Street, under Washington Street Bridge (State Route 60 and State Route 7) (Docks next to the Ohio River Museum under the Washington Street Bridge) 45750. www.valleygemsternwheeler.com. Phone: (740) 373-7862. Admission: $7.00-$14.00 (ages 3+). Tours: Narrated Public Sightseeing Cruises are available at 1:30pm Daily (July, August), plus most days in June. Saturdays only in May & September. Note: Gift and snack area on board. Heated A/C cabin. Catered meal cruises too. The Riverera is an upscale restaurant at the Gem's dock.*

The gentle splash of the paddlewheel reminds you of a bygone era, but this modern-day sternwheeler has all the amenities to make your sentimental journey tranquil and relaxing. Take the 300 passenger, 60 minute cruise on the Valley Gem where the captain points out historic interests. See who can find the large stone blocks spelling "Marietta" on the landing welcoming steamboats. Why was the boat named after a piano company?

RED, WHITE AND BLUES

Marietta - Downtown. www.mariettaohio.org. A full day of parades, rides, entertainment & fireworks. (July 4th)

PUMPKIN MAZE PLAYLAND

Marietta - Sweetapple Farm, 149 Sweetapple Rd,CR 805. Pumpkin Patches / Hayrides / Corn Mazes / Fall Playland - Admission (average $6.00). Plan on at least two hours playtime. Open weekends, some weekdays (by appointment) & weeknights. www.sweetapplefarm.com (September - early November).

BIG MUSKIE BUCKET/ MINER'S MEMORIAL PARK JESSE OWENS STATE PARK

McConnelsville - *4470 E SR 78. 43756. Phone: (330) 222-1712. http://parks.ohiodnr.gov/jesseowens*

The Miner's Memorial is a monument to the achievements of the men and women of AEP and its subsidiary Central Ohio Coal Company, located along State Route 78. One of the main attractions of this memorial is the Big Muskie, which is the largest dragline ever built. This "bucket" moved more than 483 million cubic yards of material while in operation from 1969 to 1991. Two school buses (side by side) or an entire marching band could fit inside the bucket! Guilford Lake State Park is a quiet fishing lake located in northeastern Ohio on the west fork of the Little Beaver Creek.

The State Park is the newest and largest in Ohio. The rolling hills of Jesse Owens State Park and Wildlife Area are a success story in environmental stewardship, conservation and reclaiming land for outdoor recreation. Located in Morgan County and surrounded by thousands of acres of land open to public use, the 5,735-acre park and wildlife area is teeming with wildlife as well as ponds and waterways full of paddling, boating and fishing opportunities.

Nelsonville

HOCKING VALLEY SCENIC RAILWAY

Nelsonville - *33 Canal Street (Off US 33) 45764. Phone: (740) 470-1300 or (800) HOCKING. (513) 753-9531 (Saturday and Sunday). www.hvsry.com. Hours: Weekends 11am and 3pm, (Memorial Day weekend-early November). Special Holiday Schedule. Admission: $16.00-$25.00 general (age 3+). Upgrade at the depot to first class seating, in newly-restored luxury coach with toilet and air conditioning, by paying $2.00 more per person.*

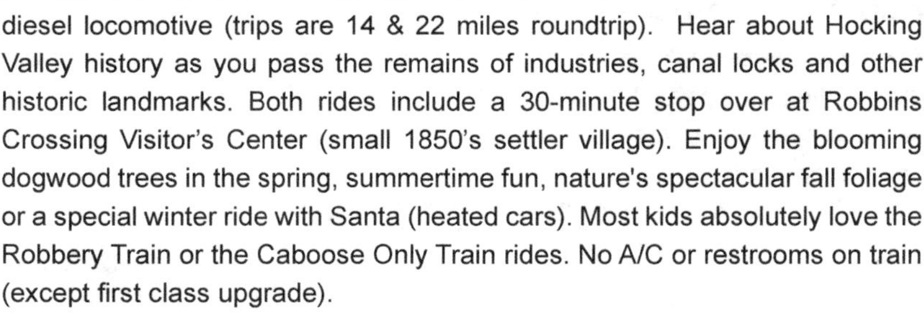

Ride through the hills of scenic Hocking Valley on an authentic 1916 steam locomotive or a 1950 diesel locomotive (trips are 14 & 22 miles roundtrip). Hear about Hocking Valley history as you pass the remains of industries, canal locks and other historic landmarks. Both rides include a 30-minute stop over at Robbins Crossing Visitor's Center (small 1850's settler village). Enjoy the blooming dogwood trees in the spring, summertime fun, nature's spectacular fall foliage or a special winter ride with Santa (heated cars). Most kids absolutely love the Robbery Train or the Caboose Only Train rides. No A/C or restrooms on train (except first class upgrade).

EASTER EGG HUNTS

Nelsonville – Hocking Valley Scenic Railway. Easter Bunny appearance, treat stations, egg hunts, and kids entertainment and crafts. Admission. (usually held the Saturday before Easter)

SANTA TRAIN

Nelsonville – Hocking Valley Scenic Railway. Train trip in decorated coaches with Santa. Songs and treats. Dress warmly. Admission. (select weekend dates in December)

PAUL BUNYAN SHOW

Nelsonville - Hocking College Campus. (740) 753-3591 or www.ohioforest.org. Ohio's largest forestry exposition features lumberjack competitions, forestry displays, guitar pickers championship and chainsaw sculpting. Admission. (first weekend in October)

ROCKY BOOTS OUTDOOR GEAR STORE & THE BOOT FACTORY GRILL

Nelsonville - off US 33 (downtown). www.rockyboots.com. Home of the world's best-selling work boots, this three story complex has 1000s of items at clearance prices plus local products at reasonable prices. All that shopping may get exhausting (esp if trying on dozens of boots) so you'll want to rest and grab something to eat. The Boot Factory Grill has a rustic, casual dining setting with some very reasonable gourmet lunch specials. If you're "game" try a bison burger.

JACKSON LAKE STATE PARK

Oak Hill - *35 Tommy Been Road (2 miles West of Oak Hill on State Route 279) 45656. Phone: (740) 682-6197. http://parks.ohiodnr.gov/jacksonlake*

The park's serene lake is a focal point for excellent fishing and provides the ideal setting for a peaceful walks. 200 foot sand beach provides recreation for swimmers and sunbathers. 335 acres of camping, boating, fishing, swimming and winter sports.

SERPENT MOUND

Peebles - *3850 State Route 73 (six miles north of State Route 32) 45660. Phone: (937) 587-2796 or (800)752-2757. www.greatserpentmound.com Hours: Museum open Daily 10:00am-4:00pm (April-October). Weekends only (November-March). Closed Jan/Feb. Park open year-round 10:00am-5:00pm. Admission: $8.00 per car. Note: Profile of the "cyptoexplosion" doughnut shape can be seen off State*

Route 770 - East of Serpent Mound.

The largest earthwork in the United States, it measures 1335 feet from head to tail and is about 15 feet high. The mound appears as a giant serpent uncoiling in seven deep curves. The oval doughnut at one end probably represents the open mouth of the snake as it strikes. The museum contains exhibits on the effigy mound and the geology of the surrounding area.

Portsmouth

PORTSMOUTH MURALS

Portsmouth - ***State Route 23 South, Front Street (Washington Street to Ohio River - follow green mural signs) 45662. www.ohiorivertourism.org. Educators: although the murals keep the attention of the kids best, you may consider adding a tour of the SOUTHERN OHIO MUSEUM, the 1810 HOUSE MUSEUM, or the STONE HOUSE. Visitors come in close contact with the past by walking through an actual home where residents lived for decades instead of looking through glass panes and roped-off areas.***

About 10 years ago, a committee was formed to begin a project that would take a 20 foot floodwall that protected its city from the Ohio River and transform it into 2,200 feet of magnificent art. Each mural tells the story of the history of Ohio and its people - beginning in the year 1730 and ending in 2002. Artist Robert Dafford (internationally known muralist) for years could be seen working on new murals. Our two favorites were Chillicothe Street 1940's (a very colorful, tremendously detailed, cartoon-like mural) and Twilight (a modern day view of the bridge over the river, looks like a photograph). What talent to be able to see a picture and then paint it to scale on a rough outdoor surface!

FORKED RUN STATE PARK

Reedsville - ***63300 State Route 124 (3 miles Southwest of Reedsville off State Route 124) 45772. Phone: (740) 378-6206. http://parks.ohiodnr.gov/forkedrun***

Located in the heart of Appalachia, colorful history, riverboats, scenic vistas and abundant wildlife give the park its rural charm. 400-foot sand beach offers enjoyment for swimmers and sunbathers. 817 acres of camping, hiking, low power boating and rentals, fishing, swimming, winter sports and food service. A disc golf course is on the property. Shade River State Forest (hiking trails) is adjacent (740) 554-3177.

BOB EVANS FARM

Rio Grande - *State Route 588, 791 Farmview Drive (off US 35 to State Route 325 South) 45614. Phone: (800) 994-FARM. www.bobevans.com. Hours: Daily 10:00am-4:00pm (May-October). Adm: FREE for tour - Activities additional.*

Begin or end your visit at the restaurant, once named "The Sausage Shop" - Bob's first restaurant. Then, wander 'round to visit the Farm (implements of yesteryear farms) and small animal barn yard, plus the Homestead (an old stagecoach stop and former home of Bob and Jewel Evans). At the Homestead Museum, sit at the reconstructed counter of the original Steak House owned by Bob Evans, view (on an old television console) commercials that were hosted by Bob and Jewell Evans in their own kitchen. See through the lens of an actual television camera of the era a setting of Bob and Jewell "at work" filming the ads and tour many other displays which form a life-sized "scrapbook of the business." Nearby in Bidwell (State Route 50/35) is Jewel Evan's Mill where you can view millstones grinding flour. Also in the area are good horseback riding stables and canoe liveries.

To make the bean soup for each Farm Festival, it takes 3.2 million beans (2,000 pounds)

FARM FESTIVAL

Rio Grande - Bob Evans Farm. Down on the farm feeling with over 100 craftspeople, country music, square dancers, homestyle foods and contests such as apple peeling, cornshelling, cow chip throwing and hog calling. Admission. (mid-October weekend)

LAKE WHITE STATE PARK

Waverly - *2767 State Route 551 (4 miles Southwest of Waverly on State Route 104) 45690. Phone: (740) 947-4059. http://parks.ohiodnr.gov/lakewhite*

Part of Lake White State Park includes the remains of the old canal channel. 358 acres of camping, unlimited power boating, fishing, swimming/beach and wintersports.

BUCKEYE FURNACE

Wellston - *123 Buckeye Park Road (two miles south of SR 124 on Buckeye Furnace Road in Jackson County) 45692. www.ohiohistory.org/visit/museum-site-locator/buckeyefurnace. Phone: (740) 384-3537. Hours: Park is open daylight hours. Museum is only open weekends from Noon-4:00pm (June - October). Group tours may make an appointment for weekdays. Admission: FREE, donations accepted. Educators: Excellent gradeschool aged lesson plans (self guided tour) are linked to ohiohistoryteachers.org site.*

Visit Ohio's only restored charcoal furnace which remains from the original 80 furnaces in Ohio. In the mid – 1800's, this industry took root as large trees were converted into charcoal to make iron for railroads and ammunition. The self-guided tour of the furnace shows you where raw materials (charcoal, iron ore, etc.) were brought to the top of the hill and poured into the furnace to be heated to 2700 degrees F. Impurities (slag) stayed on the top while liquid iron (which is heavier) flowed to the base. The reconstructed company store serves as a visitor orientation area. There are two nature trails.

LAKE ALMA STATE PARK

Wellston - ***Rte. 1 (3 miles Northeast of Wellston on SR 349) 45692. Phone: (740) 384-4474. http://parks.ohiodnr.gov/lakealma***

A quiet lake and a gentle creek meandering through a wooded valley provide a restful setting for park visitors. 2 public beaches are located on the north side of the lake. Approximately 3.5 miles of trail traverse hilltops and valleys offering hikers a scenic view of the park. A 1-mile paved walkway/bicycle path begins at the park entrance and ends at the park exit. 279 acres of camping, hiking, boating, fishing and swimming.

SHAWNEE STATE PARK

West Portsmouth - ***4404 State Route 125 (8 miles West of Portsmouth on State Route 125) 45663. Phone: (740) 858-6652. http://shawneeparklodge.com. Note: Watch out for thousands of ladybugs visiting each mid-October.***

Lodge rooms are furnished with American Indian and Appalachian furnishings and the restaurant serves an extensive children's menu (even steak), plus many good sandwiches and entrees. Many seasonal events include hayrides, hikes, campouts and cookouts (Autumn: Cornbread and Beans Black Pot Supper Days). Their one mile hiking trails are unpaved and just right for families. Public beaches are situated on Roosevelt Lake and Turkey Creek Lake, which offers vending machines. Nature programs, acres of camping, boating and rentals, fishing, swimming, winter sports and food service. Family cabins, lodge with indoor/outdoor pools, sauna, whirlpool, fitness center, tennis and basketball.

SHAWNEE STATE FOREST: 62,583 acres in Scioto and Adams counties. Ohio's largest state forest. Backpack trails (60 miles) with 8 walk-in camp areas (self-registration permit - no fee), Bridle trails (75 miles), horse campground (no fee), 5 small forest lakes, 8000 acre wilderness area. Shawnee State Park is adjacent.

Chapter 8 South West Ohio

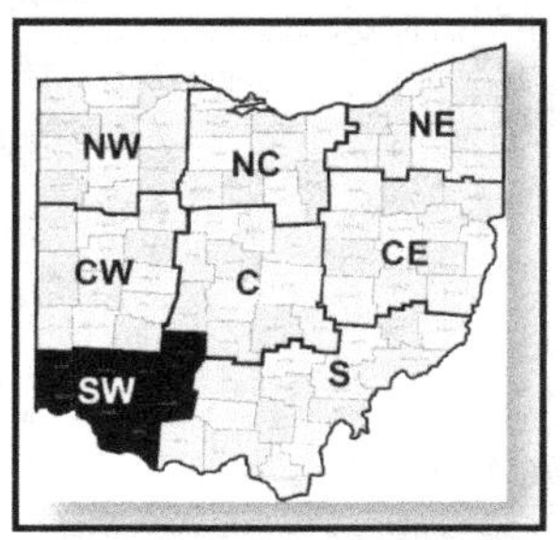

Bethel

- East Fork State Park

Cincinnati

- All American Birthday Party
- Carew Tower
- Cincinnati Art Museum
- Cincinnati Fire Museum
- Cincinnati History Museum
- Cincinnati Sports
- Cincinnati Symphony Orchestra
- Cincinnati Zoo And Botanical Gardens
- Coney Island
- Covedale Center For The Performing Arts
- Duke Energy Children's Museum
- Garfield Suites Hotel
- Krohn Conservatory
- Museum Of Natural History And Science
- National Underground Railroad Freedom Center
- Oktoberfest-Zinzinnati
- Parky's Farm
- Stowe House, Harriet Beecher
- Taft Museum Of Art
- Taft National Historic Site, William Howard
- United Dairy Farmers

Cincinnati (Covington, Ky)

- BB Riverboats

Cincinnati (Fairfield)

- Jungle Jim's International Market

Cincinnati (Loveland)

- Loveland Castle

Cincinnati (Milford)

- Cincinnati Nature Center
- Pumpkin Maze Playland

Cincinnati (Sharonville)

- Heritage Village Museum
- Homewood Suites By Hilton

Cincinnati (West Chester)

- Entertrainment Junction

Clarksville

- Pumpkin Maze Playland

College Corner

- Hueston Woods State Park

Corwin

- Little Miami State Park

Georgetown

- Glass Refactory
- Grant Boyhood Home

Hamilton

- Pumpkin Maze Playland
- Pyramid Hill Sculpture Park

Harveysburg

- Ohio Renaissance Festival

Hillsboro

- Rocky Fork State Park
- Thunder In The Hills Race

Kings Mills

- Kings Island & Boomerang Bay

Lebanon

- Lebanon Mason Monroe Railroad
- Pumpkin Maze Playland
- Warren County Historical Society Museum

Mason

- Great Wolf Lodge
- The Beach Waterpark

Middletown

- Light Up
- Middfest International

Okeana

- Governor Bebb Preserve

Oregonia

- Fort Ancient

Oxford

- McGuffey Museum

Pleasant Plain

- Stonelick State Park

Point Pleasant

- Grant Birthplace

Ripley

- Rankin House

Trenton

- Pumpkin Maze Playland

Waynesville

- Caesar Creek State Park

Wilmington

- Banana Split Festival
- Cowan Lake State Park

Hand-Picked Favorites Around...

South West Ohio

The first major-league pro baseball team was the Cincinnati Red Stockings, but the Cincinnati area has many more "major-league" attractions to offer. Spend the weekend exploring four great places in one historic building at the **Cincinnati Museum Center** at Union Terminal. Walk through the Ice Age and a recreated limestone cave at the **Museum of Natural History and Science** or let kids explore The Woods, an interactive adventure in the wilderness, at the Duke Energy **Children's Museum**. A Hands-on History Museum and an IMAX theatre are located here, too.

But that's not all there is to do for family fun. In the city you can climb down a real fire pole (**Cincinnati Fire Museum**). On the water you can **Ride the Ducks** and get Quacky with it. In the water, the greater Cincinnati area has two indoor waterparks and two outdoor waterparks.

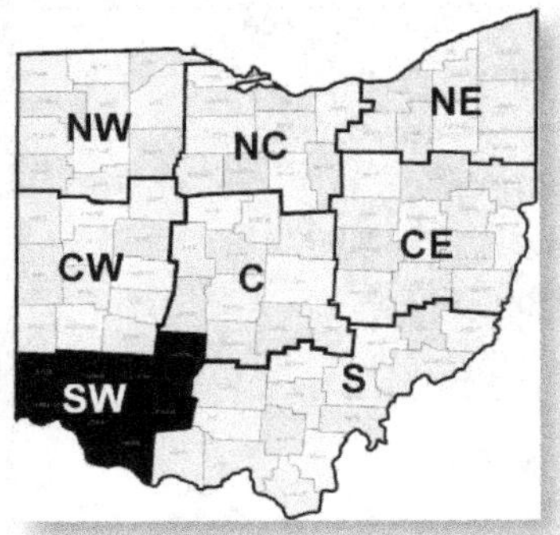

There are some pretty neat places just a little ways north of downtown Cincinnati that are so worth fitting into your next trip. A small pioneer village bustles with activity most every weekend at **Heritage Village** in Sharonville. Try your hand at churning butter or marching a Civil War battle drill at special events throughout the year. A hidden gem is **Loveland Castle** – a real castle over the spring and in the woods – that you can play like a knight or princess. You can pretend to be an engineer or a taste tester on tour at the giant **United Dairy Farmers** ice cream and milk factory. The reward for your icy cold adventure tour is freshly made ice cream sundaes at the end! Off the northern tip of the outerbelt you'll find a grocery store adventure at **Jungle Jim's**. This store is a supermarket that's a tourist attraction in Fairfield. Foodies and kids love the animals that greet you outside and the whimsical dioramas inside. Look for the Amish buggy, a shrimp boat, the Big Cheese, Elvis, a fire truck and even a walk through Sherwood Forest.

Finally, if you want to get away from the big city and wander a while in the woods, head for **Hueston Woods State Park Resort** in Oxford (home of Miami University). Stay overnight at the lodge or in a cozy cabin and in the morning head over to the Nature Center with programs including nature crafts, movies, fossils and animals – especially raptors in the rehab center.

Sites and attractions are listed in order by City, Zip Code, and Name. Symbols indicated represent: Restaurants Lodging

EAST FORK STATE PARK

Bethel - ***3294 Elklick Road (4 miles Southeast of Amelia off SR 125, I-275 exit 63 or 65) 45106. Phone: (513) 734-4323. http://parks.ohiodnr.gov/eastfork***

East Fork offers a great diversity of recreational opportunities and natural history only 25 miles from Cincinnati. The park's terrain includes both rugged hills and open meadows. There are 2,160 acres of water and unlimited horsepower boating with access available at six launch ramps. A 1,200-foot swimming beach features change boots with showers, restrooms and a vending area. 32-mile Steven Newman Worldwalker Perimeter Trail circles the park and is available for hikers, backpackers, and horsemen. 10,580 acres of camping, hiking, boating, fishing, swimming and winter sports.

CINCINNATI SPORTS

Cincinnati

When you're in the birthplace of professional baseball, you know you're in a place where sports are special. Have a major league experience at the Great American Ball Park - home of the Cincinnati Reds. Or experience the famous tailgating before, during or after a Cincinnati Bengals game.

CINCINNATI BENGALS - (513) 621-3550 or www.bengals.com. (I-75 exit 1A follow the 2nd Street signs) Be part of the jungle. Professional football at Paul Brown Stadium (downtown, riverfront). Join the Bengals Kids Club for great novelty items (August – December).

CINCINNATI REDS - www.cincinnatireds.com. (513) 421-REDS or (877) 647-REDS. (I-75 exit 1A follow the 2nd Street signs). Professional Major League baseball at the Great American Ball Park. First professional baseball team. Several family-friendly ticket days and fun promotions for kids on game days. ($5.00 - $25.00+) (April – September)

CAREW TOWER

Cincinnati - *441 Vine Street (5th and Vine, across from Fountain Square, Downtown, I-75 exit 1C) 45202. Phone: (513) 241-3888. www.cincyusa.com/attractions/carew-tower. Hours: Monday-Thursday 9:30am-5:30pm, Friday 9:00am-6:00pm, Saturday/Sunday 10:00am - 7:00pm.*

An 1930's Art Deco building that is the tallest building downtown. The building itself is a study in old and new. Modern elevators passing renovated plush office floors transport guests only as high as the 45th floor. A trip to the observation deck requires a ride in a rickety, phone booth-sized elevator to the 48th floor. The Observation deck has a panoramic view. Small admission fee per person ($1.00-2.00).

CINCINNATI ART MUSEUM

Cincinnati - ***953 Eden Park Drive 45202. www.cincinnatiartmuseum.org. Phone: (513) 721-ARTS. Hours: Tuesday-Sunday 11:00am-5:00pm. Extended Wednesday evening hours. Closed Thanksgiving, Christmas and New Years. Admission: FREE admission daily except for special exhibits.***

Art collection presents 5000 years of visual arts. Favorites include the Syrian Damascus Room, Blue glass chandelier, old musical instruments, Andy Warhol's Pete Rose and the futuristic robot (good size Contemporary Art Section). Family First Saturdays. Museum shop and café.

FIRE MUSEUM OF GREATER CINCINNATI

Cincinnati - ***315 West Court Street, near Plum, Downtown (I-75 exit 1C follow signs for 5th Street) 45202. Phone: (513) 621-5553. www.cincyfiremuseum.com. Hours: Tuesday-Saturday 10:00am-4:00pm. Closed holidays. Admission: $8.00 adult, $7.00 senior (65+), $6.00 child (7-17).***

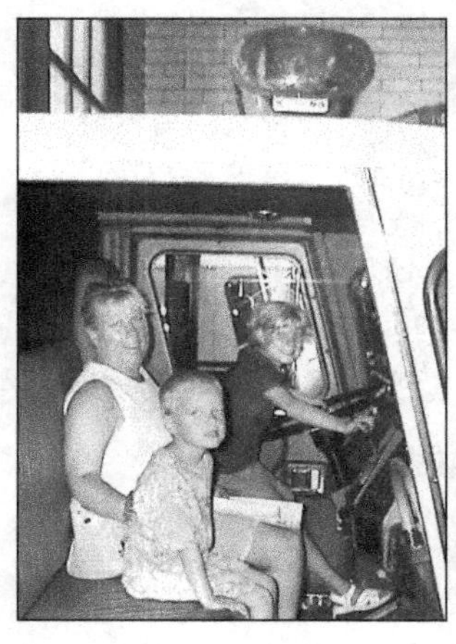

From the minute you walk in the restored fire station, the kids will be intrigued by the nation's first professional fire department exhibits. Displays chronicle fire fighting history from antique equipment to the cab of a newer fire truck where you can actually pull levers, push buttons, ring bells, operate the siren and flash emergency lights. The history of Cincinnati in frontier days comes to life as the children participate in a "hands-on" bucket brigade and take a turn on an old style hand pumper. The museum has an emphasis on fire safety with "Safe House" models (touch and demo area) and a video about fire fighting dangers. Before you leave be sure you slide down the 5-foot fire pole or ring the old fire bell. Let's Stop, Drop and Roll. Everyone can do it! This is the most kid-friendly fire museum in the Midwest!

GARFIELD SUITES HOTEL

Cincinnati , - 2 Garfield Place. 45202. www.garfieldsuiteshotel.com. Going to the city for some museum hopping with the kiddos? While you might be hesitant to stay downtown because of the normal upscale hotels offered (not kid-friendly), we have found one that caters to families. The Garfield Suites Hotel is just that- all suites! Every room rented is complete with a living room (w/ sofa sleeper) and at least one

separate bedroom. But the best part for families is the spaciousness of the living spaces and the full kitchen! While we could have gone down to the restaurant for breakfast and Starbucks each morning, we opted to cook a full course breakfast in our room. We grabbed lunch out n about but either re-heated leftovers or went to Cafe Martin for dinner. Cincinnati seems to be crazy for Angus beef burgers and sliders so we tried both and loved the flavor. When you're chilling in the suite after a long day at the zoo, amusements, or a variety of museums, we found relaxing in the suite, popping popcorn, watching a movie was a great winddown. Specials run starting ~$100 per night - with downtown adjacent parking at only $5.00 per day!

KROHN CONSERVATORY

Cincinnati - *950 Eden Park Drive (I-71 North to the Reading Road exit #2. Turn right at the end of the exit/traffic light onto Eden Park Drive) 45202. Phone: (513) 421-4086. www.cincinnatiparks.com/krohn. Hours: Daily 10:00am-5:00pm.*

A rainforest full of 5000 varieties of exotic desert and tropical plants. The Palm, Tropical, Desert and Orchid houses exhibit permanent displays of exotic plants in natural settings, complete with a 20 foot rainforest waterfall. One of the nation's largest - check out their seasonal displays. FREE, admission for special exhibits like the Enchanted Garden or Butterflies of Morocco.

CHRISTMAS OPEN HOUSE

Cincinnati – Krohn Conservatory. Buildings decorated for holidays, Santa visit, entertainment and light refreshments served. Great way to expose younger ones to historical homes that might be boring otherwise. Admission. (mostly first weekend of December)

NATIONAL UNDERGROUND RAILROAD FREEDOM CENTER

Cincinnati - *50 East Freedom Way (Cincinnati waterfront, I-71 exit 2nd street, I-75 exit 1A) 45202. Phone: (513) 333-7500. www.freedomcenter.org. Hours: Tuesday-Saturday 10:00am-5:00pm, Sunday-Monday Noon-5:00pm. Admission: $15.00 adult, $13.00 senior (60+) and students with ID, $10.50 child (3-12). Nearby parking can be pricey so look at options to park a little ways away and walk or get a shuttle. Note: Audio tours, one for adults and another for children, are available free of charge with paid admission. North Star Cafe.*

Ohio's involvement in guiding slaves to freedom is commemorated in a museum that helps tell the story of the Underground Railroad. The Center is made up of three buildings that symbolize the cornerstones of freedom - it's a warm art museum with an historical twist.

A dynamic presentation, the "moving painting" titled "Suite for Freedom" takes visitors on an emotional journey from freedom to un-freedom. Next, move on to the Slave Pen - used to "warehouse" slaves being moved further south for sale. ESCAPE! This child-friendly gallery uses storytelling and hands-on interaction. Probably the only area designed for kids, time can be spent listening to choices slaves must make, then testing YOUR decisions as a computer-interactive slave yourself. From Slavery to Freedom takes the visitor on a journey from the slaves' arrival in the New World through the Colonial period to the Civil War. The Concluding Experience area is designed to help each visitor put into personal perspective all that he or she has just experienced. What does freedom mean today? Visitors can participate in individual polling based on "what would you do" scenarios. This is serious stuff, be sure your children are prepared to think about their reactions to the material. (The site would be an excellent student post-study of Pre-and-Post Civil War era history).

TAFT MUSEUM OF ART

Cincinnati - ***316 Pike Street (Broadway to Fifth to Pike Sts, I-75 exit 1C) 45202. Phone: (513) 241-0343. www.taftmuseum.org. Hours: Wednesday-Sunday 11:00am-4:00pm, weekends open until 5:00pm. Admission: Online $10 adult, $8 senior (60+) and youth (12-17). Kids are FREE. The museum is FREE to all on Sundays. Educators: Lesson plans online under Education icon. Note: Café and gift shop.***

See works of European and American painters, Chinese porcelains, Limoges enamels displayed in a federal period mansion. At the greeter's desk on the second floor, pick up one of the Family Gallery Guides (ex. Animals, Children). Select Saturdays "Families Create!" programs combine storytelling and games with art-making activities. If you need an action break, Lytle Park is across the street and is a great play space.

CINCINNATI HISTORY MUSEUM

Cincinnati - ***1301 Western Avenue, Cincinnati Museum Center (I-75 south exit 2A; I-75 north exit 1G) 45203. www.cincymuseum.org. Phone: (513) 287-7000 or (800) 733-2077. Hours: Daily 10:00am-5:00pm. Closed Thanksgiving and Christmas. Admission: $10.50-$14.50 per person. Toddler (age 1-2) rates are 1/2 price. Combo prices with other museums available. Parking fee. Note: Gift Shops. OmniMax Theatre on premises has several shows daily (a movie fee is charged per person). Educators: look for a wide list of pdf Teachers Guides on current and past exhibits on the online icons: www.cincymuseum.org/educators/resources/***

As you enter the museum, your eyes will race around the Cincinnati in Motion model of the city (from 1900-1940) with interactive computer booths. Most of the transportation moves (planes, trains, cars, etc). Next, you'll visit with The Flynns talking about life at home during World War II. Hop on board a streetcar with the conductor telling news of the war. Now, walk through a life-like forest with shadows and birds wrestling and singing. Then, walk through re-created streets of Cincinnati. Visit the Fifth Street Market and Millcreek Millery - try on hats of the early 1900's and then shop next door at the pretend open air market. The kids can play in a miniature cabin and flat boat, then actually board a steamboat and pretend you're the captain. Very authentically presented, clever displays throughout the whole museum.

DUKE ENERGY CHILDREN'S MUSEUM

Cincinnati - *1301 Western Avenue, Cincinnati Museum Center (I-75 south exit 2A; I-75 north exit 1G) 45203. www.cincymuseum.org. Phone: (513) 287-7000 or (800) 733-2077. Hours: Monday-Saturday (& Holidays) 10:00am-5:00pm, Sunday 11:00am-6:00pm. Closed Thanksgiving and Christmas. Admission: $8.50-$10.50 per person. Toddler (age 1-2) rates are lower. Combo Museum center passes available. Parking fee. Note: Museum stores (great kids gift ideas). Snack Bar.*

Start in the Woods, kiddies. The dim lighting adds mystery to the slides, tunnels, rope climbing mazes and walls, and treehouses. The Energy Zone has kids move plastic balls along a conveyor to a gigantic dump bucket. It's actually a gigantic physics experiment in this Zone - lots of machines and tubes to move balls. Other highlights are the Little Sprouts Farm (age 4 and under), Water Works, Kids Town (pretend town), or Animal Spot (lots of unusual skeletons). We liked how most areas required friend's/parent's participation to complete a task.

MUSEUM OF NATURAL HISTORY AND SCIENCE

Cincinnati - *1301 Western Avenue, Cincinnati Museum Center (I-75 south exit 2A; I-75 north exit 1G) 45203. www.cincymuseum.org. Phone: (513) 287-7000 or (800) 733-2077. Hours: Daily 10:00am-5:00pm. Closed Thanksgiving and Christmas. Admission: $10.50-$14.50 per person. Toddler (age 1-2) rates are lower. Combo prices with other museums. Parking fee. Note: Gift Shops - Worth a good look! OmniMax Theatre on premises has several shows daily (a movie fee is charged per person). Educators: look for a wide list of pdf Teachers Guides on current and past exhibits: www.cincymuseum.org/educators/resources.*

Want to know a lot about the Ohio Valley's Natural and Geological history? The Cave simulated area is a wonderful walk-thru reproduction that is so real, it's almost spooky. The simulated Limestone Cavern with underground waterfalls and a live bat colony (behind glass!). (There are two routes - one that is challenging and involves much climbing and navigating, and the other that is wheelchair or stroller accessible). Look for lots of dino skeletons in Dinosaur Hall. Find out about Space Exploration as you aim for the stars. See if you have the right stuff, like John Glenn, or follow in the small steps and giant leaps of Neil Armstrong. This exhibit features a 360° theater experience and artifacts that can only be seen in Cincinnati. Plan a few hours at this extremely well done museum - we promise it will engage you and you'll learn many new things!

CINCINNATI SYMPHONY ORCHESTRA

Cincinnati - ***1241 Elm Street 45210. www.cincinnatisymphony.org. Phone: (513) 381-3300. $10-$25.00 tickets.***

The CSO presents soloists, pops concerts and an artist series in Music Hall. Young People's Concerts introduce students to orchestral music and performance with stimulating prep activities done beforehand. Lollipop Concerts are themed concerts with instrument demos and hands-on activities. CSO RiverBend Music Center hosts Symphony/Pops Orchestra, plus contemporary artists (May-September).

UNITED DAIRY FARMERS

Cincinnati - ***3955 Montgomery Road, 45212. Phone: (513) 396-8700 - Ask for Consumer Relations. Admission: FREE. Tours: Mondays and Fridays, 9:30am-1 ½ hours, Ages 6 and up. Maximum 25 persons. Advice: They only book tours on Nov 1st for Jan-June of the next year and on May 1st for July-December of the current year. I was also told that you have to start calling at 8:00am on those days because the tours book up for the 6 month time period in just a few hours!!! Certainly not for the impromptu, but it's worth the effort!***

Who wouldn't love a visit to a giant science factory that makes ice cream? In 1938 Carl H. Lindner Sr. had an idea to start a small dairy in Norwood, Ohio. At a time when almost all milk was home-delivered and paid for on a weekly or monthly basis, Carl Sr. had a new concept: he would process milk and other dairy products and sell them, cash-and-carry, at his own dairy store. Begin your tour, as a group, weighing yourselves on their giant truck scale! See milk being filled in containers (and the large vats where they store raw and treated milk). The plastic bottles are also made on the premises from tiny pellets of plastic melted, blown up and compressed (see it up close). Next, stop in and visit with the Food Scientists in the Flavor Lab (maybe help pick a new flavor). Best of all, watch ice cream packed and frozen (you even get to step inside the deep-freeze room!). Get a free ice cream sundae (flavor of the day - right off the production line) as a souvenir. We have found this to be one of the best organized, interesting and fun factory tours around!

STOWE HOUSE, HARRIET BEECHER

Cincinnati - ***2950 Gilbert Avenue (corner of MLKing Drive) (SR 3 and US 22) 45214. Phone: (513) 751-0651. http://stowehousecincy.org/index.html. Hours: Thursday-Saturday 10am-4pm & Sunday Noon-4pm. Admission: $3.00-$6.00***

The home of the author of "Uncle Tom's Cabin" novel that brought attention to the evils of slavery. Displays describe the Beecher family, the abolitionist movement and the history of African-Americans. Request the video about the story of the book. Mrs. Stowe's journal is available for viewing, as are photo quilts of slave faces. This museum is best visited after some study of the anti-slavery roots along the Ohio River. The videos are long, but helpful.

HIGHFIELD DISCOVERY GARDEN

Cincinnati - ***10397 Springfield Pike 45215. www.greatparks.org/parks/glenwood-gardens/the-highfield-discovery-garden Phone: (513) 771-8733. Hours: Wednesday-Saturday 9:30am-5pm, Sunday Noon-5:00pm. Admission: Admission: $5.00/ person. $2.00/person in winter.***

This 12-acre garden is a delight for any age. Along with the 25-foot Discovery Tree, there are seven smaller gardens to explore within the Garden: Frog & Toads Garden - Look closely between those lily pads and you'll see they are surrounded by frogs. Wizard's Garden - Pass the purple hat, don't wake the dragon and take the bouncy bridge to the fairy garden. Trolley Garden - Four small scale trains run on tracks surrounding some of your favorite storybook characters. Vegetable Garden - Raised beds will put you eye level with common and unusual vegetables. Grandma's Scent Garden - You'll be surrounded by smelly plants for your pretend tea party in this garden. Morph Garden - The caterpillars in this garden are huge! Butterfly Garden - This garden is shaped like its favorite resident.

TAFT NATIONAL HISTORIC SITE, WILLIAM HOWARD

Cincinnati - ***2038 Auburn Avenue (I-71S, take Exit 3 (Taft Road). Go 3/4 mile to Auburn Avenue. Turn left and go 1/2 mile to the home) 45219. Phone: (513) 684-3262. www.nps.gov/wiho. Hours: Daily 8:30am-4:45pm. Closed Thanksgiving, Christmas and New Year's. Admission: FREE - Donations accepted. Note: Check out the orientation video first in the Education Center adjacent. Tours every 30 minutes on the hour and half hour.***

Visit the birthplace and boyhood home of a US President and Chief Justice. Four of the rooms are furnished to reflect Taft's family life 1857-77. Other exhibits depict his public service career. The signature exhibit of the center is an animatronic figure of the President's Son, Charlie Taft. Charlie tells stories about different family members. Children's group tours give kids the opportunity to dress up from a trunk of period hats and over-garments and play with old fashioned toys. This really helps the children understand life for a young person in the mid-1800's.

CINCINNATI ZOO AND BOTANICAL GARDENS

Cincinnati - ***3400 Vine Street (I-75 to exit 6, Mitchell Ave) 45220. Phone: (513) 281-4700 or (800) 94-HIPPO. www.cincinnatizoo.org. Hours: Daily 9:00am-6:00pm (Summer); 9:00am-5:00pm (Winter). Admission: $18.00 adult, $13.00 child (2-12). Children's Zoo and rides are $2.00-$6.00 additional. Parking Fee $10.00. Look for online specials. Note: Safari Restaurant. Concessions. Tram and train rides, 4D Theater, & Carousel (additional fee), Children's Zoo & Animal Nursery. Wildlife Theatre. Stroller rentals. FREEBIES: Self-Guided Scavenger Hunts.***

Recognized by Child Magazine as one of the "10 Best Zoos for Kids."

Ranked one of the top 5 zoos in the United States, its highlight is the successes in breeding white Bengal tigers and other rare wild animals. Komodo dragons (10 feet long and 300 lbs!) and endangered Florida Manatees are some of the large, unusual animals there. Visitors can pass into the underwater world of the manatee in a freshwater spring habitat. The Lords of the polar bears on land and nose-to-nose through underwater glass panels, too. Dramatic waterfalls and a polar bear cave, with educational interactives complement the exhibit. The zoo added to its furry family the first-ever Mexican wolf pups born in 2007 - now exploring Wolf Woods in the Children's Zoo. And you'll also find a new eye level experience - Giraffe Ridge. This 27,000 square-foot exhibit, complete with an elevated viewing platform, provides an amazing

interactive experience, bringing guests eye-to-eye with a herd of giraffes. Their landscaped gardens duplicate the animals' world and the Jungle Trails exhibit even has a tropical rainforest. The first Insectarium (you guessed it!) in the nation is also here.

EASTER CELEBRATION

Cincinnati – Cincinnati Zoo & Botanical Gardens. Easter Bunny appearance, treat stations, egg hunts, Zoo Blooms, and animal enrichment. Admission. (Easter weekend and/or weekend before)

FESTIVAL OF LIGHTS

Cincinnati – Cincinnati Zoo & Botanical Gardens. Ice Skating, decorated villages, and Santa. All include hundreds of thousands of lights & holiday / storybook characters. Daily, evenings. Admission. (Thanksgiving - January 1)

CONEY ISLAND

Cincinnati - *6201 Kellogg Avenue (Off I-275 East) 45228. Phone: (513) 232-8230. www.coneyislandpark.com. Hours: Daily: Pool 10:00am-8:00pm, Rides 11:00am-9:00pm (Memorial Weekend-Labor Day). Admission: $11.95-$20.95 pricing for pool OR rides day pass. Online discount. Discount combo park passes (Ages 5+). Tikes pricing around $7.95. Discount prices after 4:00pm. Parking $8.00 per vehicle.*

Sunlite, the world's largest re-circulating pool (200' x 401' and holding more than three million gallons of water!) with a huge slide and 6 diving boards, is one of the many fun attractions. Also, The Challenge Zone, Zoom Flume water toboggan, Pipeline Plunge tube water slide, Typhoon Tower playspace, Giant Slide, kiddie rides, classic rides (Scrambler, Ferris Wheel, Tilt-a-whirl, etc) miniature golf, bumper boats, pedal boats and picnic areas.

PARKY'S FARM

Cincinnati - *10073 Daly Road (Winton Woods Park) (Winton Road & Lake Forest Drive) 45231. www.greatparks.org/parks/winton-woods/parkys-farm Phone: (513) 521-PARK. Hours: Winton Park open daily during daylight hours. Farm open daily (late morning to late afternoon) but activities only open daily during the summer and weekends (including Fridays) in the Spring and Fall.*

The park has a 3-mile paved hike-bike trail (bike rental is available), bridle trail and riding center on the south side of Winton Lake.

The park also has picnic areas, a 1-mile fitness trail, a boathouse, nine shelters and an 18-hole Frisbee golf course and a regular golf course. At Parky's Farm explore orchards and crops plus farm animals. Pony rides, Wagon Rides and PlayBarn (farm theme play pits with plastic apples and eggs to jump in) cost $3.00 each. Note, some parts of farm are open only in the summer.

COVEDALE CENTER FOR THE PERFORMING ARTS

Cincinnati - *4990 Glenway Avenue (I-75 to Harrison Ave exit. Follow signs to Queen City Ave, take that 2 miles. Left on Sunset Ave. Right on Glenway) 45238. Phone: (513) 241-6550. www.cincinnatilandmarkproductions.com/ccpa/. Hours: Thursday-Saturday 8:00pm, Sunday 2:00pm (mid-April-mid-October). Additional shows on Wednesdays and Sundays on the Majestic. Weekends (November, December seasonal shows).*

Contemporary and classic musicals, comedies and dramas. Choose venues from the Showboat Majestic - live riverfront shows (moored at Broadway St landing); Cincinnati Young Peoples Theatre - end of summer drama; or the Covedale Center Performances - including a Christmas Carol. average $25.00 for tickets.

ALL AMERICAN BIRTHDAY PARTY

Cincinnati – Sawyer Point , downtown. A full day of parades, rides, entertainment and fireworks. (July 4th)

OKTOBERFEST-ZINZINNATI

Cincinnati - Fifth Street, downtown. www.oktoberfest-zinzinnati.com. The nation's largest authentic Oktoberfest featuring seven areas of live entertainment, food and a children's area. FREE. (third weekend in September)

BB RIVERBOATS

Cincinnati (Covington, KY) - *Covington Crossing, just over the blue suspension bridge (I-75 exit 192 to Riverboat Row) 45202. Phone: (800) 261-8586. www.bbriverboats.com. Admission: $24 and up. Basically, double the cost if meal served. Children nearly half price. Tours: 1 1/2 hour sightseeing cruises on the Ohio River. Several times daily (best to call for schedule). Reservations Required (May-October). Concessions on board.*

Docked at the foot of Madison Street see the Modern "Funliner", "Mark Twain" sternwheeler or steamboat "Becky Thatcher". Also theme cruises like Lock and Dam, River Pirates, or year-round holiday tours. Many cruises offer additional lunch, brunch and dinner cruise options with live entertainment.

JUNGLE JIM'S INTERNATIONAL MARKET

Cincinnati (Fairfield) - ***5440 Dixie Highway (Route 4) (I-75 exit 16 west on I-275 to exit 41 north) 45014. Phone: (513) 674-6000. www.junglejims.com. Hours: Open daily 8:00am-10:00pm.***

A grocery store is an adventure? This store, selling exotic foods is! This Fairfield, Ohio landmark is as popular a supermarket as it is a tourist attraction. Ohio's Famous Playground for Food Lovers (Foodies) allows customers to shop in four acres of food from all around the world all under one roof. Plastic animals and giant fruits greet you. Once inside, the store is divided into theme areas. Visit Amish Country, The Ocean, Europe, South America, India and the Middle East. Does the Big Cheese ever change? Try some new food like medallions of alligator! Their fish are so fresh, they keep them in holding ponds and tanks in the store until they are ready to be purchased. You can view this tanks and a mezzanine walkway near the indoor ponds. Spicy food is inside a walk-thru firetruck - hot. Food from England lies under a moving display of Robinhood and friends in the Sherwood Forest. Even Elvis is here and will occasionally sing a tune while you choose pastries.

A replica of the SS Minnow in a supermarket? Be sure to allow lots of time to explore here!

LOVELAND CASTLE

Cincinnati (Loveland) - ***12025 Shore Road (2 miles South of Kings Island) 45140. Phone: (513) 683-4686. www.lovelandcastle.com. Hours: Daily 11:00am-5:00pm (April-October). Weekends only (Nov – March). Admission: $5.00 general admission (age 6+). Self-guided tour. Higher fee for special events. Tours: Guided tours are weekdays, by appointment (warm weather season). Groups must have 20+. 35-40 minute tours. Note: Only authentically built medieval castle in the United States. Call for directions. Dads: Any man of high ideas who wishes to help save civilization is invited to become a member of the Knights of the Golden Trail, whose only vows are the Ten Commandments.***

This is a real hidden castle and a huge family favorite!

Chateau LaRoche was the vision of Harry D. Andrews and construction spanned some 50 years beginning in 1929. He actually did 99% of the work himself!

The castle is authentic in its rugged structure with battlement towers, a princess chamber, a dungeon, narrow passageways, tower staircases, a "king's" dining room, and tower bedrooms. Over 32,000 hand-made (cast in milk cartons donated by neighbors) bricks were used to build parts of the structure (ask to see a sample). Learn a lot about castle building and why the front door has over 2500 nails in it. A real Knight of the Golden Trail (or Lady) will greet you and answer any questions throughout your visit. If you're brainy, try some of the challenging games and puzzles that Harry and his Knights designed. Curious about Harry and his Knights? Look for the 10 Commandments Creed in the Chapel and the video interviews with Harry playing continuously upstairs. If you have time, plan to bring a picnic, they have many tables scattered near the garden or the water below. Don't miss this real adventure that your children and you will love (maybe even play pretend - bring along dress up clothes)!

CINCINNATI NATURE CENTER

Cincinnati (Milford) ***- 4949 Tealtown Road, 45150. www.cincynature.org. Phone: (513) 831-1711. Hours: Open all year, dawn to dusk. Visitor Center: daily 9am-5pm. Admission: $9.00 adult, $6.00 senior (65+), $4.00 child (4-12).***

This original Cincinnati Nature Center site boasts 18 miles of hiking trails for visitors to explore and enjoy. Educational programs for people of all ages take place in this outdoor classroom. Hike a trail through pristine natural habitat at Rowe Woods, Milford or Long Branch in Goshen. Or, explore the children's garden and farmyard at Gorman Heritage Farm, Evendale (www. gormanheritagefarm.org). Some properties are only open for events.

PUMPKIN MAZE PLAYLAND

Cincinnati (Milford) - Shaw Farm, I-275 & Rte 131 due north. Pumpkin Patches / Hayrides / Corn Mazes / Fall Playland - Admission (average $6.00). Plan on at least two hours playtime. Open weekends, some weekdays (by appointment) and weeknights. Weekday educational tours learning how farm grown products reach your supermarket. www.shawfarmmarket.com. (late September - late October).

HERITAGE VILLAGE MUSEUM

Cincinnati (Sharonville) - *11450 Lebanon Pike, Sharon Woods Park (I-75 exit 16 east to US 42, 1 mile south of I-275 exit 46) 45241. www.heritagevillagecincinnati.org. Phone: (513) 563-9484. Hours: Wed-Sat 10am-5pm, Sun 1-5pm. (May-Sept). Wed-Fri 10am-4pm (Oct-April). Guided Tours: $7 adult, $3 child (5-11). Educators: Click on the Teachers Page under Education Programs. Note: Dressed interpreters. Bicycle rental, hiking trails. $2.00 entry into Sharon Woods park (per vehicle). Many picnic & shelter areas, mostly wooded for shade. General Store with many pioneer hand-make items.*

See 18th Century Ohio. Nine actual buildings from Southwest Ohio including: The Elk Lick House - "fancy house", learn about the Gothic Ohio clock and why the "mouse ran up the clock"; the Train Station - with its treasure trunk hands-on pieces to play with; Kemper Log House - look for Isabella's sampler (Little House on the Prairie theme here) and the "Y" staircase; the kitchen and smokehouse - during festivals they cook here; and the medical office - see Civil War medical and pharmaceutical equipment-amputation city! Their Kids History Camps are wonderfully organized.

CIVIL WAR DAYS

Cincinnati (Sharonville) - Heritage Village Museum becomes the backdrop for fascinating civil war adventures in an authentic 19th-Century setting. Demonstrations of military and civilian activities, military drills, inspections, Calvary units and general camp life, with many hands-on activities for all ages. Admission. (second or third weekend in May)

HARVEST FEST

Cincinnati (Sharonville) - Heritage Village Museum. The weekend is full of heritage games, crafts, activities, entertainment, demos and refreshments. Included in the bountiful Harvest Fest are "pioneer chores", candle dipping, sack races, tug-o-war, scarecrow making, hearth cooking, etc. In addition, the Village hosts guided tours of its 19th-century buildings. Admission. (last wkend in September)

HOLLY DAYS

Cincinnati (Sharonville) - Heritage Village Historic 1800s Village decorated with the old fashioned tastes of gingerbread, molasses cookies, candy, & bread pudding. One of the historic houses in the Village interprets Hanukah in the mid 1800's where guests taste latkes and other traditional Jewish foods. Music and song plays through out the village. Village Train Station has Forest of Christmas Trees. Admission. (first two weekends of December)

HOLIDAY IN LIGHTS

Cincinnati (Sharonville) - Sharon Woods. www.holidayinlights.com. (mid-November thru December)

ENTERTRAINMENT JUNCTION

Cincinnati (West Chester) - *7379 Squire Court (I-75 exit 22 toward Mason) 45069. Phone: (513) 898-8000. www.entertrainmentjunction.com. Hours: Monday-Saturday 10:00am-6:00pm, Sunday Noon-6:00pm. Closed only Easter, Thanksgiving and Christmas. Admission: $14.95 adult, $11.95 senior (65+) and child (3-12). There is a separate charge of $2.50 for the Kids' Express hand-cranked locomotives (open seasonally June-Labor Day), weather permitting. Seasonal Journey prices run $9.95 extra.*

EnterTrainment Junction offers the largest interactive indoor G-scale layout known, with more than two miles of track and 90 trains, depicting every era of American railroading (called the Train Journey). Start in the early days (pre-Civil War) up to the present. Each train car (over 1,200 of them!) is about the size of a loaf of bread. Even though they're big, they're not all at eye level - some are below and some even high in the air. Actual water flows through canals and rivers into a large lake with a huge waterfall backdrop. Lots of tunnels, small towns, trestles and trains shine with lights. There's also an American Railroading Museum and a 5,000-square-foot play area for kids called "Imagination Junction," that includes a climbing structure and interactive games.

SEASONAL JOURNEY:

- FUNHOUSE (January - September): old-time amusement park fun house.
- JACK-O-LANTERN JUNCTION (fall): well-lit mazes through an old Victorian village that is slightly haunted. Mirror mazes, clown rooms, chain-link mazes, and a wind tunnel.
- CHRISTMAS AT THE JUNCTION (winter): walk-thru either A Christmas Carol scene or a Journey to the North Pole.

The Junction also offers train displays of all different sizes, as well as exhibits on railroading and model railroading.

PUMPKIN MAZE PLAYLAND

Clarksville - Bonnybrook Farms, 3779 SR 132. Pumpkin Patches/ Hayrides / Corn Mazes / Fall Playland. www.bonnybrookfarms.com. Admission (average $6.00). Plan on at least two hours playtime. Open weekends, some weekdays (by appointment) and weeknights. (late September - late October).

HUESTON WOODS STATE PARK

College Corner - ***6301 Park Office Road (5 miles North of Oxford off State Route 732) 45003. http://huestonwoodslodge.com/. Phone: (513) 523-6381 or (800) 282-7275 reservations.***

A big feature of this park is the Nature Center with programs including their nature crafts, movies, fossils, and fabulous animals (like bobcat, cougar, bunny, snakes, turtles). The Raptor Rehab Center is where they care for injured animals, nursing them back to health (hawks, owls, etc). At the park is also a Rent-a-Camp, biking and rentals, camping, hiking/bridle trails and rentals, boating and rentals, fishing, swimming and winter sports. Kids/Family activities include swimming pool games, candy crafts, guided hikes (fossil hunts) and the ever popular, Bingo games. Evening hikes and bonfire/marshmallow roasts, too. There are cute, cozy, newly remodeled family cottages and a lodge with overnight rooms, indoor / outdoor pools, sauna and fitness areas.

MAPLE SYRUP FESTIVAL

College Corner – Hueston Woods State Park. Meet at the main beach parking area. Explore the process of maple sugaring from the methods used by Native Americans to the modern methods used today. Pancake breakfast is offered for a small fee. Tour the sugar bush. (first and second weekend in March)

LITTLE MIAMI STATE PARK

Corwin - ***(North of Corwin) 45068. Phone: (513) 897-3055. http://parks.ohiodnr.gov/littlemiami.***

As the river twists and bends, visitors will discover many natural wonders such as steep rocky cliffs, towering sycamores and elegant great blue herons on the wing. Little Miami State Park introduces a new concept to the state park system--a trail corridor. This non-traditional approach focuses on offering numerous recreational pursuits--bicycling, hiking, cross-country skiing, rollerblading, backpacking and horseback riding. The corridor also provides access to canoeing the Little Miami River. Three staging areas (Loveland, Morrow and Corwin) have been located along the developed portion of the park. These include parking lots, restrooms, public phones and trail access points.

Georgetown

GLASS REFACTORY

Georgetown - *9262 Mt. Orab Pike 45121. www.glassrefactory.com. Phone: (888) 291-5690. Admission: FREE. Tours: By appointment, Tuesday-Friday 9:00am-5:00pm. Minimum group size is 8, maximum is 75. Must be at least 6 years old.*

Recycling with a twist...recycling bottles into pieces of art. First collect used glass, melt it and form it into suncatchers. Custom designed molds and some whimsical. Some of their items are sold in the gift shop at places like the National Underground Railroad Freedom Center. Plan to bring $6.00-$10.00 to purchase one at the shop.

GRANT BOYHOOD HOME

Georgetown - *219 East Grant Avenue (one block west of SR 125) 45121. Phone: (937) 378-4222. www.usgrantboyhoodhome.org Hours: Wednesday-Sunday Noon-5:00pm (May-October). Admission: $3.00-$5.00 per adult or student. Educators: a bio of Grant is on the link to ohiohistorycentral.org.*

The Grant Boyhood Home in Georgetown was the home of Ulysses S. Grant, 18th president of the United States, from 1823, when Grant was one year old, until 1839, when he left to attend West Point. Ulysses Grant lived in this home longer than any other during his lifetime. Ulysses worked in his father's tannery and, from the ages of about six to thirteen, he attended classes in the little schoolhouse on Water Street. The home was restored and furnished, with one room which is dedicated to Grant and Georgetown memorabilia.

PYRAMID HILL SCULPTURE PARK

Hamilton - *1763 Hamilton-Cleves Road (I-275 to SR 27 to SR 128) 45011. Phone: (513) 868-8336. www.pyramidhill.org. Hours: Daily 10:00am-5:00pm (until 6:00pm weekends April-October). Admission: $8 adult, $3 child (6-12).*

Pyramid Hill is an outdoor museum focusing on monumental pieces of sculpture in an environment of meadows, forests, and various gardens. Their mission is to have a collection which will demonstrate the complete history of sculpture, making Pyramid Hill the only art park in the world working on the accomplishment. This park currently has 50 titled sculptures. Especially noticeable is "Abracadabra" by internationally famous sculptor, Alexander Liberman. Many passengers flying into Cincinnati can see the 2 ½ story high, bright red contemporary walk-thru sculpture from above.

Isn't Rockababy Moon sweet? The Baroque Trajectory arrived the summer of 2002. This piece survived the September 11 attack - it stood just 3 blocks away in New York City!

HOLIDAY LIGHTS ON THE HILL

Hamilton – Pyramid Hill Sculpture Park. Hundreds of thousands of lights & holiday / storybook characters. Daily, evenings (unless noted). Admission. (Thanksgiving - January 1)

PUMPKIN MAZE PLAYLAND

Hamilton - Neiderman Farm, 5110 Lesourdsville West Chester Rd. Pumpkin Patches / Hayrides / Corn Mazes / Fall Playland - Admission (average $6.00). Plan on at least two hours playtime. Open weekends, some weekdays (by appointment) and weeknights. www.niedermanfamilyfarm.com. (late September - late October).

OHIO RENAISSANCE FESTIVAL

Harveysburg - 5 miles East of Waynesville on SR-73. www.renfestival.com. (513) 897-7000. The recreation of a 16th century English Village complete with costumed performers, strolling minstrels, may pole dances, full-armored jousting, sword play or feast on giant turkey legs and hearty bread bowls. Two Student Days (Wednesdays) are open special each year: (This is the recommended time to attend with families) Interview Sessions with Queen Elizabeth, Puppet Theatre, Experiment with Historical Games & Rides, Pirate Invasions on the 65-foot Pirate Ship, Combat Demonstrations, Knighthood & Chivalry Discussions, Scottish Dance & Bagpipe Demonstrations, Music Workshops. Admission average $8-15.00 (age 5+). (weekends beginning end of August through mid-October)

ROCKY FORK STATE PARK

Hillsboro - *9800 North Shore Drive (6 miles Southeast of Hillsboro off State Route 124) 45133. Phone: (937) 393-4284. http://parks.ohiodnr.gov/rockyfork*

Unlimited horsepower boating allows for excellent skiing on the lake which also provides catches of bass, muskellunge and walleye. A scenic gorge, dolomite caves and natural wetlands add to the popularity of this recreation area. A 1.5 mile hiking trail takes visitors through cool woodlands, scenic gorges and moist wetlands. A short trail near the campground takes nature lovers to an observation station where excellent birdwatching can be pursued. A two-mile mountain bike trail is also popular with park visitors. 3,464 acres of camping, hiking, boating rentals, and swimming.

RUMBLE IN THE HILLS HYDROPLANE RACE

Hillsboro - Rocky Fork Lake State Park. www.facebook.com/rockyforklakeoh/?hc_location=ufi. Hydroplane boat racing, 2nd largest race in the country. FREE. (mid-Sept)

KINGS ISLAND & SOAK CITY

Kings Mills - ***I-71 to Exit 25A or 24 (24 miles North of Cincinnati) 45034. Phone: (513) 754-5700. www.visitkingsisland.com. Hours: Daily 10:00am-Dark (Late April-Late August). Weekends Only (September, October). Park closed for maintenance first two weeks of September. Admission: Gate Price: ~$72.00 general, ~$45.00 child (3-6) and senior (60+). Ticket includes both the amusement park and the waterpark. Good discounts available at area hotels, online and at local stores. Online tickets can save up to $21. Check local tourism site. Parking Fee $12.00. Note: Three restaurants plus 60 fast food areas. Local favorites like LaRosa's Pizza, Graeter's Ice Cream, Montgomery Inn Ribs and Skyline Chili. Kings Island is smoke-free (except in designated areas).***

Some of the 80+ featured attractions at King's Island are: SOAK CITY Water Park Resort - The Aussie-themed resort area has more than 50 water activities, including 30 water slides, tropical lagoons, rushing rivers, surfable waves, three family activity areas and careening waterfalls. ACTION ZONE – The Beast (longest wooden coaster), The Crypt (1st indoor coaster to catapult in the dark at high velocity), Thunder Alley (racing car simulator of high speed stock car racing), Backlot Stunt Coaster, Whitewater Rides; the Racer (the Racer is also notable for its appearance in an episode of The Brady Bunch, filmed at the park in 1973), Adventure Express mine ride - journey into ancient temples, proceed thru chambers and strap into a vehicle to make a daring escape. Kings Island has the greatest variety of children's attractions, including four kids' coasters (more than any park in the world), a collection of 20 rides and the fun, live stage shows including: PLANET SNOOPY includes a total of 18 rides and attractions bringing to life Peanut's popular character celebrities and adventures. Most popular with school age kids. Family rides of all types. Live shows throughout the park, too.

Lebanon

LEBANON MASON MONROE RAILROAD

Lebanon - ***(two depots: Cincinnati Riverfront - 1901 River Rd (west of downtown) & Lebanon - 198 South Broadway/US 42) 45036. Phone: (513) 398-8584 or (513) 933-8022 info line. www.lebanonrr.com. Departures: Late Morning, Noon, Early Afternoon. Thursday-Sundays (peak) and weekends year-round. Admission:***

$14.00 adult, $10.00 senior (62+), child (2-16). Special rates for theme train rides for the holidays and Day Out with Thomas. Note: Station Depot with Gift Shop. The passenger cars do not have restrooms and are not heated or air-conditioned. You are permitted to bring snacks and beverages on the trains. Refreshments are also available for purchase on specific rides.

LEBANON: The one-hour rides depart from Historic downtown Lebanon and travel along the original CL&N line. Trains operate with a restored 1950s-era GP-7 diesel-electric locomotive, open window commuter coaches built in 1930 and a popular open-air gondola car on the rear of the train allows you to enjoy a panoramic view of the countryside. Besides the holiday trains, they have fun theme train rides like: Meet Daniel Tiger, Princess and Snow Sisters Trains. So fun you probably can't just do one!

CINCINNATI: Climb aboard their 1950's / 1960's vintage stainless steel High-Level streamliner coaches and settle back for a nostalgic journey. You'll be treated to a unique High Level experience as you ride up above the surrounding terrain. Most excursions are half or whole day long.

EASTER TRAIN

Lebanon – Lebanon MM Railroad. Easter Bunny appearance, treat stations, egg hunts, and kids' entertainment and crafts. Admission. (usually held the Saturday before Easter)

PUMPKIN TRAIN

Lebanon – Lebanon MM Railroad. Take your little ones on a delightful train ride to the Pumpkin Patch where they can choose their special pumpkin to be transported back to the station on the flatbed car attached to the train. Ride the train to Schappacher Farm where you can pet animals, select a pumpkin and play in the hay before heading back. Small admission fee for ride and for pumpkin. (October weekends)

SANTA TRAIN

Lebanon – Lebanon MM Railroad. Train trip in decorated coaches with Santa. Songs and treats. Dress warmly. Admission. (Thanksgiving weekend thru weekend before Christmas)

WARREN COUNTY HISTORICAL MUSEUM

Lebanon - *105 South Broadway, 45036. www.wchsmuseum.org. Phone: (937) 932-1817. Hours: Tuesday-Saturday 9:00am-4:00pm, Sunday Noon-4:00pm. Admission: $2.00-$4.00.*

The Museum contains artifacts from prehistoric eras to the 1830s and mid-20th century periods. In its Village Green exhibit, antiques are displayed in re-created store fronts. They have the largest collection of Shaker furniture. The Golden Lamb (Ohio's oldest inn) is open for lunch/dinner. Many Presidents have spent the night here. Historical rooms.

PUMPKIN MAZE PLAYLAND

Lebanon - Irons Fruit Farm, 1650 Stubbs Mills Road. Pumpkin Patches / Hayrides / Corn Mazes / Fall Playland - Admission (average $6.00). Plan on at least two hours playtime. Open weekends, some weekdays (by appointment) and weeknights. Applefest in September. www.ironsfruitfarm.com. (late September - late October).

Mason

GREAT WOLF LODGE

Mason - *2501 Great Wolf Drive (I-71 Western Row Rd exit 24) 45040. Phone: (800) 913-9653. www.greatwolf.com/mason. Hours: Waterpark generally open 10:00am-8:00pm off peak days. Open until 10:00pm peak days. Admission: Basically a family stay package (includes waterpark passes) begins at around $120 but plan on double that during peak breaks or weekends. Day Pass = $70.00.*

It's always a balmy 84 degrees inside the resort's mammoth, 78,000 square-foot indoor waterpark. Bear Track Landing puts the emphasis on fun with 11 waterslides, six pools and a four-story treehouse waterfort. Besides the basics, try the new water roller coaster ride and cannon bowl tube ride or one of six pools: Gigantic wave pool, recreation pool, zero-depth entry children's pool, lazy river, adult whirlpool and family whirlpool. Supervised yet independent kid-friendly fun gives parents time to relax with children in sight.

Check out the Triple Twist - prepare yourself for a five-story drop into huge funnel followed by twists, turns and two more funnels before splashing down. And at night, the Triple Twist takes it up a notch as you are immersed ina full-sensory LED lighting experience. (ride is first of its kind in the world)

Great Wolf Lodge provides a comprehensive package of destination lodging amenities, including: 401 all-suite guest rooms; Camp Critter Bar & Grille, a themed family restaurant and bar; The Loose Moose Cottage, a gourmet buffet; Elements Spa featuring Scooops Kid Spa (an ice cream themed spa); MagiQuest game that immerses guests into a world of fantasy using a techno wand to solve the challenges around the resort; Cub Club children's craft and activity room; an animated Great Clock Tower; Northern Lights Arcade; Iron Horse Fitness Room; Bear Claw Café and confectionery, pizza, coffee and gift shops.

THE BEACH WATERPARK

Mason - ***2590 Waterpark Drive (I-71 Exit 25B - 20 miles North of Cincinnati) 45040. Phone: (513) 398-SWIM or (800) 886-SWIM. www.thebeachwaterpark.com. Hours: Daily opens 10:00am-Closing varies (usually at dark). (Memorial Wkend to mid-September). Admission: $20.00-$29.00 Children–Senior–General. Discounts after 4:00pm. Discount general admission tickets online. Parking fee $8. Note: Food Service. No outside food or drink allowed into the park. Bags checked.***

Over 40,000 square feet of beach and two million gallons of water and waves await you! As a tropical themed adventure for the whole family and the largest stand alone waterpark in Ohio, The Beach is situated on 35 acres of rolling wooded terrain that provides lots of shade and lush ambiance. Real live palm trees, real white ocean sand, real waterfalls and crashing waves help set the scene and Reggae music and sand volleyball reinforce the tropical island experience. Favorites include the Pearl leisure heated tropical spa pool, Aztec Adventure watercoaster, Thunder Beach Wave Pool and the Lazy Miami River inner tube ride. The young children's water area has Splash Mountain with warm water and Jolly Mon non-water areas!

MIDDFEST INTERNATIONAL

Middletown - One Donham Plaza, downtown. www.facebook.com/middfest/. Exhibits, music, authentic ethnic dances & menus from many countries. Youth Park. International sports and games, ethnic craft demos, food prep and customs. (October weekend)

LIGHT UP

Middletown - Smith Park, downtown off Rte. 73 / Rte. 4. Hundreds of thousands of lights & holiday / storybook characters. Drive thru. Daily, evenings. www.lightupmiddletown.org. Admission. (Thanksgiving - January 1)

GOVERNOR BEBB PRESERVE

Okeana - *1979 Bebb Park Lane (follow SR 129 (Hamilton-Scipio Road) about 8 miles. Turn left on California Road then right on Cincinnati-Brookville Road) 45053. Phone: (513) 867-5835 or (877) PARK-FUN. www.yourmetroparks.net/parks/governor-bebb-metropark Hours: Saturday and Sunday 1:00-5:00pm (summer). Park open daily from 8:00am-dark. $5 permit/vehicle.*

Visit the small 1812 village with the restored log cabin (birthplace of William Bebb - born in 1802). He was the governor of Ohio from 1846 - 48 and a trial lawyer noted for his emotional zeal. There is an 1850's covered bridge, picnic sites, a group picnic shelter, playgrounds, nature trails, restrooms and an on-site park ranger. Rustic family campsites, youth group campsites and a reservable cabin are also available. Good to visit during special events.

FORT ANCIENT

Oregonia - *6123 State Route 350 and Middleboro Road (I-71 to Rt. 123 to State Route 350) 45054. www.fortancient.org. Phone: (513) 932-4421 or (800) 283-8904. Hours: Tuesday-Saturday 10am-5:00pm, Sunday Noon-5:00pm (April-October). Weekends only (rest of year). Admission: $7.00 adult, $6.00 student (6-17).*

The Museum at Fort Ancient contains 9000 sq. ft. of exhibits, including many interactive units, focusing on 15,000 years of American Indian history in the Ohio Valley. Ohio's entire Indian heritage is displayed from prehistoric to modern times. The 100 acre field is where graves and artifacts were found and is also home to the second largest earthwork in the nation (constructed by Hopewell Indians between 300 BC - 600 AD). Great to visit during Indian Celebration weekends, Children's Day (games and chores) or Night Hiker evenings. Hiking trails.

MCGUFFEY MUSEUM

Oxford - *410 Spring St, Spring & Oak Sts. (Miami University campus area) 45056. Phone: (513) 529-2232 or (513) 529-1809 campus tours. www.miamioh.edu/cca/mcguffey-museum. Hours: Thursday-Saturday 1:00-5:00pm (Except Campus holidays and breaks). Campus tours are at your leisure during University hours of operation. Admission: FREE. Note: Points of interest around campus are: Gardens, Anthropology & Zoology Museums (Upham Hall), Geology Museum (Shideler Hall on Patterson), the Library and the Chapel.*

See an original collection of McGuffey Readers (lesson books on the three R's and morality, i.e. brotherly love, honesty and hard work). The First Eclectic Readers, published in 1836, started the series of books that was to educate five generations of Americans by 1920. They are still in print and still used today. The home, (built in the early 1830's) is where William Holmes McGuffey wrote his readers while preparing class work for children. On display is Professor McGuffey's lectern and traveling 3-part secretary/bookcase. Check out his eight-sided desk! Recently, they've added some activities for kids ages 3-12 (or so) - reproduction 19th-century costumes (for boys and girls), a butter-making activity in the Kitchen, readers to look at in the Library, and a reproduction stereoscope and cards to view in the Parlor. (yeah! we love when museums add more "hands-on" history).

STONELICK STATE PARK

Pleasant Plain - ***2895 Lake Drive (1 mile South of Edenton off State Route 727) 45162. Phone: (513) 625-7544. http://parks.ohiodnr.gov/stonelick***

An interesting feature of the Stonelick landscape is the significance of sweet gum trees. Normally, sweet gum is a subordinate tree but co-dominates the woodlands of Stonelick with beech and maple. Also, colonies of dense flying star, purple fringeless orchid and Virginia mountain mint - all uncommon wildflowers in Ohio - can be found in the park. 5+ miles of hiking trails provide opportunities for exercise and nature study. Hiking trails are also open to mountain bikes. A 500-foot public beach is located on the lake's south shore. 1,258 acres of camping, hiking trails, boating, fishing, swimming & winter sports.

GRANT BIRTHPLACE

Point Pleasant - ***219 East Grant Avenue (off US 52) 45157. Phone: (513) 553-4911 or (800) 283-8932. www.usgrantbirthplace.org Admission: $1.50-$3.00 per adult or student. Tours: Wednesday – Saturday 10am – 5:00pm, Sunday 1-5pm (May-September). Closed for lunch each day (except Sunday). 5th grade and above.***

Civil War General and 18th President's birthplace cottage with period furniture. This restored one-story, three-room cottage, which was built in 1817, was next to the tannery where Grant's father worked. At one time the birthplace made an extensive tour of the United States on a railroad flatcar and was also temporarily displayed on the Ohio State fairgrounds. The small white home has no heat and is sparsely lit – daytime in comfortable weather is best.

RANKIN HOUSE

Ripley - ***6152 Rankin Road, Rankin Hill (Northeast off US 52, Race Street or Rankin Road) 45167. www.ripleyohio.net/htm/rankin.htm Phone: (937) 392-1627 or (800) 752-2705. Hours: Wednesday-Saturday 10:00am-5:00pm, Sunday Noon-5:00pm (April - October). Admission: $2.00-$4.00 per adult or student. Educators: Lesson plans on Abolishanists is on the link to ohiohistoryteachers.org.***

This restored home of Reverend John Rankin (early Ohio abolitionist) was part of the Underground Railroad and home to Eliza, a character in "Uncle Tom's Cabin", who found refuge off the Ohio River. A lighted candle in an upstairs window of the Rankin House signaled slaves that it was safe to proceed on the route to freedom. They sheltered (along with neighbors) more than 2,000 slaves escaping to freedom. In this modest home, there were as many as 12 escapees hidden at one time. Winding roads lead to the remote cabin hidden in a clearing in the woods.

PUMPKIN MAZE PLAYLAND

Trenton - Barn N Bunk Farm Market, SR 73 & Wayne-Madison Road. Pumpkin Patches / Hayrides / Corn Mazes / Fall Playland - Admission (average $6.00). Plan on at least two hours playtime. Open weekends, some weekdays (by appointment) and weeknights. www.barnnbunk.com. (late September - late October).

Waynesville

CAESAR CREEK STATE PARK

Waynesville - *8570 East State Route 73 (State Route 73, 6 miles West of I-71, near Waynesville) 45068. Phone: (513) 897-3055. http://parks.ohiodnr.gov/caesarcreek*

The park's excellent fossil finds give testimony to the life of this long vanished body of water. The Caesar Creek area was named for a black slave captured by the Shawnee on a raid along the Ohio River. The Shawnee adopted Caesar and gave him this valley as his hunting ground. Caesar lived in this area during the time Blue Jacket was war chief and was said to have gone on many raids with him. Caesar Creek's clear waters and 1,300-foot beach offer excellent swimming opportunities. The park's nature center houses interesting displays of the cultural and natural history of the area. Naturalist programs are offered year round. The pioneer village (open seasonally for special events) features 15 historic buildings depicting life in the early 1800s. Bridle trails. 10,771 acres of camping, hiking trails, boating, fishing and winter sports.

MAPLE SYRUP WEEKEND

Waynesville – Caesar Creek State Park. Syrup making demos. Pancake dinners/ breakfasts. Sugarbush tours by foot on a woodland walk and learn how trees are drilled to collect sap for making syrup. (third weekend in February)

Wilmington

COWAN LAKE STATE PARK

Wilmington - *1750 Osborn Road (5 miles South of Wilmington off US 68) 45177. Phone: (937) 289-2105. http://parks.ohiodnr.gov/cowanlake*

The limestone near Cowan and other parts of the exposed arch are some of the most famous fossil hunting fields in the world. (Collection of fossils requires a permit from the Chief). American Lotus, a brilliant water lily, is abundant in the lake's shallow areas. It is unusual to find such a large colony of lotus on an inland lake. The plant's leaves grow up to two feet in diameter supporting large yellow flowers. Swimming, fishing, sailing and canoeing are popular on the lake. Meandering trails through mature woodlands compliment the natural features of this scenic park. Nature programs. Bike Rental. 1,775 acres of camping, boating and rentals, winter sports and family cabins.

BANANA SPLIT FESTIVAL

Wilmington - Memorial Park, SR 3 / US 22, downtown. www.bananasplitfestival. com. Celebrate the birthplace of the banana split (first made at Hazzard's Drug Store in 1907). If you love a good old-fashioned festival, set to the tune of the fabulous 50s and 60s, then you've come to the right place. Just think drive-in movies, poodle skirts, sock hops, Dick Clark's American Bandstand, hula hoops, classic cars, and roadside diners. The highlight is the "build your own" banana split booth. (second weekend in June)

AMUSEMENTS

ANIMALS & FARMS

HISTORY

MUSEUMS

OUTDOOR EXPLORING

OUTDOOR EXPLORING *(cont.)*

SEASONAL & SPECIAL EVENTS

SEASONAL & SPECIAL EVENTS *(cont.)*

SCIENCE

SPORTS

SUGGESTED LODGING & DINING

THE ARTS

TOURS

CPSIA information can be obtained
at www.ICGtesting.com
Printed in the USA
LVHW041934300322
714844LV00011B/1202

9 781733 506953